MORE LOST BOOKS OF THE BIBLE:

PISTIS SOPHIA

*A Gnostic miscellany: being for the most part extracts
from the books of the Savior to which are added
excerpts from a cognate literature.*

*Translated into English, with an Introduction
and Annotated Bibliography
by*
G.R.S. MEAD

the apocryphile press
BERKELEY, CA
www.apocryphile.org

a p o c r y p h i l e   p r e s s
BERKELEY, CA

Apocryphile Press
1700 Shattuck Ave #81
Berkeley, CA 94709
www.apocryphile.org

First published in 1921 by John M. Watkins, London.
Apocryphile Press Edition, 2006.

Printed in the United States of America
ISBN 1-933993-20-0

CONTENTS

INTRODUCTION

PISTIS SOPHIA

TRANSLATION

DIVISION I.

THE FIRST BOOK OF PISTIS SOPHIA

CONTENTS

PISTIS SOPHIA

CONTENTS

THE NOTE OF A SCRIBE

Division II.

Superscription :

THE SECOND BOOK OF PISTIS SOPHIA

PISTIS SOPHIA

END OF THE STORY OF PISTIS SOPHIA

CONTENTS

SUB-SCRIPTION :

A PORTION OF THE BOOKS OF THE SAVIOUR

PISTIS SOPHIA

DIVISION III.

THE CONCLUSION OF ANOTHER BOOK

A THIRD BOOK

CONTENTS

A FOURTH BOOK

PISTIS SOPHIA

SUB-SCRIPTION :

A PORTION OF THE BOOKS OF THE SAVIOUR

CONTENTS

PISTIS SOPHIA

PREFACE

In the Introduction (pp. xxxv f.) to the first edition (1896), the translator wrote :

" In presenting the following translation to the English-reading public, I may say that I should not have ventured on such an undertaking if any Coptic scholar had undertaken the task, or I had heard that such a task was contemplated. In a matter of so great difficulty every possible liability to error should be eliminated, and it stands to reason that the translation of a translation must needs be but an apology for a first-hand version. Nevertheless I am not without predecessors. The Coptic MS. itself is in the first place a translation, so that even Coptic scholars must give us the version of a translation. I am persuaded also that the anonymous and very imperfect French translation (1856) in the Appendix to Migne's *Dictionnaire des Apocryphes* (vol. i.) is made from Schwartze's Latin version (1851) and not from the Coptic text. C. W. King in *The Gnostics and their Remains* (2nd ed., 1887) has also translated a number of pages of the Pistis Sophia from Schwartze. Some three or four years ago Mr. Nutt, King's publisher, sent out a notice proposing the publication of the whole of King's translation,

but the project fell through. Last year (1895) I
offered to edit this translation of King's, but was
informed that the literary legatee of the deceased
scholar was of the opinion that it would be unfair
to his memory to publish a MS. that was in so
incomplete a condition.

" In 1890 I had already translated Schwartze's
Latin version into English and published pages
1 to 252, with comments, notes, etc., in magazine-
form from April 1890 to April 1891. But I
hesitated to put it forward in book-form, and
should not have done so, but for the appearance
of Amélineau's French translation in 1895. I
then went over the whole again and checked it by
Amélineau's version. I was further induced to
venture on this undertaking, because the narrative, though dealing with mystical and therefore
obscure subjects, is in itself exceedingly simple,
and therefore mistakes cannot so readily creep in
as into a difficult philosophical work. I, therefore, present my translation with all hesitation,
but at the same time think that the English
public, which is steadily increasing its interest
in mysticism and allied subjects, will be better
satisfied with half a loaf than with no bread."

A quarter of a century has rolled away ; much
water has flowed under the bridges of scholarly
research whence the general stream of Gnosticism has been surveyed with greater accuracy,
and much good work been done on the special
subject of the Coptic Gnostic documents. Though
the first edition of this book was quickly exhausted
and many requests were made for a second, I

had hitherto refused to accede to this demand,
still hoping that some English Coptic scholar
would take the matter in hand.   Indeed, at one
time I was in high expectation that this would
be achieved.   Shortly before the War a friend,
whom I had interested in the work, completed a
version of the fine Untitled Apocalypse of the
Bruce Codex, and was next to have attempted
a translation of the P.S.   But pressing interests
and activities of a totally different nature connected with the War and its aftermath have
absorbed all my friend's energies, and the version
of the P.S. has been definitely abandoned.   Nor
can I hear of any other project of translation.
This being the case, and as the utility of even
a translation of a translation is evidenced by
the keen demand for the volume in the second-
hand market, I have at last decided to repeat
my venture.

Nevertheless a reprint of the first edition was
not to be thought of.   Introduction and translation needed revision in the light of twenty-five
years' further study of the work of specialists.
To this end the most valuable help, not to speak
of his long labours on the allied documents, is
afforded by Carl Schmidt's admirable German
translation of the P.S. (1905).

Schwartze's Latin translation was good for its
date (1851), and scholars still quote it to-day ;
Amélineau's French rendering (1895) was somewhat of an improvement ; but Schmidt's version
is unquestionably the best.   I have therefore
revised my prior Englishing from the former

two by the finer work of the latter. Schmidt is exceedingly careful throughout, and not only have I taken his decision where Schwartze and Amélineau differ, but have generally preferred him for consistency in phrasing. In my humble opinion it will be long before we have a better rendering than that of this ripe Coptic scholar.

But not only has the Translation been thoroughly revised; the Introduction has been entirely rewritten and the Annotated Bibliography corrected and brought up to date. The second edition is practically a new book.

The Schwartze-Petermann marginal pagination, which is the usual scheme of reference, and which in the first edition was shown in brackets in the text, is now indicated at the side of the page. I have also adopted Schmidt's division into chapters as an additional convenience for more general reference, and have numbered the verses of the Psalms and of the Odes of Solomon for easier comparison with the Repentances and Songs of Sophia. It should, of course, be understood that the detailed paragraphing does not exist in the original, which runs on for the most part monotonously without break.

G. R. S. M.

Kensington,
July 1921.

INTRODUCTION

THE unique MS. of the Coptic Gnostic document commonly called ' Pistis Sophia ' was bought by the British Museum in 1785 from the heirs of Dr. Askew, and is now catalogued as MS. Add. 5114. The title on the back of the modern binding is ' *Piste Sophia Coptice.*' On top of the first page of the MS. is the signature ' A. Askew, M.D.' On the first page of the binding is the following note, probably in the hand of Woide, the most famous Coptic scholar of those days and Librarian of the Museum :

" *Codex dialecti Superioris Ægypti, quam Sahidicam seu Thebaidicam vocant, cujus titulus exstat pagina* 115 : *Pmeh snaou ñtomos ñtpiste Sophia—Tomos secundus fidelis Sapientiæ—deest pagina* 887–844."

The title ' Piste Sophia ' is incorrect. Nowhere is this form found in the very numerous instances of the name in the text, and the hastily suggested 'emendation' of Dulaurier and Renan to read ' Piste Sophia ' thoughout has perforce received no support.

Woide, in a letter to Michaelis (Bibliography, 4), says that Askew bought the MS. from a bookseller (apparently in London) ; its previous history is unknown. Crum informs us in an official description (Bib. 46, p. 178) that at the end of a copy in the B.M. of the sale-catalogue of Askew's MSS. is the entry : ' Coptic MS. £10. 10. 0.,' and that this refers presumably to our Codex—a good bargain indeed !

The best descriptions of the MS. are by Schmidt (Introd. to his Trans., Bib. 45, pp. xi f.), and Crum (*l.c.*). The Codex is of parchment and contains 178 leaves=356 pages 4to (8¾×6½ in.). The writing is in two columns of from 30 to 34 lines each. There are 23 quires in all ; but the first has only 12 and the last 8 pages, of which the last page is left blank. It is, as a whole, in an exceptionally well-preserved state, only 8 leaves being missing (see ch. 143, end).

The Scripts. The writing as a whole is the work of two scribes, whose entirely different hands are very clearly distinguishable. The first (MS. pp. 1–22, 196–354) wrote a fine, careful, old uncial, and the second (MS. pp. 23–195) in comparison a careless, clumsy hand with signs of shakiness which S. thinks might suggest the writing of an old man. They used different inks and different methods both of paging and correction, not to speak of other peculiarities. These scribes must have been contemporaries and divided the task of copying fairly equally between them. So far Crum and Schmidt are in complete agreement ; they differ only as to the handwriting of a note on MS. p. 114, col. 2, of the superscription on p. 115 and of the last page (see pp. 105, 106 and 325 of Trans.).

From an external point of view the contents fall The Con-
into 4 main Divisions, generally referred to as ^{tents.}
Books i.–iv.

i. The first extends to the end of ch. 62, where
in the MS. more than a column and a half
has been left blank, and a short, but entirely
irrelevant, extract has been copied on to the
second column, presumably from some other
book of the general allied literature.

There is no title, either superscription or sub-
scription, to this Div. Why the second scribe
left a blank here in his copying is a puzzle, for
the text which follows on MS. p. 115 runs straight
on without a break of subject or incident.

ii. The next page is headed ' The Second
Book (or Section) of Pistis Sophia.' Crum assigns
this superscription to the second hand, and the
short extract on the second column of the preceding page to the first. But Schmidt thinks
that both are later additions by another hand,
and this is borne out both by the colour of the ink
and also by the very important fact that the
older Coptic MSS. have the title at the end and
not at the beginning of a volume, conserving the
habit of the ancient roll-form. And as a matter
of fact we find at the bottom of MS. p. 233,
col. 1, the subscription : 'A Portion of the Books
(or Texts) of the Saviour ' (see end of ch. 100).

iii. There follows a short piece on the Gnosis
of the Ineffable (ch. 101), which is without any
setting and entirely breaks the order of sequence
of ideas and is the end of a larger whole. It is
clearly an extract from another ' Book.'

After this again with ch. 102 we have a very distinct change of subject, though not of setting, from the ending of ii., so that, in my opinion, it is difficult to regard it as an immediate continuation. Later, at ch. 126, occurs another abrupt change of subject, though not of setting, preceded by a lacuna in the text. At the end of ch. 135 (bottom of MS. p. 318, col. 1) we have again the subscription: 'A Portion of the Books of the Saviour.'

iv. The last piece has no title, either superscription or subscription. From the change of setting in its introduction and the nature of its contents it is generally assigned to an earlier phase of the literature. Here again a complete change of subject occurs with ch. 144, after a lacuna of 8 leaves. Finally, on the last page is an appendix, somewhat in the style of the Mark-conclusion, beginning quite abruptly in the middle of a sentence and presumably part of a larger whole. The contents, measurements and writing make it almost certain that it formed no part of the original copy. At the very end two lines surrounded by ornamentation are erased. These may have contained the names of the owner or scribes, or possibly a general subscript title.

The Title.   From the above indications and from a detailed study of the contents it is evident that, though the episode of the adventures of Pistis Sophia, her repentances and songs and their solutions (chh. 30–64), occupy much space, it is by no means the principal theme of the collection; it is rather an incident. The blundering heading of a later scribe, 'The Second Book of Pistis Sophia,' some two-thirds of the way through this episode, has misled earlier scholars and set up the bad habit of referring to the whole document as the 'Pistis Sophia'—a habit it is now too late to change. If there is any general title to be derived from the MS. itself, it should be rather 'A Portion' or 'Portions of the Books of the Saviour.' Whether this title can be made to cover Div. iv. is an open question. In any case we have before us extracts from a more extensive literature which belonged to the same group, and of which there were at least two strata. The contents of the Askew Codex are thus a collection or a miscellany, and not a single consistent work. It is very difficult, therefore, to distinguish the contents by any consistent nomenclature. I have followed the usual custom of calling the whole 'Pistis Sophia,' and let Divv. i. and ii. stand as Books i. and ii., as is usually done, though this is clearly improper, judged from the point of view of contents. Thereafter I have distinguished the extracts in Div. iii. as being from two different 'Books' (apart from the short insertion at the beginning), and again those in Div. iv. as being from two different 'Books,' these 'Books' meaning simply subdivisions of or excerpts from larger wholes.

It seems highly probable that our scribes did not do the extracting themselves, but found it already done in the copy which lay before them.

The date of our MS. is undecided, owing to The Date the difficulty of making exact judgments in of the MS.

Coptic paleography. The general view assigns it with Schmidt to the 5th century. It may be noted that Woide (Bib. 8) assigned it to the 4th, and Crum seems to agree with him. Hyvernat (Bib. 21) suggests the 6th, and Wright (Bib. 16) the 7th. Amélineau (Bib. 35) goes to a ridiculous extreme by placing it in the 9th or 10th century, but his too radical views have been severely criticized.

Translated from the Greek. The Coptic of the P.S. is in pure Sahidic—that is, the dialect of Upper Egypt,—preserving many features of antiquity. It is, however, clearly not the original language in which the extracts were written. These, like the rest of the extant Coptic Gnostic documents, were originally composed in Greek. This is shown by the very large number of Greek words, not only names, but substantives, adjectives, verbs, adverbs, and even conjunctions, left untranslated, on well-nigh every page, and this applies to the O.T. and N.T. quotations equally with the rest. The Schwartze-Petermann Latin version preserves every Greek word throughout untranslated, and Schmidt's German translation invariably adds them in brackets. In the P.S. a large number of abstract qualificative general names of exalted super-æonic orders is given, such as ' Unapproachables,' ' Uncontainables,' which could not possibly be native to Coptic diction. In a number of passages again, where the translator had difficulty, he slavishly follows the Greek construction. Frequently also he gives alternative renderings. The fact of translation from the Greek is well-nigh universally

acknowledged ; and indeed we now possess decisive objective proof, for one of the documents
in the Berlin Codex, which presents identical
linguistic phenomena, lay before Irenæus in its
Greek original form (Bib. 47). Nevertheless
Granger (Bib. 44) and Scott-Moncrieff (Bib. 56)
have questioned this fact of translation, and
quite recently Rendel Harris (Bib. 60), after
accepting the general consensus of opinion (Bib.
49), has changed his mind and thinks that the
matter should be reinvestigated. None of these
scholars, however, has set forth any objective
grounds for his opinion. It is difficult to believe
that any one who has laboured through the
versions line by line and word by word can have
the slightest doubt on the matter. The whole
style of the work is foreign to the Coptic idiom,
as may be seen from Amélineau's Introduction to
his French version (Bib. 85), where he writes (p. x):
" Whoever has any knowledge of the Coptic
language knows that this idiom is foreign to long
sentences ; that it is a tongue eminently analytic
and by no means synthetic ; that its sentences
are composed of small clauses exceedingly precise,
and almost independent of each other. Of course
all Coptic authors are not equally easy, some of
them are even exceedingly difficult to understand ;
but this much is certain, that never under any
circumstances in Coptic do we come across those
periods with complicated incidental sentences,
of three or four different clauses, whose elements
are synthetically united together so that the
sense of the entire sentence cannot be grasped

before we arrive at the last clause.   Nevertheless, this is just what the reader meets with in this work.   The sentences are so entangled with incidental and complicated propositions, that often, indeed very often, the Coptic translator has lost the thread, so to say, and made main propositions out of incidental clauses. . . .   The one thing that it conclusively proves is that the book was originally written in a learned language."

Amélineau makes rather too much of the abstruse nature of the subject ; for, though many passages are transcendental or mystical, nevertheless the whole is conceived in a narrative or descriptive style.   There is no attempt at philosophical argument, no really involved logical propositions. We may then take it as sufficiently established that Greek originals underlay the whole contents of the Askew Codex.   It is on this basis at any rate that rests every methodical attempt which has hitherto been made to determine the most probable place and date of origin and to discover the school or circle to which the P.S. miscellany can be referred.

Originals composed in Egypt.   Amid much else that is uncertain no one has questioned that the immediate place of origin must be sought in an Egyptian environment.   In other words, the ' Books ' of the miscellany were all composed or compiled in Egypt, though where precisely it is impossible to conjecture. But the clearly Egyptian elements are not the more numerous ; moreover, they do not seem to be the most fundamental, but are blended with, or rather superimposed upon, others which clearly did not originate in Egypt.

The date of composition is a difficult problem, and is bound up with the more puzzling question of the sect to which the P.S. literature should be ascribed. There is as yet no certainty; it is a matter of cumulative probabilities at best.

The earlier view ascribed the P.S. to Valentinus, who died probably about the middle of the 2nd century, or a decade later, or alternatively to an adherent of the Valentinian school. We may call it the 2nd-century theory. A succession of scholars were of this opinion, among whom may be mentioned Woide, Jablonski, La Croze, Dulaurier, Schwartze, Renan, Révillout, Usener and Amélineau. This earlier view can hardly be said to have been supported by any great show of detailed argument, except by the French Egyptologist and Coptic scholar Amélineau, who was its most stalwart supporter. Seven years prior to his translation of P.S. in 1895, Amélineau devoted 156 pp. of a voluminous essay (Bib. 19), in which he sought to prove the Egyptian origins of Gnosticism—a general thesis which can hardly be maintained in the light of more recent research, —to a comparison of the system of Valentinus with that of the P.S.

Meantime in Germany, shortly after the appearance of Schwartze's Latin version in 1851, the careful analysis of the system of the P.S. by Köstlin in 1854 gave rise to or confirmed another view. It abandoned the Valentinian origin, and pronounced generally in favour of what may be

Date : The 2nd-century Theory.

The 3rd-century Theory.

called an ' Ophitic ' derivation. Köstlin placed
the date of the P.S. in the 1st half of the 3rd century, and Lipsius (Bib. 15) and Jacobi (Bib. 17)
accepted his finding. We may call this alternative general view the 3rd-century theory.

In 1891 Harnack, accepting Köstlin's analysis
of the system, attacked the problem from another
point of view, basing himself chiefly on the use of
scripture, as shown in the quotations from the
O.T. and N.T., and on the place of the doctrinal
ideas and stage of the sacramental practices in
the general history of the development of Christian dogma and rites. He pointed out also one
or two other vague indications, such as a reference
to persecution, from which he concluded that it
was written at a date when the Christians were
' lawfully ' persecuted. These considerations led
him to assign the most probable date of composition to the 2nd half of the 3rd century. Schmidt
in 1892 accepted this judgment, with the modifi-
cation, however, that Div. iv. belonged to an older
stratum of the literature, and should therefore
be placed in the 1st half of the century. This
general view has been widely adopted as the more
probable. In Germany it has been accepted by
such well-known specialists as Bousset, Preuschen
and Liechtenhan; and in France by De Faye.
Among English scholars may be mentioned chiefly
E. F. Scott, Scott-Moncrieff and Moffat.

The only recent attempt to return to the earlier
2nd-century view is that of Legge in 1915 (Bib. 57),
who roundly plumps for Valentinus as the author.
In order to do this he thinks it necessary first of

all to get out of the way Harnack's parallels in P.S. with the fourth gospel. They may just as well, he contends, be compilations from the synoptics. One clear parallel only can be adduced, and this may be due to a common source. I am not convinced by this criticism; nor do I think it germane to Legge's general contention, for it is precisely in Valentinian circles that the fourth gospel first emerges in history. In the Introduction to the first edition of the present work I registered my adhesion to the Valentinian hypothesis, but, as I now think, somewhat too precipitously. On general grounds the 3rd-century theory seems to me now the more probable; but, even if Harnack's arguments as a whole hold, I see no decisive reason why the P.S. may not equally well fall within the 1st half as within the 2nd half of the century.

The question of the sect or even grouping to The 'Ophitic' which the P.S. literature should be assigned is Background. still more difficult. To call it 'Ophitic' is nebulous at best. Ophitism in Gnosticism is ill-defined, if not chaotic, owing to the confusing indications of the Church Fathers. They called Ophitic or classed as Ophitic very different sects who never used the name for themselves. It ought to mean people either who worshipped the serpent or in whose symbolism or mythology the serpent played the most characteristic or dominant rôle. But most of what we are told of the views and doctrines of circles directly referred to under this opprobrious designation (as it is clearly intended to be by the heresiologists) and of those brought into close connection with them, has not the slightest reference to what by hypothesis should have been their chief cult-symbol. *Sed et serpens* is conspicuous by its absence. All that we can legitimately say is that along this confused line of heredity we have to push back our researches in any endeavour to discover the earliest developments of Gnosticism in Christian circles. These took place unquestionably first on Syrian ground, and doubtless had already a long heredity behind them, former phases of syncretism, blendings of Babylonian, Persian, Semitic and other elements. The ' Ophitic ' elements in P.S. are of Syrian origin, but developed on Egyptian soil. If there is also a slight Hellenistic tinging, it is not of a philosophizing nature.

Three vague Pointers.

Can we, however, find any indications in the P.S. which might be thought to direct us whither to search in the jumble of sects which the chief heresiological Fathers bring into an ' Ophitic ' connection? There are three vague pointers : (1) Philip is declared pre-eminently (chh. 22, 42) to be the scribe of all the deeds and discourses of the Saviour, but with him are associated Thomas and Matthew (ch. 43) ; (2) in Div. iii. Mary Magdalene stands forth as the chief questioner, no less than 39 of the 42 questions being put in her mouth ; (3) in Div. iv. a foul act of obscene sorcery is condemned as the most heinous of all sins (ch. 147).

Now, Epiphanius (writing about 374–377 A.D.) groups together certain sects under the names

Nicolaïtans, Gnostics, Ophites, Cainites, Sethians
and Archontics ; these possessed a rich apocalyptic literature.   Among the titles of their
books reference is made to a *Gospel of Philip*
(*Hær.* xxvi. 13) and *Questions of Mary*, both
The Great and *The Little* (*ib.* 8).   A quotation
is given from the former, and several from the
latter.   But in both cases they are of an obscene
nature and have clearly nothing whatever to do
with P.S. in any way.   It is true that the more
abundant quotations are from *The Great Questions*, and this has led Harnack and others to
assume that *The Little Questions* may have been
of a different and even ascetic character.   But
Epiphanius classes the two writings together
without distinction ; and even if the title
Questions of Mary could be legitimately given to
part of the contents of P.S., surely these would
be more appropriately styled *The Great* and not
The Little Questions ?   Finally, the document
from which Epiphanius quotes belongs to a
different type of setting.   Mary questions apart,
is alone with Jesus.   She is not with the rest of
the disciples, as in the P.S.

In describing these sects Epiphanius repeatedly
dwells on certain unspeakably foul rites and
practices which he would have us believe were
widely spread among them.   P.S. condemns with
even greater severity a similar obscene abomination, introducing this stern reprobation with
the solemn words, the only instance of such an
outbreak in the whole narrative : " Jesus was
wroth with the world in that hour and said unto

Thomas : ' Amēn, I say unto you : This sin is more heinous than all sins and all iniquities.' " There is, however, no indication that in the experience of the writers of the P.S. such a practice was widespread ; on the contrary, it would seem for them to have been a rare occurrence—indeed, the most horrible thing of which they had ever heard. If Epiphanius is to be relied on here, it is vain to look for the Gnostics of the P.S. in such an environment. But Epiphanius has no great reputation for accuracy in general, and it is very difficult to believe in such widespread iniquity of so loathsome a nature. In any case he is writing at a later date. Liechtenhan's hypothesis (Bib. 41), that a certain common body of literature was rewritten—on the one hand to serve libertinist propensities, and on the other in the interest of ascetic tendencies,—though more or less accepted by Harnack, seems to me to be too facile a generalization to meet the special difficulty with which we are confronted. Epiphanius in his youth had certain unfortunate experiences with the adherents of a libertinist sect in Egypt, and the moral shock it gave him seems to have warped his judgment as a historian in this part of his work ; it led him to collect every scrap of evidence of obscenity he could lay hands on and every gross scandal that had come to his ears, and freely to generalize therefrom.

The Severiana.   Into relation with the above-mentioned Epiphanian group of names Schmidt brings the ascetic Severians ; these, according to our heresiologist (xlv.), still in his own day maintained a miserable existence in the upper Thebaid. To them S. would specifically refer the P.S. But, in my opinion, it is very difficult indeed to fit in what Epiphanius tells us so sketchily of these people, however skilfully it is analyzed, with the main doctrines and practices in the P.S.

With nothing but Patristic indications before us, no matter what pains are taken to submit them to microscopic critical inspection, it seems impossible to place the P.S. precisely. But our Codex does not stand in isolation as the only directly known Christian Gnostic document—that is to say, as coming straight from the hands of the Gnostics themselves, though by way of translation. We have first of all the two MSS. of the Bruce Codex in the Bodleian, Oxford. One of these, *The Book of the Great Logos according to the Mystery,* is closely connected with the literature from which the P.S. miscellany is excerpted, especially with Div. iv. We can say with a high degree of confidence that it belonged to the same tradition, though whether to an earlier or later stratum is not quite decided. There are, however, no indications in it which will further help us as to date or name of sect. The second MS., a lofty apocalypse, which unfortunately bears no title, is of another line of tradition or type of interest. Schmidt, in the Introduction to his translation (p. xxvi, Bib. 45), thinks he can refer it with certainty to the Sethian-Archontic group, placing it in the 1st half of the 3rd century, instead of, as previously (Bib. 28), in the last quarter of the 2nd. His reason for this change

The Bruce Codex.

of view may be seen from the following obser-
vations, which introduce us to the third extant,
but unpublished, collection of Coptic Gnostic
works.

On July 16, 1896, Schmidt surprised and delighted students of Gnosticism by reporting, at a
sitting of the Royal Prussian Academy of Sciences,
on the contents of a precious Coptic Gnostic
Codex which had in January of the same year
been procured by Dr Reinhardt at Cairo from a
dealer in antiquities from Akhmīm, and is now
in the safe custody of the Berlin Egyptian
Museum (*Sitzungsberichte d. k. p. Akad. d. Wissensch. zu Berlin,* xxxvi). This notice and a more
detailed study of one of the treatises by S. in 1907
(Bib. 47) give us all the information we possess
so far concerning this very important Codex.
In 1900 I summarized S.'s first notice in the first
edition of my *Fragments of a Faith Forgotten*
(pp. 579–592). The Codex consists mainly of
three original Greek Gnostic works in Coptic
translation: (1) *The Gospel of Mary*; (2) *The
Apocryphon of John*; (3) *The Wisdom of Jesus
Christ.* At the end there is an extract from *The
Acts of Peter*, which are also of Gnostic origin,
setting forth an episode from the healing wonders
of the Apostle.

The Gospel of Mary relates visions of John and
Mary Magdalene, but Schmidt gives us none of
their contents. He is equally reserved as to the
contents of *The Wisdom of Jesus Christ*, giving
only the introduction. After the resurrection
the twelve disciples and seven women-disciples

of Jesus go into Galilee to a certain mountain
(as in Div. iv. of P.S.). To them Jesus appears
as a great angel of light and bids them lay all
their questions before him. The disciples bring
forward their questions and receive the desired
replies. Schmidt must have told Harnack more
about the contents, for in an appendix to the
report, the latter ventures on the suggestion
that it may possibly be found that this treatise
is the lost book of Valentinus referred to under
the title of *Wisdom*.

It is the second treatise, *The Apocryphon of* The so-
John, to which S. devotes most of his attention Barbēlō-
in both the papers to which we are referring, the Gnostics.
titles of which are respectively, ' A Pre-irenæic
Gnostic Original Work in Coptic ' and ' Irenæus
and his Source in *Adv. Hær.* i. 29,' S. proves
beyond a shadow of doubt that the Greek original
of this Gnostic apocryphon lay before Irenæus
(*c.* 190 A.D.), and that the Church Father's method
of quotation and summarizing is, to say the least
of it, misleading, for it practically makes nonsense
of what is by no means absurd. The treatise tells
us much of interest concerning the part played
by Barbēlō, ' the perfect Power,' ' the Æon perfect in glory ' ; the system is of the philosophized
type and by no means inconsistent. Hitherto
the clumsy treatment of it by Irenæus has been
generally referred to as descriptive of the tenets
of the Barbēlō-Gnostics, and to them Scott (Bib.
54) and Moffat (Bib. 58) have sought variously
to ascribe the P.S. These Gnostics are brought
by Irenæus into a confused relationship with

some of the sects of the group on which Epiphanius two centuries later animadverted so severely.

The Sethians.

Schmidt, however, has shown that the document in question belongs immediately to the literature of the Sethians, to whom also he now ascribes the Untitled Apocalypse of the Bruce Codex. *The Apocryphon of John* is clearly imbued with a very similar spirit of philosophizing to that of the Valentinian school, and Schmidt promises to compare the two systems in detail, so as to determine their relationship, when he publishes his translation of these new documents, which are of so great importance for the history of the Christianized Gnosis.

The present Position of the Enquiry.

What precise light the publication of Schmidt's labours will throw, directly or indirectly, on the puzzling question of the exact placing of the P.S. literature, we must wait to see; it is highly probable, however, that it will throw some light on its problems. But from what we glean so far from the above indications it may be again suggested that, though the Valentinian hypothesis will have to be definitely abandoned, there seems nothing to compel us to lean to the 2nd rather than to the 1st half of the 3rd century for the date. Here the view of Lipsius (Bib. 20) and Bousset (Bib. 48), that similar features in the P.S. and the religion of Mani are in a more primitive form in the former than in the latter, has to be considered. Manichæism emerged somewhere about 265 A.D., but it is very difficult to say what was its precise original form. The similarities in the two systems may of course be due to their coming from a common source.

What is certain is that we have in the contents of the Askew, Bruce and Berlin Codices a rich material which hands on to us valuable direct information concerning what I have called ' The Gnosis according to its Friends,' in distinction from what previously used to be our only sources, the polemical writings of the heresiological Fathers, which set forth ' The Gnosis according to its Foes.' We have thus at last a new standpoint from which to review the subject, and therewith the opportunity of revising our impressions in a number of respects ; a considerably different angle of vision must needs change the perspective of no little in the picture. The new and the old Perspective in Gnostic Studies.

The chief business or interest of the orthodox Fathers was to select and stress what appeared to them to be the most bizarre points and elements, all that was most absurd in their judgment, in the many Gnostic systems, and of course, and rightly, everything that could be thought to be ethically reprehensible. Good, bad and indifferent were only too frequently lumped together. It was of no interest to this polemic to mention similarities in belief and practice between the heretics and their opponents, to dwell on the lofty faith of numbers of these Gnostics in the transcendent excellence and overmastering glory of the Saviour, or on many signs of spiritual inwardness, and especially of high virtue, in which they were at the least not less scrupulous than their critics. Doubtless there were sects and groups whose tenets were absurd at any valuation, and some whose laxity of ethics demanded severe reprobation. But the majority could not be accused on the score of moral delinquency, indeed no few were rigidly ascetic; and some of their speculations again have a sublimity of their own, and in a number of cases anticipated Catholic dogma. If we turn to our direct sources in Coptic translation, we find that the ethic is admirable, even if we are averse from over-asceticism in the religious life, and that their whole-souled devotion to and worship of the Saviour is unbounded.

It is no part of the plan of this translation to attempt anything in the nature of a commentary. That would mean a second volume, and would in any case be an unsatisfactory performance; for much would still remain obscure, even if every ray of light shed on this or that special point by those who have most deeply studied the subject, were gathered together. One or two very general remarks, however, may be ventured.

The Ministry of the First Mystery. In the P.S. Jesus is everywhere pre-eminent and central. He is here revealed as Saviour and First Mystery, who knows all and unveils all, infinite in compassion. As such he is pre-existent from eternity, and his ministry is not only earthly, but cosmic and supercosmic; indeed, it is the chief feature in the divine economy. Yet nowhere is he called the Christ. If this is intentional, no reason seems to be assignable for such an abstention. There is no sign of antagonism to Judaism or to the O.T. On the contrary, the psalms and other utterances which are quoted, are validated by the theory that it was the Power of the Saviour which so prophesied of old through the mouth of a David, a Solomon, or an Isaiah.

The whole setting is post-resurrectional. In Divv. i.–iii. Jesus has already, for eleven years after the crucifixion, been instructing his disciples, men and women, in the Gnosis. The scene now depicts the disciples as gathered round the Saviour on the Mount of Olives on earth. The range and scope of this prior teaching may be seen in Div. iv., where the introductory words speak of it as taking place simply after the crucifixion. In this stratum the scene is different. The sacramental rite is solemnized on earth ; it takes place, however, on the Mount of Galilee and not on the Mount of Olives. But the scene is not confined to earth only, for the disciples are also taken into some of the regions of the invisible world, above and below, have vision there conferred upon them, and are instructed on its meaning. Now in Divv. i.–iii. Jesus promises to take the disciples into the spheres and heavens for the direct showing of their nature and quality and inhabitants, but there is no fulfilment of this promise in the excerpts we have from ' The Books of the Saviour.' It is not to be supposed, however, that Div. iv. is part of the fulfilment of the high promise made in the prior extracts ; for in it we move in an earlier phase of the instruction and in an atmosphere of lesser mysteries than those indicated in the preceding part.

Divv. i.–iii. throughout proclaim the revelation of higher mysteries. This is only now made

The post-resurrectional Setting.

possible by the supremely joyous fact that in
the twelfth year of the inner-teaching-ministry
a great, if not supreme, moment in the life of the
Saviour has been accomplished: his earthly
ministry is now achieved, and he is invested with
the full radiance of his triple robe of glory,
which embraces the whole powers of the universe.
He ascends into heaven in dazzling light which
blinds the disciples. After thirty hours he re-
turns again, and in compassion withdraws his
blinding splendour, so as to give his final teaching
to his faithful in his familiar form. This means
that 'The Books of the Saviour' purport to
contain not only a post-resurrectional teaching,
and therefore a Gnostic revelation supplementary
to the public preaching before the crucifixion,
but also a still higher and more intimate unveiling
within the post-resurrectional instruction already
current in the tradition. If there had been
apocalyptic elements and visions in the prior
literature, there were to be still more transcendental revelations now on the completion of
the ministry. Until the investiture, or rather
reinvestiture, had taken place according to the
divine command, it had not been possible for the
Saviour to speak in utter openness face to face
on all things; now it is possible. Such is the
convention.

In Divv. i.–iii. there is presupposed throughout
a system of æons and the rest, which is already
highly complex and shows manifest signs of consisting of stages once severally at the summit of
earlier systems, but now successively subordin-

ated. It is clear then that, if still loftier hierarchies are to be brought on to the stage, it can
only be by again reducing what had previously
been regarded as ' the end of all ends ' to a sub-
ordinate position. This is the method adopted,
and we lose ourselves in the recital of the designa-
tions and attributes of ever more transcendental
beings and spaces and mysteries.

In all of this, however, there is no sign of The Sophia
Episode.
interest in metaphysical speculation ; there is
no philosophizing.· It is then not any element of
Hellenic thought proper in the æonology, which
is said to have been so strongly the case with the
teaching of Valentinus himself, that has led so
many to conjecture a Valentinian derivation.
It is rather the long episode of the sorrowing
Sophia which has influenced them. This episode
reflects on a lower level of the cosmic scale somewhat of the *motif* of the ' tragic myth ' of the
world-soul, the invention of which is generally
ascribed to Valentinus himself, though he may
possibly have transformed or worked up already
existing materials or notions. It is this long
Sophia episode and its skilfully inverted mystical
exegesis and allegorical interpretation, following
the methods developed by Alexandrine contem-
platives, which haš produced the impression on
many that it was of fundamental importance for
the system of the P.S.

It is certainly an indication of the deep interest The ethical
Interest.
of the circle in repentance and the penitential
psalms. But the interest is here ethical rather
than cosmological. Pistis Sophia would seem·to

be intended to represent the type of the faithful repentant individual soul. Throughout, the chief interest is in salvation and redemption. This is to be acquired by repentance and by renunciation of the world, its lures and cares, but above all by faith in the Saviour, the Divine Light, and his mysteries. The first requisite is sincere repentance. The chief topic round which all the ethical teaching naturally centres, is sin, its cause and its purification, and the revelation of the mystery of the forgiveness of sins and of the infinite compassion of the First Mystery. Though there is very much also concerning the complex schematology of the invisible worlds and the hierarchies of being, much concerning the soul and its origin, of how it comes to birth and departs from earth-life, much of the light-power, the spiritual element in man,—all is subordinated to the ethical interest in the first place, and in the second to the efficacy of the high mysteries of salvation.

The Mysteries.

The whole is set forth in terms of these mysteries, which are now conceived in a far more vital way than was apparently the case in the earlier literature. On the lower side the mysteries still in some respects keep in touch with the tradition of words-of-power, authentic and incorruptible names, and so forth, though there is little of this specifically in Divv. i.–iii. But it is evidently intended that the higher mysteries should now be conceived in the light of the fact that the Saviour himself is in himself concretely the First Mystery and indeed the Last Mystery, and that

the mysteries are not so much spiritual powers
as substantive beings of transcendent excellence.
The light-robe is a mystery of mysteries, and they
who have received of the high mysteries become
light-streams in passing from the body. The
mysteries are closely intertwined with the lore of
the glory and its modes.

One of the main elements in the lower sche- The astral
matology is the ancient astral lore, those ground-
conceptions of sidereal religion which dominated
the thought of the times and upheld their sway
directly and indirectly for long centuries after.
But here again our Gnostics, while retaining the
schematology for certain purposes, placed it low
in the scale. Moreover, while not denying that
previously there was truth even in the astro-
logical art, they reduced the chances of the
horoscope-casters to zero, by declaring that the
Saviour in the accomplishment of his cosmic
ministry had now drastically changed the revolu-
tion of the spheres, so that henceforth no calcu-
lations could be counted on ; these were now of
no more value than the spinning of a coin.

Our Gnostics were also transmigrationists ; Trans-
transcorporation formed an integral part of their corporation.
system. They found no difficulty in fitting it
into their plan of salvation, which shows no sign of
the expectation of an immediate end of all things
—that prime article of faith of the earliest days.
So far from thinking that reincarnation is alien to
gospel-teaching, they elaborately interpret certain
of the most striking sayings in this sense, and
give graphic details of how Jesus, as the First

Mystery, brought to rebirth the souls of John the
Baptizer and of the disciples, and supervized the
economy of his own incarnation.   In this respect
the P.S. offers richer material for those interested
in this ancient and widespread doctrine than can
be found in any other old-world document in the
West.

The magical
Element.
A far more distressingly puzzling immixture is
the element of magic.   In Div. iv. especially there
are invocations and many names which resemble
those found in the Greek magical papyri and
other scattered sources.   But no one has so far
thrown any clear light on this most difficult
subject of research in general, much less on its
relation to the P.S.   It is evident that the writers
of Div. iv. and of the first treatise of the Bruce
Codex set a high value on such formulæ and on
authentic names ; nor are these entirely absent
from the excerpts from 'The Books of the Saviour,'
as witness the five words written on the light-
robe.   Our Gnostics unquestionably believed in a
high magic, and were not averse from finding in
what was presumably its most reputable tradition,
material which they considered to be germane to
their purpose.   In this tradition there must have
been a supreme personage possessing character-
istics that could be brought into close connection
with their ideal of the Saviour, for they equate a
certain Aberamenthō with him.   The name occurs
once or twice elsewhere ; but who or what it
suggested, we do not know.   In any case, as
they utilized and attempted to sublimate so
much else which was considered by many in those

days to be most venerable, in order that they might the more extend and exalt the glory of the Saviour and take up into it what they considered the best of everything, so did they with what was presumably the highest they could find in the hoary tradition of magical power, which had enjoyed empery for so long in the antique world and still continued to maintain itself even in religio-philosophical circles, where we should, from the modern standpoint, least expect to find it.

As to the setting of the narrative,—if we had not such an abundance of instances of pseudo-historic and pseudo-epigraphic scripture-writing, if this were not, so to speak, the commonplace, not only of apocryphal and apocalyptic literature, but also of no little that falls within the borders of canonical sanction, we might be more surprized than we are at the form in which the composers or compilers have framed their work.   It is clear that they loved and worshipped Jesus with an ecstasy of devotion and exaltation ; they do not fall short in this of the greatest of his lovers. What sort of authority, then, could they have supposed they had for conceiving the setting of their narrative in the way they have ?

Objective physical history, in the rigid sense in which we understand it to-day, was of secondary interest to them, to say the least ; indeed, it was apparently of little moment to the Gnostics of any school, and their opponents were not infrequently rowing in the same boat.   The Gnostics were, however, less disingenuous ; they strenuously declared their belief in continued

History and psychic Story.

revelation, they delighted in apocalyptic and in psychic story. The belief in a post-resurrectional teaching had doubtless existed for long in many forms in Gnostic circles. It must have been widespread ; for, as shown by Schmidt quite recently (Bib. 59), a Catholic writer in Asia Minor found himself compelled to steal the fire of the Gnostics and adopt the same convention in an orthodox document that was intended to be a polemic against Gnostic ideas, somewhere in the 3rd quarter of the 2nd century. However they arrived at their conviction, it seems highly probable that the writers of the P.S. must have sincerely believed they had high authority for their proceeding, and were in some way emboldened by ' inspiration ' to carry out their task. As far as they were concerned, they do not by any means seem conscious of belonging to a decadent movement or of deterioration in the quality of the ideas they were attempting to set forth, as so many modern critics would have it. On the contrary, they thought they were depositories or recipients of profound mysteries never hitherto revealed, and that by a knowledge of these mysteries they could the more efficiently evangelize the world.

The P.S. a reserved Document.

It is evident, however, that the P.S. was never intended to be circulated as a public gospel. Certain things are to be preached or proclaimed to the world, but only certain things. Certain mysteries, again, the recipients were to bestow under certain conditions, but others were to be reserved. The ' Books of the Saviour ' are, therefore, to be regarded as apocrypha in the original sense of the word—that is, 'withdrawn' or 'reserved' writings. As such they fell within the proscriptions of artificial secrecy common to all the initiatory institutions of the time and of all time. And artificial secrecy can with difficulty, if ever, avoid the moral and intellectual hazard of its innate obscurations. The P.S. was intended for already initiated disciples, for chosen learners, though no pledge of secrecy is mentioned. It was intended, above all, for would-be apostles, for those who should go forth to proclaim what was for them the best of good news ; it is clearly the inner instruction of a zealously propagandist sect.

If 'The Books of the Saviour' in their full Its general original form—for in the extant P.S. we have but selections from them and the formulæ of the higher mysteries are omitted,—and if what is given of the lower mysteries in Div. iv. were held back from public perusal owing partly at least to the fear of the unworthy making improper use of them, there is little danger to-day on this score, for this part of the miscellany remains so far the most securely incomprehensible. And indeed no little else remains obscure, even when we are of those who have made a protracted study of the psychical elements in mysticism and of the general psychology of religious experience. But there is much also in our Codex which has a charm of its own. There are things of rare, if exotic, beauty, things of profound ethical significance, things of delicate spiritual texture.

In any case, however all these very various elements and features in the syncretism be judged and evaluated, the Pistis Sophia is unquestionably a document of the first importance, not only for the history of Christianized Gnosticism, but also for the history of the development of religion in the West.

A Skeleton of the Scheme of the System. In conclusion, a skeleton of the scheme underlying the P.S. is added. It may prove of service generally to assist the reader in the maze of details.

The Ineffable.

The Limbs of the Ineffable.

I. The Highest Light-world or Realm of Light.
    i. The First Space of the Ineffable.
    ii. The Second Space of the Ineffable, or The First Space of the First Mystery.
    iii. The Third Space of the Ineffable, or The Second Space of the First Mystery.

II. The Higher (or Middle) Light-world.
    i. The Treasury of the Light.
        1. The Emanations of the Light.
        2. The Orders of the Orders.
    ii. The Region of the Right.
    iii. The Region of the Midst.

III. The Lower Light or Æon-world, or The Mixture of Light and Matter.
    i. The Region of the Left.
        1. The Thirteenth Æon.
        2. The Twelve Æons.

3. The Fate.
4. The Sphere.
5. The Rulers of the Ways of the (Lower) Midst.[1]
6. The Firmament.
   ii. The World (Kosmos), especially Mankind.
iii. The Under-world.
1. The Amente.
2. The Chaos.
3. The Outer Darkness.

Finally, the bibliography which follows is not simply a list of authors' names and of the titles of their contributions to the subject, but is furnished with notes which may serve briefly to indicate the chief moments in the development of the literature and in the history of opinion. There doubtless are a few articles hidden away in the back numbers of periodicals which should be added fully to complete the list; but they cannot be of any importance, or they would have been referred to by some one or other of the subsequent writers.

---

[1] I have printed this without a capital in the text to distinguish it from the higher Midst above.

ANNOTATED BIBLIOGRAPHY

1. 1770.   Art. in *Brittische theol. Magazin* (?) ; see Köstlin below, 13.
2. 1773.   Woide (C. G.).   Art. in *Journal des Savants* (Paris).
3. 1778.   Woide (C. G.).   Art. in J. A. Cramer's *Beyträge zur Beförderung theologischer und ` andrer wichtigen Kenntnisse* (Kiel u. Hamburg), iii. 82 ff.

It was by W. that the New Testament, according to the text of the famous Codex Alexandrinus, was edited, in uncial types cast to imitate those of the MS., in 1786. In an Appendix to this great undertaking, in 1799 (see below, 5), he added certain fragments of the New Testament in the Thebaico-Coptic dialect, together with a dissertation on the Coptic version of the New Testament. The date of the C.A. is generally assigned to the 5th cent., and, with the exception of the Codex Vaticanus and the Codex Sinaiticus, which are sometimes assigned to the 4th cent., is the oldest extant MS. of the New Testament. This being the case, it is of interest to quote from the *Beiträge* W.'s opinion on the date of the MS. of P.S., which was lent to this careful scholar by Dr. Askew and which he copied from the first word to the last :

" It [P.S.] is a very old MS. in 4to on parchment in Greek uncial characters, which are *not so round* as those in the Alexandrine MS. in London, and in the Claromontain MS. in Paris [Codex Regius Parisiensis, also an Alexandrine text]. The characters of the MS. [P.S.] are somewhat longer and more angular, so that I take them to be *older* than both the latter MSS., in which the letters eta, theta, omicron, rho and sigma are much rounder."

Thus W. would date the MS. towards the end of the 4th cent.

4. 1794.   Buhle (J. G.).   *Literarischer Briefwechsel von Johann David Michaelis* (Leipzig), 3 vols., 1794–96, iii. 69.

Under date 1773 there is a letter from Woide to Michaelis, in which the former says in reference to the P.S. Codex that Askew had picked it up by chance in a book-shop. There follows a description of the MS.

lii

5. 1799. Woide (C. G.). *Appendix ad Editionem Novi Testamenti Græci e Codice MS. Alexandrino . . . cum Dissertatione de Versione Bibliorum Ægyptiaca quibus subjictur Codicis Vaticani Collatio* (Oxford), p. 137.

W. gives the date of the P.S. Codex as about the 4th cent., and considers the writer of the Greek original to have been Valentinus.

6. 1812. Münter (F.). *Odæ Gnosticæ Salomoni Tributæ, Thebaice et Latine, Prefatione et Adnotationibus philologicis illustratæ* (Hafniæ).

Bishop Münter, a learned Dane, probably got his text from Woide's copy. His brief pamphlet is of no particular importance ; nevertheless it was solely upon these few selections, the five Odes of Solomon, that, with the exception of Dulaurier, scholars formed their opinion of the P.S. up to the time of the publication of Schwartze's translation in 1851. Münter believed that the original treatise belonged to the 2nd cent. For Odes of Solomon see below, 49, 53 and 60.

7. 1838. Dulaurier (É.). Art. in *Le Moniteur* (sept. 27).

8. 1843. Matter (J.). *Histoire Critique du Gnosticisme et de son Influence sur les Sectes religieuses et philosophiques des six premiers Siècles de l'Ère chrétienne* (Paris), 2nd ed., ii. 41 ff., 350 ff. The first edition appeared in 1828 and contains no reference to P.S. In Dörner's German translation the references are ii. 69 ff. and 163 ff.

M. rejects the authorship of Valentinus, though he bases himself otherwise entirely on Woide. He vaguely places the date of the original treatise between the end of the 2nd and the end of the 5th cent., but gives no opinion as to the school to which it belongs (p. 352).

9. 1847. Dulaurier (É.). Art. in the *Journal Asiatique*, 4ᵉ série, tom. ix., juin, pp. 534–548, ' *Notice sur le Manuscript copte-thébain, intitulé La Fidèle Sagesse ; et sur la Publication projetée du Texte et de la Traduction française de ce Manuscript.*'

D. had prepared a translation of the P.S. He writes : " The translation of the Pistis Sophia and the glossary which forms a complement to it are finished, and will be sent to the printers, when I have convinced myself that I have fulfilled the requirements that this task imposes, taking into consideration the present state of science and my own capabilities. The MS. from which 1 have made my translation is a copy which I have taken from the original, during my stay in England in 1838–1840, when I was charged by MM. de

Salvandy and Villemain, successive ministers of public
instruction, with the commission of proceeding to London to
study this curious monument " (p. 542). D., however, did
not publish his labours, nor have I as yet come across any
record of the fate of his MS. He ascribes the treatise to
Valentinus.

10. 1851. Schwartze (M. G.). *Pistis Sophia, Opus Gnosticum Valentino
            adjudicatum, e Codice Manuscripto Coptico Londinensi
            descriptum.* Latine vertit M. G. Schwartze, edidit
            J. H. Petermann (Berlin).

In 1848 Schwartze made a copy of the Codex in London,
but unfortunately died before the completion of his labours on
the P.S., and the MS. translation he left behind contained a
number of blanks and passages which he intended to fill up
and correct. His friend Petermann confined himself in his
notes strictly to verbal corrections and suggestions as to
variæ lectiones. The consequence is that we have a translation without the notes of the translator and without a word
of introduction. P. says the task of editing was so severe
that he frequently suffered from fits of giddiness. In spite
of numerous blemishes this first edition is said to be 'an
outstanding achievement.' S. considers the original treatise,
as we see from the title of his work, to have been written
by Valentinus ; but P. is of the opinion that it is the work of
an Ophite, and promises to set forth his reasons at length in a
treatise, which has unfortunately never seen the light. A
review of S.'s work appeared in the *Journal des Savants* of
1852 (p. 333).

11. 1852. Bunsen (C. C. J.). *Hippolytus und seine Zeit, Anfänge und
            Aussichten des Christenthums und der Menschheit* (Leipzig),
            i. 47, 48. *Hippolytus and his Age* (London, 1852), i. 61,
            62.

" Great, therefore, were my hopes in 1842, that the ancient
Coptic manuscript of the British Museum, inscribed Sophia,
might be a translation, or at least an extract, from that lost
text-book of Gnosticism [the work quoted by Hippolytus,
sub Valent.]: but unfortunately the accurate and trust-
worthy labours of that patient and conscientious Coptic
scholar, Dr. Schwartze, so early taken away from us, have
proved to me (for I have seen and perused his manuscript,
which I hope will soon appear), that this Coptic treatise is a
most worthless (I trust, purely Coptic) offshoot of the
Marcosian heresy, of the latest and stupidest mysticism about
letters, sounds and words."

B.'s Marcosian theory has been partially revived by Legge (below, 57), but is supported by no one else, and we doubt whether B. could have read Schwartze's MS. with any great care.

12. 1853. Baur (F. C.). *Das Christenthum und die christliche Kirche der drei ersten Jahrhunderte* (Tübingen), notes on pp. 185, 186, and 205, 206.

B. evidently added these notes at the last moment before publication. On page 206 he leans to the idea of an Ophite origin.

13. 1854. Köstlin (K. R.). Two arts. in Baur and Zeller's *Theologische Jahrbücher* (Tübingen), xiii. 1–104 and 137–196, '*Das gnostische System des Buches Pistis Sophia*.'

K. was the first to make an exhaustive analysis of the contents of the treatise, with the special object of setting forth the system of P.S., and his labours were used later by Lipsius in his art. in Smith and Wace's *Dictionary of Christian Biography* (below, 20). He assigns its date to the first half of the 3rd cent., and thinks that it is of Ophite origin. In a note to page 1, K. writes :

" The MS. from which the work is published belongs to the collection of MSS. collected by Dr. Askew of London during his travels in Italy and Greece, of which *The British Theological Magazine* (*Das Brittische theol. Magazin*) for the year 1770 (vol. i. part 4, p. 223) gives more particulars."

We know nothing of these travels, and there is no such magazine in the catalogue of the British Museum. *The Theological Repository* for 1770 contains no information on the subject ; and no permutation of names solves the mystery. There were very few magazines published at that early date, so that the choice is limited.

14. 1856. An Anonymous Translation in Migne's *Dictionnaire des Apocryphes*, tom. i. app. part. ii. coll. 1181–1286 ; this tome forms vol. xxiii. of his third *Encyclopédie Théologique*.

The translation is a sorry piece of work, more frequently a mere paraphrase from Schwartze's version than translation ; there are also frequent omissions, sometimes as many as 40 pages of Schwartze's text ; *e.g.* pp. 18, 19, 36 ff., 50, 51, 72, 73, 86–90, 108–135, 139, 157–160, 162, 171, 179, 180, 184–186, 221–243, 245–255, 281–320, 324–342. These are some of the omissions ; but there are many more. It is, therefore, entirely useless to the student. The anonymous

writer vaguely suggests a late date for the treatise because of
the complicated nature of the system.

15. 1860. Lipsius (R. A.).   Art. 'Gnosticismus,' in Ersch and Gruber's
                    Encyclopädie, separately published at Leipzig, 1860,
                    pp. 95 ff. and 157 ff.

L. considers P.S. an Egypto-Ophite treatise, and with
Köstlin assigns its date to the first half of the 3rd cent.
See his Art. in Dict. of Christ. Biog. (1887).

16. 1875-1883. The Palæographical Society, Facsimiles of MSS. and
                    Inscriptions, Oriental Series, ed. by William Wright
                    (London).

Plate xlii.   The editor says that the original is later than
Valentinus, and places the MS. in the 7th cent.   There is a
careful analysis of the text from the technical standpoint,
and the facsimile is of f. 11 a.

17. 1877. Jacobi (H.).   Art. 'Gnosis,' in Herzog's Theolog. Real Encyclo-
                    pädie (Leipzig), 2nd ed., 1888 ; Translation (New York),
                    1882, 1883.

J. believes in an Ophite origin.

18. 1887. King (C. W.).   The Gnostics and their Remains, Ancient and
                    Mediæval (London); 2nd ed. The first ed. appeared in
                    1864, but contains no reference to P.S.

K. regards the P.S. as the most precious relic of Gnosticism.
Besides many references scattered throughout the volume,
there are translations from Schwartze of pages 227-239,
242-244, 247-248, 255-259, 261-263, 282-292, 298-308,
341, 342, 358, 375.   K. does not venture an opinion on either
the date or author.

19. 1887. Amélineau (E.).   Essai sur le Gnosticisme égyptien, ses
                    Développements et son Origine égyptienne, in Annales du
                    Musée Guimet (Paris), xiv.
                    See the third part for system of Valentinus and of
                    P.S., pp. 166-322.

20. 1887. Lipsius (R. A.).   Art. 'Pistis Sophia,' in Smith and Wace's
                    Dict. of Christ. Biog. (London), iv. 405-415.

A still valuable study.   "We may regard ourselves as
justified in assigning (with Petermann and Köstlin) the book
Pistis Sophia to one of the large groups of Ophite sects,
though nevertheless the system it contains is not identical
with any one of the other Ophite systems known to us."   Of
importance is L.'s suggestion that P.S. may be indirectly
one of the sources of the Manichæan religion.   In any case,

ANNOTATED BIBLIOGRAPHY lvii

" it may be assumed as probable that the book Pistis Sophia was written before the time of the Manichæan system, and therefore before A.D. 270. Moreover, as the system contained in it is evidently more recent than the other Ophitic systems known to us, we shall have, with Köstlin, to assign its composition to the first half of the 3rd cent." (p. 414b).

21. 1888. Hyvernat (H.). *Album de Paléographie Copte* (Paris–Rome).

Pl. ii. is a reproduction of a page of our Codex, showing the work of the second scribe. H. dates it " about the end of the 6th cent.," but without a word of justification for this ascription.

22. 1889. Harnack (A.). Crit. of Amélineau's *Essai* (above, 19), in *Theolog. Literaturzeitung* (Leipzig), viii. 199–211.

23. 1890. Amélineau (E.). Art. ' *Les Traités gnostiques d'Oxford ; Étude critique,*' in the *Revue de l'Histoire des Religions* (Paris), xxi. no. 2. 178–260.

Practically the Introduction to his publication of the Text and Translation of the Bruce Codex (24, below). In it A. sets forth the results of "the researches and studies, the hypotheses and convictions of seven years " of labour (p. 4 offprint).

24. 1891. Amélineau (E.). *Notice sur le Papyrus gnostique Bruce, Texte et Traduction,* in *Notices et Extraits des Manuscripts de la Bibliothèque Nationale et Autres Bibliothèques* (Paris), xxix. pt. i. 65–305.

These views have been severely criticized, especially by Schmidt (below, 28 ; also 25–27).

24a. 1891. Harnack (A.). *Über das gnostische Buch Pistis-Sophia* (Leipzig). (*Texte u. Untersuch.* vii. 2.)

A study (144 pp.) of the first importance, in which this high authority on the history and chronology of early Christian literature and the history of the development of dogma submits the contents of the Latin version of Schwartze to a careful analysis, and gives 8/9 reasons for placing the P.S. in the second half of the 3rd cent. H. is mainly valuable in his analysis of the Biblical references in the P.S., especially the uses it makes of the N.T., and in his estimate of the stage of development of the general Christian and Catholic elements in P.S. H. thinks that Div. iii. should be called ' Questions of Mary ' (pp. 94, 108). Unknown to H., Renan (*Marc Aurèle,* p. 120) had already hazarded the suggestion that the whole P.S. might be identical with the *Little Questions*

of Mary, mentioned by Epiphanius. But R. shows (p. 145)
that he has no direct acquaintance with the subject. H.
assigns the P.S. to an ' Ophitic ' sect, but not the ' Ophites '
in the narrower meaning, for here, as elsewhere often in the
use of the name, no sign of the worship of the serpent is
found (p. 110). He brings the P.S. sect into close connection
with the Syrian Ophitic group, which had offshoots in Egypt,
and opens up those investigations into the statements of
Epiphanius which Schmidt has surveyed in greater detail in
his edition of the Codex Brucianus (below, 28). In fact these
two scholars have been in close touch with one another in
their work on the P.S. as to its origin, date and place. The
concluding remark of H. on the general religious status of
the P.S.—that is to say, its bearing on Early Christian and
Catholic religion, in other words its place within the general
history of Christianity—is noteworthy. He writes (p. 114) :
" In this respect the P.S. is a document of first rank, for we
possess no second work which brings before our eyes so
clearly the previous history of Catholic sacramentism.
What we meet with here more sharply brought out and at
one stroke among the Gnostics of the end of the third century, was accomplished by the Catholic Church toilsomely
and gradually in the following century. This Gnosticism is
not the father of Catholicism, but rather an elder brother
who gained by assault what the younger brother attained
subsequently amid a thousand exigencies."

25. 1891. Schmidt (C.). *Götting. Gelehrte Anzeigen* (Göttingen), Nr.
xvii. 640-675.

A very damaging review of Amélineau's edition of the
Bruce Codex (above, 23).

26. 1891. Amélineau (E.). Art. '*Le Papyrus Bruce : Réponse aux
Göttingische Gelehrte Anzeigen,*' in *Revue de l'Histoire des
Religions* (Paris), xxiv. no. 3. 376-380.

A.'s reply to Schmidt's criticisms.

27. 1892. Schmidt (C.). *Götting. Gelehrte Anzeigen* (Göttingen), Nr. 6.
201-202.

S.'s further rejoinder to A.

28. 1892. Schmidt (C.). *Gnostische Schriften in koptischer Sprache aus
dem Codex Brucianus* (Leipzig), 692 pp. (*T. u. U.* viii.)

S.'s masterly edition entirely supersedes that of Amélineau,
who worked on Woide's copy of the confused heap of leaves
preserved in the Bodleian. His minute examination of the

original discovered that the chaos could first of all be sorted out into two totally different MSS. The larger work is entitled *The Book of the Great Logos according to the Mystery*. The contents fall naturally into two divisions, which S. calls respectively ' The First ' and ' The Second Book of Jeû.' The system is closely related to that of the P.S. miscellany. S. devotes pp. 334–538 to a penetrating study of this relationship, in which he makes a most valuable contribution to the analysis of the contents of the P.S. His labours here are practically an Introduction to his subsequent translation of the P.S. in 1905 (below, 45). Among much else of the greatest value he gives us a minutely detailed investigation of the system of the P.S., which supersedes Köstlin's painstaking pioneer effort (1854). S. is rightly of opinion that P.S. is a more or less happy compilation from other works (p. 318), as Köstlin had already pointed out (p. 344). He seems to think little of the possible objection that, whereas the ' Two Books of Yew,' mentioned twice in the P.S., are said to have been dictated to Enoch by Jesus before the Flood and hidden away, the contents of the first document of the C.B. are revealed by Jesus himself to the disciples (p. 343). The statement in the P.S. is in keeping with common apocalyptic claims, and in any case the sect as a matter of fact did possess two Yew Books, and the contents of C.B. I. are what we should expect from the references in the P.S., while the intimate relationship between P.S. Div. iv. and C.B. I.b is patent to the most casual reader. He agrees with Harnack as to the date of the P.S.—namely, the latter half of the 3rd cent. for Divv. i.-iii., and a few decades earlier for Div. iv. C.B. I. is thus to be placed in the first half of the 3rd cent. (pp. 540, 598). C.B. II. is a work without a title, the contents of which have roused S. to enthusiasm (pp. 34, 35). It is plainly of an earlier date, and so S. here conjectures for it about 160-200 A.D. (p. 542) ; but he has subsequently changed his view as to date (see 47, below).

After a close methodical investigation, in which in particular he submits the statements of Epiphanius to a searching criticism, S. thinks that everything points to the Severians as being most probably the sect to which the writings contained in P.S. and C.B. I. can be attributed (p. 596). C.B. II., he concludes, may be assigned to Sethian-Archontics (p. 659). But the whole question bristles with difficulties when precise names are in question. It is to be noted that in his researches

S. lays under contribution as very pertinent to the inquiry his prior labours on the puzzling problem of the Gnostics of Plotinus, in his treatise *Plotin's Stellung zum Gnosticismus und kirchlichen Christentum* (Leipzig), 1900, 168 pp. (*T. u. U. N.F.* v. 4.). There is much criticism of Amélineau's work and views scattered throughout this C.B. volume.

29. 1892. Schmidt (C.). *De Codice Bruciano seu de Libris gnosticis qui in Lingua coptica extant Commentatio* (Leipzig), Pars i., 30 pp.

No other part has been published, and there is nothing in it, as far as I am aware, which has not appeared in C.'s larger works.

30. 1893. Crum (W. E.). *Coptic Manuscripts brought from the Fayyum by W. M. Flinders Petrie* (London).

C. seems almost to allow that the copy of P.S. might have been made in the 4th cent. (p. 24).

31. 1893. Legge (G. F.). Art. 'Some Heretic Gospels' in *The Scottish Review* (London), xxii. 133–162.

Pp. 134–157 are devoted to P.S., the rest to the documents of the Bruce Codex. L.'s *Forerunners* (1915) gives his maturer views (see below, 57).

32. 1893. Harnack (A.). *Geschichte der altchristlichen Literatur bis Eusebius* (Leipzig), I. i. 171 f.

A summary description of the contents of the P.S. and Cod. Bruc. from his important study, *Über d. gnost. Buch P.S.* (above, 24a), based on Schwartze's Latin version.

33. 1894. Preuschen (E.). Rev. of Schmidt's *Gnostische Schriften in k. S. aus d. Cod. Bruc.* (1892), in *Theolog. Literatur-zeitung* (Leipzig), Nr. vii. 183–187.

P.'s main criticism is that S.'s identification of the two parts of the first treatise of the Bruce Codex with 'The Books of Yew' mentioned in P.S. is mistaken.

34. 1894. Schmidt (C.). '*Die in dem koptisch-gnostischen Codex Brucianus enthaltenen "Beide Bücher Jeû" in ihrem Verhältnis zu der Pistis Sophia*,' in *Zeitschr. f. wissen-schaft. Theolog.* (Leipzig), xxxvii. 555–585.

S.'s reply to P.'s criticism.

35. 1895. Amélineau (E.) *Pistis-Sophia, Ouvrage gnostique de Valentin, traduit du copte en français, avec une Introduction* (Paris), xxxii + 204 pp.

A. advocates strongly the Valentinian origin of the treatise,

and leans almost exclusively to an Egyptian origin of the
ideas. These views have been severely criticized, especially
by Schmidt. The MS. itself, however, A. places very late,
writing on page xi of his Introduction as follows :—" After
an examination of the enormous faults which the scribe has
committed, 1 cannot attribute to the MS. which has preserved
the Pistis-Sophia to us, a date later than the ninth or tenth
century, and that too the minimum. For this I have several
reasons. Firstly, the MS. is written on parchment, and
parchment was hardly ever commonly used in Egypt before
the sixth or seventh century. Secondly, the writing, which
is uncial, though passable in the first pages of the MS.,
becomes bastard in a large number of leaves, when the
scribe's hand is fatigued ; no longer is it the beautiful
writing of the Egyptian scribes of the great periods, but
slack, inconsistent, almost round and hurried. Thirdly, the
faults of orthography in the use of Greek words evidently
show that the scribe belonged to a period when Greek was
almost no longer known."

In a footnote Amélineau says that he is perfectly aware
that this opinion of his will ' raise a tempest,' and begs for a
suspension of judgment till he has published his reasons,
especially as to the late use of parchment, at greater length.
The storm broke, and no one has accepted A.'s arguments.
Among other things he failed to notice that in the first place
the Askew Codex is the work of two scribes, and not of one,
and that the various portions of their common task can be
unquestionably assigned to each. The parchment argument
has never seen the light, as far as I am aware.

36. 1896. Mead (G. R. S.). *Pistis Sophia : A Gnostic Gospel* (*with
Extracts from the Books of the Saviour appended*), originally translated from Greek into Coptic and now for the
first time Englished from Schwartze's Latin Version of the
only known Coptic MS. and checked by Amélineau's
French Version (London).

The first edition of the present work.

37. 1898. Schmidt (C.). *Götting. Gelehrte Anzeigen* (Göttingen), Nr. vi.
436–444.

A severely critical review of Amélineau's Introduction to
his Translation of P.S. (above, 35).

38. 1899. Crum (W. E.). *Egyptian Exploration Fund, Archæological
Reports*, 1897/1898 (London), p. 62.

Description of MS. of P.S., which is, however, improved
upon below (46).

39. 1900. Mead (G. R. S.). *Fragments of a Faith Forgotten : Some Short Sketches among the Gnostics* (London), 1st ed. (2nd ed. 1906), 'The Gnosis according to its Friends.' pp. 451–602.

'The Askew and Bruce Codices' (pp. 453–458) ; 'Summary of the Contents of the So-called Pistis Sophia Treatise' (pp. 459–506) ; 'Summary of the Extracts from the Books of the Saviour' (pp. 507–517) ; 'Selections from the Untitled Apocalypse of the Codex Brucianus' (pp. 547–566) ; 'Notes on the Contents of the Bruce and Askew Codices' (pp. 567–578) ; 'The Akhmîm Codex' [now called the Berlin Codex] (pp. 579–592).

40. 1901. Rahlfs (A.). *Die Berliner Handschrift des sahidischen Psalters* (Berlin). *Abhandl. d. königl. Gesellschaft d. Wissenschaft zu Göttingen. Philol. hist. Kl. N.F.* Bd. iv. Nr. 4.

On p. 7 R. calls attention to a remarkable difference in the versions of the Psalms quoted in the P.S. While the citations in pp. 53–82 and 111–181 (Schw.-Pet. ed.) vary relatively only slightly from the usual Sahidic version, those in pp. 86–110 are so totally different that they must be an independent translation from the Greek. If this is so, we are confronted by the high probability that Repentances 8–13 are a later addition, and that there were thus originally only 7 Repentances. If this hypothesis stands, it is of great importance for the internal analysis of the literature. R.'s view is criticized by Rendel Harris (below, 60).

41. 1901. Liechtenhan (R.). '*Untersuchungen zur koptisch-gnostischen Literatur*,' in *Zeitschr. f. wissenschaft. Theologie*, Bd. xliv. H. ii. 236–253.

In his analysis of the composition of the P.S., L. introduces a novelty. He thinks that pp. 128 (ch. 64)–175 (end of ch. 80), subsequent to the thirteen Repentances, are a later insertion in the Sophia-episode, and regards the opening lines of ch. 81 ("It came to pass after all this") as a redactor's connecting paragraph.

With regard to the appropriateness of the suggested title, 'The Questions of Mary,' for Div. iii., and of 'The Gospel of Philip' (P.S. ch. 42) as a possible title for Divv. i. and ii.,—he tries to get over the difficulty that those two titles are mentioned by Epiphanius among the books of a group of sects to which the Church Father ascribes the most filthy, blasphemous and obscene rites, in the following conjecture (p. 242) :—" A Gnostic sect in Egypt possessed a rich, apocalyptic literature, among which was to be found a *Gospel of Philip* and *Questions of Mary*. This sect was divided into an ascetic and a libertinist branch, and each group worked over the sacred literature which had come down to them." Epiphanius (*Hær.* xxvi.) got hold of the libertinist redaction ; the ascetic is preserved for us in P.S., Divv. i.–iii.   Div. iv. is an earlier stratum.   ' The Books of Yew ' mentioned in P.S. are said to have been revealed to Enoch ; accordingly, like Preuschen, he thinks that these cannot be the treatise of the Bruce Codex to which Schmidt has assigned this title, for the latter is revealed to the Disciples (p. 251).

42. 1904.   Harnack (A.).   *Die Chronologie der altchristlichen Literatur* (Leipzig), II. ii. 193–195, ' *Die Pistis Sophia und die in Papyrus Brucianus Sæc. V. vel. VI. enthaltenen gnostischen Schriften.*'

H. repeats, from his detailed study (above, 24a), his reasons for assigning the contents of P.S. Divv. i.–iii. to the latter half of 3rd cent.   He says that Liechtenhan's final opinion (above, 41) on ' The Questions of Mary ' problem is not far from his own view.   Why H. assigns the treatises of the Bruce Codex to the 5th or 6th cent. (!) is not set forth.

43. 1904.   Liechtenhan (R.).   Art. ' *Ophiten*,' in *Schaff-Herzog's Real-encycl. f. protest. Theologie*, 3rd ed., vol. xiv.

L. (p. 405) includes the P.S. among a score of sects which he brings together under this too general heading of ' Ophites.' (A shortened form of the above appears in *The New Schaff-Herzog Encyclopædia of Religious Knowledge* (New York), 1910, vol. viii.)

44. 1904.   Granger (F.).   Art. 'The Poemandres of Hermes Trismegistus,' in *The Journal of Theological Studies* (London), v. 395–412.

G. (p. 401) questions whether the P.S. is a translation from the Greek ; but the only reason he advances is the hazardous statement that : " The Egyptian Gnostic writings of the third century exhibit the same qualities of style as the Coptic biographies and apocalypses of the fourth and following centuries."

45. 1905.   Schmidt (C.).   *Koptisch-gnostische Schriften.*   Bd. I. *Die Pistis Sophia.   Die beiden Bücher des Jeû.   Unbekanntes altgnostisches Werk* (Leipzig), xxvii + 410 pp.

Bd. II. is to contain the three unpublished works of the Berlin Codex entitled : (1) *The Gospel of Mary* ; (2) *The Apocryphon of John* ; (3) *The Wisdom of Jesus Christ.* (See my *Fragments of a Faith Forgotten*, 2nd ed., London, 1906, pp. 579–592, for a summary of Schmidt's notice of the Codex, published in *Sitzungsber. der Königl. Preuss. Akademie d. Wissensch.*, Berlin, 1896 pp. 839 ff., entitled '*Ein vorirenaeisches gnostisches Original-werk in koptischer Sprache.*') This long-expected second volume has not yet seen the light. The contents are of great value, for *The Apocryphon of John*, in its original Greek form, lay before Irenæus, and in an appendix to Schmidt's notice Harnack ventures the query : Can *The Wisdom (Sophia) of Jesus Christ* possibly be the lost famous writing of Valentinus so entitled ?

In the Introduction (pp. ix–xviii) S. sums up the results of his prior studies. The Translation of the P.S. occupies pp. 1–254, and is deserving of the highest praise.

46. 1905. Crum (W. E.). *Catalogue of the Coptic MSS. in the British Museum* (London), p. 173.

The B.M. official description of the Askew Codex.

47. 1907. Schmidt (C.). Art. '*Irenäus und seine Quelle in Adv. Hær. I. 29,*' in *Philotesia. Paul Kleinert zum LXX. Geburtstag dargebracht von Adolf Harnack, u.s.w.*, pp. 317–336.

This is a very important study, in which S. again treats of *The Apocryphon of John* in the unpublished Coptic Gnostic Berlin Codex, on which he had already specially dwelt in reporting for the first time the contents of the Codex to the Prussian Academy in 1896. The Greek original is early, and a copy of it lay before Irenæus. We are thus in a position to estimate the nature of the Church Father's method of quotation and summarizing, and it is clearly proved to be unreliable. S. definitely assigns this special document to a Sethian circle in Egypt, and brings its æon-lore into close touch with Valentinian ideas. He says nothing, unfortunately, of how this document and the other two of the Codex—namely, *The Gospel of Mary* and *The Wisdom of Jesus Christ*—bear on the line of descent of the doctrines of the P.S. Doubtless he is reserving his treatment of the subject for his long-expected edition of the whole Berlin Codex, which for the first time will give us first-hand knowledge of second-century Gnosticism, and, judging by what little S. has already disclosed to us, throw a brilliant light on some of the most puzzling obscurities in the history of the development of Gnostic doctrine.

48. 1907. Bousset (W.). *Hauptprobleme der Gnosis* (Göttingen), 398 pp.

This is a study of the greatest value from the comparative

standpoint. Though Lipsius (above, 20) had already drawn
attention to the point, B. goes further by showing in
detail the close connection between some main notions of the
Manichæan religion and some features of the P.S., whereas
Schmidt (1892, pp. 375, 404, 417, 564) had previously drawn
attention to isolated parallels only. In dealing with the
system of the P.S. (pp. 346–350) B. writes : " There can be
no doubt at all on the affinity between the two systems.
The only possible question which remains is whether in the
P.S. and II. Jeû direct dependence on the Manichæan system
comes up for discussion, or whether a common source under-
lies both systems. The latter appears to me provisionally
to be the more probable hypothesis. Many of the kindred
ideas appear in the P.S. in their more original and purer
form, the figure of the Virgin of Light has in the P.S. meaning
and great importance, whereas in the Manichæan system she
is a shadowy form by the side of the Third Envoy. If the
latter supposition proves correct, Mani would have far less
right of claim to originality for his system than has hitherto
seemed to be the case."

49. 1909. Rendel Harris (J.).   *The Odes and Psalms of Solomon, now
            first published from the Syriac Version* (Cambridge).
            The *editio princeps* of the now recovered 42 Odes ;
            previously only the five in the P.S. were known.

R. H. devotes pp. 16–35 to treating of the use of the Odes
in the P.S. On p. 35 he writes : " The *Pistis Sophia*, in
which the Odes are imbedded, dates from the third century,
and the author of the *Pistis* had, as we have shown, the
Odes bound up with his Canonical Psalter ; at the time
intimated there was no Coptic [Thebaic] Bible from which
the extracts could have been made ; so we may be sure the
Odes were taken from a Greek Bible, and, with almost equal
certainty, that the *Pistis Sophia* itself was a Greek book."
For R. H.'s change of opinion see below, 60.

50. 1909. Arendzen (J. P.).   Art. ' Gnosticism,' in *The Catholic
            Encyclopædia* (New York), vol. vi.

P. S. is summarily and inadequately dealt with on p. 600.

51. 1910. Bousset (W.).   Art. ' Gnosticism,' in *Encyclopædia Britannica*
            (London), 11th ed.

B., following the prevailing German view, assigns P.S. to
the 2nd half of 3rd cent. ; he, however, thinks that both
treatises of the Bruce Codex are later than P.S., but does
not argue this important question.

52. 1912. Bousset (W.).   Arts. 'Gnosis' and 'Gnostiker,' in Paulys
            Real-Encyklopädie der classischen Altertumswissenschaft
            (ed. Wissowa-Kroll, Berlin).

B. here, in § 10, treats of the P.S. and the C.B. as belonging to the period when Gnosticism had got out of hand or
was running wild (' Die Verwilderung der Gnosis '). He does
not, however, repeat his view of the later date of C.B., and
says that the eschatology of the P.S. is strongly reminiscent
of Valentinian speculations.

53. 1912. Worrell (W. H.).   Art. 'The Odes of Solomon and the Pistis
            Sophia,' in The Journal of Theological Studies (London),
            xiii. 29–46.

An interesting study. Gives translations of the five Odes
from the Coptic and Syriac and seems to blame R. Harris
for using Schwartze's Latin version instead of Schmidt's
more modern rendering in his quotations from the P.S.

54. 1913. Scott (E. F.).   Art. 'Gnosticism,' in Hastings' Encycl. of
            Relig. and Ethics (Edinburgh), vi. 231–242.

" There can be little doubt that the Coptic writings (Pistis
Sophia, etc.) present a variety of the Barbelo-Gnosis "
(p. 239a). P.S. was written in Egypt at close of 3rd cent.
(p. 241b). This is by no means certain; we must wait for
Schmidt's full translation and commentary on The Apocryphon of John before any definite conclusion can be reached.

55. 1913. De Faye (E.).   Gnostiques et Gnosticisme : Étude critique des
            Documents du Gnosticisme chrétien aux IIᵉ et IIIᵉ Siècles
            (Paris).   Pt. iii. ' Écrits gnostiques en Langue copte,'
            pp. 247–311.

D. F. agrees with Harnack and Schmidt as to the most
probable date being the 2nd half of the 3rd cent. (p. 254).
He thinks that Div. iii. is the lost Little Questions of Mary,
favouring Harnack against Schmidt, whom he blames (p. 266)
for abandoning this view in the Introduction (p. xviii) to
his Translation (above, 45), after first adopting it in his
earlier work. He thinks that Schmidt has made out his
case for the two Jeû Books against the reservations of
Preuschen and Liechtenhan (p. 291). D. F. is strongly
opposed to the hypothesis of a Valentinian origin (p. 251);
he is also very critical of the general Ophite theory (p. 327) and
of the special Severian theory of Schmidt (p. 355). He has
no precise view of his own as to origin ; but, in keeping with
his general thesis, which would make most, if not all, of the
anonymous and pseudonymous systems later and degenerate

forms of the more metaphysical views of a Basilides, a Valentinus and a Marcion, he is content to leave the P.S. to a later period of degeneration. His general metaphysical test can hardly be said to be a criterion for history. Metaphysic does not come first ; philosophizing is a secondary stage, and this is certainly the case in the general development of the Gnosis which starts in a strongly mythological and apocalyptic circle of ideas.

56. 1913. Scott-Moncrieff (P. D.).   *Paganism and Christianity in Egypt* (Cambridge), pp. 148–182, ch. vii., 'Some Aspects of Gnosticism : Pistis Sophia.'

After a review of contents and literature, with regard to place of origin the author writes (p. 175): " But if of Syrian origin the scheme betrays here and there marked signs of Egyptian influence, and the fact that the work was sufficiently important to be translated into the native tongue shows without doubt that the sect which inspired it was an Egyptian branch who dwelt in Egypt." This is of course generally evident. S.-M. thinks, however, that the question of translation may be pressed too much. Without attempting any justification of his opinion, he asserts that " the Coptic text is at the earliest a fifth-century work when Gnosticism was fast dying out and could only be practised furtively." Surely the author is here confusing the probable date of the Askew Codex copy with the question of date of the original ?

57. 1915. Legge (G. F.).   *Forerunners and Rivals of Christianity ; Being Studies in Religious History from 330 B.C. to 330 A.D.* (Cambridge), 2 vols., ii. 134–202, ch. x., ' The System of the Pistis Sophia and its Related Texts.'

Divv. i. and ii. presuppose belief in a system resembling those of the Ophites and of Valentinus (p. 135). Divv. iii. and iv. are probably Marcosian in origin (p. 173), in any case later (!) than Divv. i. and ii. (p. 184). In this L. partially revives Bunsen's rejected theory (above, 11). He accepts translation from a Greek original, and continues (p. 177) : " We must . . . look for an author who, though an Egyptian and acquainted with the native Egyptian religion, would naturally have written in Greek ; and on the whole there is no one who fulfils these requirements so well as Valentinus himself. The fact that the author never quotes from the Gospel according to St. John indicates that it had not come to his knowledge." L.'s criticism (pp. 161 f.) of Harnack's parallels from this Gospel (above, 24a), however, does not seem to me satisfactory. The first commentary on the Fourth Gospel was made by a Valentinian. L.'s view of authorship of the P.S. revives the Valentinian hypothesis in its most radical form. The two books of the Bruce Codex, which Schmidt calls ' The Books of Jeû,' are not the books referred to in the P.S. " which therefore remains the parent document " (p. 194).

58. 1918. Moffat (J.). Art. ' Pistis Sophia,' in Hastings' *Encycl. of Relig. and Ethics* (Edinburgh), x. 45–48.

This is a useful, if brief, summary of contents and prior opinions. M. takes up a moderate position when he says that, though the P.S. is to be assigned to some Gnostic circles in Egypt, its particular type of Gnosticism cannot be identified. He thinks, however, on the whole that the occurrence of the name Barbelo assigns our miscellany " to some circle more or less allied to the pious theosophists of the 2nd cent. whom we know as the Ophites collectively, and as the Nicolaitans, Simonians and Barbelo-Gnostics specifically." H. thinks the Yew Books mentioned in the P.S. can hardly be the books of C.B. I.

59. 1919. Schmidt (C.). *Gespräche Jesu mit seinen Jüngern nach der Auferstehung. Ein katholisch-apostolisches Sendschreiben des 2. Jahrhunderts nach einem koptischen Papyrus des Institut de la Mission Archéolog. Française au Caire, unter Mitarbeit von Herrn Pierre Lacau . . . General Director d. Ägpt. Mus. Übersetzung des äthiopischen Texts von Dr Isaak Wajnberg* (Leipzig). (*T. u. U.* Bd. xliii.)

The external form of this interesting and important document is an Epistle, resembling that of the Catholic Epistles of the N.T. But within, it passes into the form of an apocalypse, and that too of Discourses between Jesus and his Disciples after the Resurrection. This latter characteristic is otherwise not found in Catholic documents ; it is a Gnostic peculiarity, of which the P.S. is a classical example, the other instances being what Schmidt calls the ' Two Books of Jeû ' of the Bruce Codex and of *The Gospel of Mary* and of *The Wisdom of Jesus Christ* of the Berlin Codex. *The Questions of Mary, The Great* and *The Little*, of Epiphanius' ' Gnostici ' were also of this post-resurrectional type of discourses (p. 206).

S. does not re-discuss the question of date of the P.S. by the light of this new find, but it is clearly of importance, seeing that with regard to the new document he concludes

(p. 402) : " The Epistola Apostolorum is written by a repre-
sentative of the Catholic Church with the intention of
attacking the Gnostic heresies, especially Docetism.   The
country of origin is Asia Minor, and the date is the second
half of the second century, more precisely 160–170 A.D."

60. 1920.   Rendel Harris (J.) and Mingana (A.).   *The Odes and Psalms
of Solomon*, re-edited for the Governors of the John
Rylands Library (Manchester), 2 vols.   Text, 1912 ; Tr.
and Notes, 1920.

Here R. H. entirely changes his view of P.S. being a
translation from the Greek.   He now thinks that (p. 117) :
" Unless . . . the P.S. has substituted the Sahidic [Bible]
version for some other version which lay before the author,
of which he has avoided the trouble of making a fresh translation, there is a strong presumption that the P.S. is a
genuine Coptic book, and not a rendering of some other work
(Greek or Syriac) into Coptic."   He rejects (p. 183) Worrell's
theory (above, 53) of a Gnostic Hymn- and Psalm-book, and
criticizes (pp. 186 f.) Rahlfs' discovery of two versions of the
Psalms (above, 40).   He is accordingly opposed to the general
view of translation from the Greek, and suggests (p. 186)
that the matter needs some further elucidation.   It cannot,
however, be said that his argument is in any way convincing.

As to the Odes of Solomon themselves, which have produced so large and instructive a literature since the first
edition was published, their lucky discoverer and able
editor, in reviewing the whole question, thinks we cannot
go far wrong if we conclude that they were written at
Antioch in the 1st century (p. 69).

[THE FIRST BOOK OF]
PISTIS SOPHIA

It came to pass, when Jesus had risen from the
dead, that he passed eleven years discoursing 1.
with his disciples, and instructing them only up
to the regions of the First Commandment and
up to the regions of the First Mystery, that within
the Veil, within the First Commandment, which
is the four-and-twentieth mystery without and
below—those [four-and-twenty] which are in the
second space of the First Mystery which is before
all mysteries,—the Father in the form of a dove.

And Jesus said to his disciples : " I am come
forth out of that First Mystery, which is the last
mystery, that is the four-and-twentieth mystery."
And his disciples have not known nor understood
that anything existeth within that mystery ; but
they thought of that mystery, that it is the
head of the universe and the head of all existence ;
and they thought it is the completion of all com-
pletions, because Jesus had said to them concerning that mystery, that it surroundeth the First
Commandment and the five Impressions and
the great Light | and the five Helpers and the 2.
whole Treasury of the Light.

And moreover Jesus had not told his disciples

1

The regions
of the great
Invisible.
the total expansion of all the regions of the great Invisible and of the three triple-powers and of the four-and-twenty invisibles, and all their regions and their æons and their orders, how they are extended—those which are the emanations of the great Invisible—and their ungenerated and their self-generated and their generated and their light-givers and their unpaired and their rulers and their authorities and their lords and their archangels and their angels and their decans and their servitors and all the houses of their spheres and all the orders of every one of them.

The Trea-
sury of the
Light.
And Jesus had not told his disciples the total expansion of the emanations of the Treasury, nor their orders, how they are extended ; nor had he told them their saviours, according to the order of every one, how they are ; nor had he told them what guard is at every [gate] of the Treasury of the Light ; nor had he told them the region of
3.
the Twin-saviour, who | is the Child of the Child ; nor had he told them the regions of the three Amēns, in what regions they are expanded ; nor had he told them into what region the five Trees are expanded ; nor as to the seven Amēns, that is the seven Voices, what is their region, how they are expanded.

The Light-
world.
And Jesus had not told his disciples of what type are the five Helpers, nor into what region they are brought ; nor had he told them how the great Light hath expanded itself, nor into what region it hath been brought ; nor had he told them of the five Impressions, nor as to the First Commandment, into what region they have been brought.   But he had discoursed with them generally, teaching that they exist, but he had not told

them their expansion and the order of their regions, how they are. For this cause they have not known that there were also other regions within that mystery.

And he had not told his disciples : " I have gone forth out of such and such regions until I entered into that mystery, and until I went forth out of it " ; but, in teaching them, he said to them : " I am come forth from that mystery." For this cause then they thought of that mystery, that it is the completion | of completions, and that it is 4. the head of the universe and that it is the total Fulness. For Jesus had said to his disciples : " That mystery surroundeth that universe of which I have spoken unto you from the day when I met with you even unto this day." For this cause then the disciples thought there is nothing within that mystery.

It came to pass then, when the disciples were CHAP. 2. sitting together on the Mount of Olives, speaking Jesus and of these words and rejoicing in great joy, and are seated on the exulting exceedingly and saying one to another : Mount of " Blessed are we before all men who are on the Olives. earth, because the Saviour hath revealed this unto us, and we have received the Fulness and the total completion,"—they said this to one another, while Jesus sat a little removed from them.

And it came to pass then, on the fifteenth day A great of the moon in the month Tybi, which is the day descendeth on which the moon is full, on that day then, when on Jesus. the sun had come forth in his going, that there came forth behind him a great light-power shining most exceedingly, and there was no measure to the light conjoined with it. For it came out of the Light of lights, and it came out of the

last mystery, which is the four-and-twentieth |
mystery, from within without,—those which are
in the orders of the second space of the First
Mystery. And that light-power came down over
Jesus and surrounded him entirely, while he was
seated removed from his disciples, and he had
shone most exceedingly, and there was no measure
for the light which was on him.

And the disciples had not seen Jesus because of
the great light in which he was, or which was about
him ; for their eyes were darkened because of the
great light in which he was. But they saw only
the light, which shot forth many light-rays. And
the light-rays were not like one another, but the
light was of divers kind, and it was of divers type,
from below upwards, one [ray] more excellent
than the other, . . . , in one great immeasurable
glory of light ; it stretched from under the earth
right up to heaven.—And when the disciples saw
that light, they fell into great fear and great
agitation. |

It came to pass then, when that light-power
had come down over Jesus, that it gradually surrounded him entirely. Then Jesus ascended or
soared into the height, shining most exceedingly in
an immeasurable light. And the disciples gazed
after him and none of them spake, until he had
reached unto heaven ; but they all kept in deep
silence. This then came to pass on the fifteenth
day of the moon, on the day on which it is full in
the month Tybi.

It came to pass then, when Jesus had reached
the heaven, after three hours, that all the powers
of the heaven fell into agitation, and all were set in
motion one against the other, they and all their

æons and all their regions and all their orders, and
the whole earth was agitated and all they who
dwell thereon. And all men who are in the world
fell into agitation, and also the disciples, and
all thought: Peradventure the world will be
rolled up.

And all the powers in the heavens ceased not
from their agitation, they and the whole world,
and all were moved one against the other, from
the third hour of the fifteenth day of the moon of
Tybi until the ninth hour of the morrow. And
all the angels and their archangels and all the
powers of the heïght, all sang praises to the inter-
iors of the | interiors, so that the whole world 7.
heard their voices, without their ceasing till the
ninth hour of the morrow.

But the disciples sat together in fear and were CHAP. 4.
in exceedingly great agitation and were afraid
because of the great earthquake which took place,
and they wept together, saying. "What will
then be? Peradventure the Saviour will destroy
all regions?" Thus saying, they wept together.

While they then said this and wept together, Jesus de-
then, on the ninth hour of the morrow, the heavens scendeth
again.
opened, and they saw Jesus descend, shining
most exceedingly, and there was no measure for
his light in which he was. For he shone more
[radiantly] than at the hour when he had ascended
to the heavens, so that men in the world cannot
describe the light which was on him; and it shot
forth light-rays in great abundance, and there was
no measure for its rays, and its light was not alike
together, but it was of divers kind and of divers
type, some [rays] being more excellent than
others . . .; and the whole light consisted to-

gether. It was of threefold kind, and the one
[kind] was more excellent than the other. . . .
The second, that in the midst, was more excellent
than the first which was below, and the third,
which was above them all, was more excellent than
the two which were below. And the first glory,
which was placed below them all, was like to the
light which had come over Jesus before he had
ascended | into the heavens, and was like only
itself in its light. And the three light-modes
were of divers light-kinds, and they were of
divers type, one being more excellent than the
other. . . .

And it came to pass then, when the disciples
saw this, that they feared exceedingly, and were
in agitation. Then Jesus, the compassionate and
tender-hearted, when he saw his disciples, that
they were in great agitation, spake with them,
saying : " Take courage. It is I, be not afraid."

It came to pass then, when the disciples had
heard this word, that they said : " Lord, if it
be thou, withdraw thy light-glory into thyself
that we may be able to stand ; otherwise our eyes
are darkened, and we are agitated, and the whole
world also is in agitation because of the great
light which is about thee."

Then Jesus drew to himself the glory of his
light ; and when this was done, all the disciples
took courage, stepped forward to Jesus, fell down
all together, adored him, rejoicing in great joy,
and said unto him : " Rabbi, whither hast thou
gone, or what was thy ministry on which thou hast
gone, or wherefor rather were all these confusions
and all the earth-quakings which have taken
place ? "

Then Jesus, the compassionate, said unto them : He pro-
miseth to
tell them
all things.
" Rejoice and exult from this hour on, for I have
gone to the regions out of which I had come forth.
From this day on then will I discourse with you
in openness, | from the beginning of the Truth 9.
unto its completion ; and I will discourse with
you face to face without similitude. From this
hour on will I not hide anything from you of the
[mystery] of the height and of that of the region
of Truth. For authority hath been given me
through the Ineffable and through the First
Mystery of all mysteries to speak with you,
from the Beginning right up to the Fulness, both
from within without and from without within.
Hearken, therefore, that I may tell you all things.

" It came to pass, when I sat a little removed
from you on the Mount of Olives, that I thought
on the order of the ministry for the sake of which
I was sent, that it was completed, and that the
last mystery, that is the four-and-twentieth
mystery from within without,—those which are
in the second space of the First Mystery, in the
orders of that space,—had not yet sent me my
Vesture. It came to pass then, when I had known
that the order of the ministry for the sake of
which I had come, was completed, and that that
mystery had not yet sent me my Vesture, which
I had left behind in it, until its time was completed,—thinking then this, I sat on the Mount
of Olives a little removed from you.

" It came to pass, when the sun rose in the east, CHAP. 7.
thereafter then through the First Mystery, which
existed from the beginning, on account of which
the universe hath arisen, out of which also I am 10.
myself now come, not in the time before my

crucifixion, but now,—it came to pass, through the command of that mystery, that there should

How the Vesture of Light was sent unto him.

be sent me my Light-vesture, which it had given me from the beginning, and which I had left behind in the last mystery, that is the four-and-twentieth mystery from within without,—those which are in the orders of the second space of the First Mystery. That Vesture then I left behind in the last mystery, until the time should be completed to put it on, and I should begin to discourse with the race of men and reveal unto them all from the beginning of the Truth to its completion, and discourse with them from the interiors of the interiors to the exteriors of the exteriors and from the exteriors of the exteriors to the interiors of the interiors. Rejoice then and exult and rejoice more and more greatly, for to you it is given that I speak first with you from the beginning of the Truth to its completion.

Of the souls of the disciples and their incarnation. 11.

" For this cause have I chosen you verily from the beginning through the First Mystery. Rejoice then and exult, for when I set out for the world, | I brought from the beginning with me twelve powers, as I have told you from the beginning, which I have taken from the twelve saviours of the Treasury of the Light, according to the command of the First Mystery. These then I cast into the womb of your mothers, when I came into the world, that is those which are in your bodies today. For these powers have been given unto you before the whole world, because ye are they who will save the whole world, and that ye may be able to endure the threat of the rulers of the world and the pains of the world and its dangers and all its persecutions, which the rulers of the height will

bring upon you. For many times have I said
unto you that I have brought the power in you
out of the twelve saviours who are in the Treasury
of the Light. For which cause I have said unto
you indeed from the beginning that ye are not
of the world. I also am not of it. For all
men who are in the world have gotten their souls
out of [the power of] the rulers of the æons. But
the power which is in you is from me ; your souls
belong to the height. I have brought twelve
powers of the twelve saviours of the Treasury
of the Light, taking them out of the portion of
my power which | I did first receive. And 12.
when I had set forth for the world, I came into
the midst of the rulers of the sphere and had the
form of Gabriēl the angel of the æons ; and the
rulers of the æons did not know me, but they
thought that I was the angel Gabriēl.

" It came to pass then, when I had come into Of the in-
the midst of the rulers of the æons, that I looked carnation
of John the
down on the world of mankind, by command Baptizer.
of the First Mystery. I found Elizabeth, the
mother of John the Baptizer, before she had
conceived him, and I sowed into her a power
which I had received from the little Iaō, the Good,
who is in the Midst, that he might be able to
make proclamation before me and make ready
my way, and baptize with the water of the
forgiveness of sins. That power then is in the
body of John.

" Moreover in place of the soul of the rulers That John
which he was appointed to receive, I found the was Elias in
a former
soul of the prophet Elias in the æons of the birth.
sphere ; and I took him thence, and took his
soul and brought it to the Virgin of Light, and

she gave it over to her receivers; they brought it to the sphere of the rulers and cast it into the womb of Elizabeth. So the power of the little Iaŏ, who is in the Midst, and the soul of the prophet Elias, they were bound into the body of John the Baptizer. For this cause then were ye in doubt aforetime, | when I said unto you: ' John said: I am not the Christ,' and ye said unto me: ' It standeth written in the scripture: When the Christ shall come, Elias cometh before him and maketh ready his way.' But when ye said this unto me, I said unto you: ' Elias verily is come and hath made ready all things, as it standeth written, and they have done unto him as they would.' And when I knew that ye had not understood that I had discoursed with you concerning the soul of Elias which is bound into John the Baptizer, I answered you in the discourse in openness face to face: ' If ye like to accept John the Baptizer: he is Elias, of whom I have said that he will come.' "

CHAP. 8.
Of his own incarnation through Mary.

And Jesus continued again in the discourse and said: " It came to pass then thereafter, that at the command of the First.Mystery I looked down on the world of mankind and found Mary, who is called ' my mother ' according to the body of matter. I spake with her in the type of Gabriĕl, and when she had turned herself to the height towards me, I cast thence into her the first power which I had received from Barbĕlŏ— that is the body which I have borne in the height. And instead of the soul I cast into her the power which I | have received from the great Sabaŏth, the Good, who is in the region of the Right.

" And the twelve powers of the twelve saviours

13.

14.

of the Treasury of the Light which I had received More concerning the light-powers in the disciples. from the twelve ministers of the Midst, I cast into the sphere of the rulers. And the decans of the rulers and their servitors thought that they were souls of the rulers; and the servitors brought them, they bound them into the body of your mothers. And when your time was completed, ye were born in the world without souls of the rulers in you. And ye have received your portion out of the power which the last Helper hath breathed into the Mixture, that [power] which is blended with all the invisibles and all rulers and all æons,—in a word, which is blended with the world of destruction which is the Mixture. This [power], which from the beginning I brought out of myself, I have cast into the First Commandment, and the First Commandment cast a portion thereof into the great Light, and the great Light cast a portion of that which it had received, into the five Helpers, and the last Helper took a portion of that which it received, and cast it into the Mixture. And [this portion] is in all who are in the Mixture, | as I have just said unto you."   15.

This then Jesus said to his disciples on the Mount Why they should rejoice that the time of his investiture had come. of Olives. Jesus continued again in the discourse with his disciples [and said]: " Rejoice and exult and add joy to your joy, for the times are completed for me to put on my Vesture, which hath been prepared for me from the beginning, which I left behind in the last mystery until the time of its completion. Now the time of its completion is the time when I shall be commanded through the First Mystery to discourse with you from the beginning of the Truth to the completion thereof, and from the interiors of the interiors [to the exteriors of the exteriors], for the world will be saved through you. Rejoice then and exult, for ye are blessed before all men who are on the earth. It is ye who will save the whole world."

CHAP. 9.

It came to pass then, when Jesus had finished saying these words to his disciples, that he continued again in the discourse, and said unto them : " Lo, I have then put on my Vesture, and all authority hath been given me through the First Mystery. Yet a little while and I will tell you the mystery of the universe and the fulness of the universe ; and I will hide nothing from you from this hour on, but in fulness will I perfect you in all fulness and | in all perfection and in all mysteries, which are the perfection of all perfections and the fulness of all fulnesses and the gnosis of all gnoses,—those which are in my Vesture. I will tell you all mysteries from the exteriors of the exteriors to the interiors of the interiors. But hearken that I may tell you all things which have befallen me.

16.

CHAP. 10.

The mystery of the five words on the vesture.

" It came to pass then, when the sun had risen in the east, that a great light-power came down, in which was my Vesture, which I had left behind in the four-and-twentieth mystery, as I have said unto you. And I found a mystery in my Vesture, written in five words of those from the height : *zama zama ōzza rachama ōzai*,— whose solution is this :

The solution thereof.

" ' O Mystery, which is without in the world, for whose sake the universe hath arisen,—this is the total outgoing and the total ascent, which hath emanated all emanations and all that is

therein and for whose sake all mysteries and all
their regions have arisen,—come hither unto us,
for we are thy fellow-members. We are all
with thyself ; we are one and the same. Thou
art the First Mystery, | which existed from 17.
the beginning in the Ineffable before it came
forth ; and the name thereof are we all. Now,
therefore, are we all come to meet thee at the
last limit, which also is the last mystery from
within ; itself is a portion of us. Now, therefore, have we sent thee thy Vesture, which hath
belonged to thee from the beginning, which
thou hast left behind in the last limit, which
also is the last mystery from within, until its
time should be completed, according to the
commandment of the First Mystery. Lo, its
time is completed ; put it on [thee].

" ' Come unto us, for we all draw nigh to thee The three
to clothe thee with the First Mystery and all robes of
light.
his glory, by commandment of himself, in that
the First Mystery hath given us it, consisting
of two vestures, to clothe thee therewith, besides
the one which we have sent thee, for thou art
worthy of them, since thou art prior to us, and
existeth before us. For this cause, therefore,
hath the First Mystery sent thee through us the
mystery of all his glory, consisting of two vestures.

" ' In the first is the whole glory of all the The first
names of all mysteries and all emanations of vesture.
the orders | of the spaces of the Ineffable. 18.

" ' And in the second vesture is the whole glory The second
of the name of all mysteries and all emanations vesture.
which are in the orders of the two spaces of the
First Mystery.

" ' And in this [third] vesture, which we have

just sent thee, is the glory of the name of the
mystery of the Revealer, which is the First
Commandment, and of the mystery of the five
Impressions, and of the mystery of the great
Envoy of the Ineffable, who is the great Light,
and of the mystery of the five Leaders, who are
the five Helpers.   There is further in this vesture
the glory of the name of the mystery of all orders
of the emanations of the Treasury of the Light
and of their saviours, and [of the mystery] of
the orders of the orders, which are the seven
Amēns and the seven Voices and the five Trees
and the three Amēns and the Twin-saviour, that
is the Child of the Child, and of the mystery of
the nine guards of the three gates of the Treasury
of the Light.   There is further therein the whole
glory of the name [of all those] which are in the
Right, and of all those which are in the Midst.
And further there is therein the whole glory of
the name of the great Invisible, | which is the
great Forefather, and the mystery of the three
triple-powers and the mystery of their whole
region and the mystery of all their invisibles
and of all those who are in the thirteenth æon,
and the name of the twelve æons and of all their
rulers and all their archangels and all their
angels and of all those who are in the twelve
æons, and the whole mystery of the name of all
those who are in the Fate and in all the heavens,
and the whole mystery of the name of all those
who are in the sphere, and of its firmaments
and of all who are in them, and of all their
regions.

" ' Lo, therefore, we have sent thee this vesture,
which no one knew from the First Command-

19.

ment downwards, for the glory of its light was _{The day of} hidden in it, and the spheres and all regions _{'Come unto us.'} from the First Commandment downwards [have not known it]. Haste thee, therefore, clothe thyself with this vesture and come unto us. For we draw nigh unto thee, to clothe thee by command of the First Mystery with thy two vestures [other] which existed for thee from the beginning with the First Mystery until the time appointed by the Ineffable is completed. | Come, 20. therefore, to us quickly, that we may put them on thee, until thou hast fulfilled the total ministry of the perfection of the First Mystery which is appointed by the Ineffable. Come, therefore, to us quickly, in order that we may clothe thee with them, according to the command of the First Mystery. For yet a little while, a very little while, and thou shalt come unto us and leave the world. Come, therefore, quickly, that thou mayest receive thy whole glory, that is the glory of the First Mystery.'

" It came to pass then, when I saw the mystery _{CHAP. 11.} of all these words in the vesture which was sent _{Jesus putteth on} me, that straightway I clothed myself therewith, _{his vesture.} and I shone most exceedingly and soared into the height.

" I came before the [first] gate of the firmament, _{He enter-} shining most exceedingly, and there was no _{eth the firmament.} measure for the light which was about me, and the gates of the firmament were shaken one over against another and all opened at once.

" And all rulers and all authorities and all _{The powers} angels therein were thrown all together into _{of the firma-} _{ment are} agitation because of the great light which was on _{amazed and} _{fall down} me. And they gazed at the radiant vesture of _{and adore} _{him.}

light with which I was clad, and they saw the mystery which contains their names, | and they feared most exceedingly. And all their bonds with which they were bound, were unloosed and every one left his order, and they all fell down before me, adored and said: 'How hath the lord of the universe passed through us without our knowing?' And they all sang praises together to the interiors of the interiors; but me they saw not, but they saw only the light. And they were in great fear and were exceedingly agitated and sang praises to the interiors of the interiors.

CHAP. 12.
He entereth the first sphere.

" And I left that region behind me and ascended to the first sphere, shining most exceedingly, forty-and-nine-times more brightly than I had shone in the firmament. It came to pass then, when I had reached the gate of the first sphere, that its gates were shaken and opened of themselves at once.

The powers of the first sphere are amazed and fall down and adore him.

"I entered into the houses of the sphere, shining most exceedingly, and there was no measure to the light that was about me. And all the rulers and all those who are in that sphere, fell into agitation one against another. And they saw the great light that was about me, and they gazed upon my vesture and saw thereon the mystery of their name. And they fell into still greater agitation, and were in great fear, saying: 'How hath the lord of the universe passed through us without our knowing?' |

22

And all their bonds were unloosed and their regions and their orders; and every one left his order, and they fell down all together, adored before me, or before my vesture, and all sang praises together to the interiors of the interiors, being in great fear and great agitation.

" And I left that region behind me and came to the gate of the second sphere, which is the Fate. Then were all its gates thrown into agitation and opened of themselves. And I entered into the houses of the Fate, shining most exceedingly, and there was no measure for the light that was about me, for I shone in the Fate forty-and-nine times more than in the [first] sphere.

" And all the rulers and all those who are in the Fate, were thrown into agitation and fell on one another and were in exceeding great fear on seeing the great light that was about me. And they gazed on my vesture of light and saw the mystery of their name on my vesture and fell into still greater agitation; and they were in great fear, saying: ' How hath the lord of the universe passed through us without our knowing?' And all the bonds of their regions and of their orders and of their houses were unloosed; they all came at once, fell down, adored before me and sang praises all together | to the interiors of the interiors, being in great fear and great agitation.

" And I left that region behind me and ascended to the great-æons of the rulers and came before their veils and their gates, shining most exceedingly, and there was no measure for the light which was about me. It came to pass then, when I arrived at the twelve æons, that their veils and their gates were shaken one over against the other. Their veils drew themselves apart of their own accord, and their gates opened one

over against the other.   And I entered into the
æons, shining most exceedingly, and there was
no measure for the light that was about me,
forty-and-nine times more than the light with
which I shone in the houses of the Fate.

The powers
of the æons
are amazed
and fall
down and
adore him.
" And all the angels of the æons and their
archangels and their rulers and their gods and
their lords and their authorities and their tyrants
and their powers and their light-sparks and their
light-givers and their unpaired and their invisibles and their forefathers and their triple-
powers saw me, shining most exceedingly, and
there was no measure for the light which was
about me.   And they were thrown into agitation
the one over against the other and great fear
fell upon them, when they saw the great light
that was about me.   And in their great agitation
and their great fear they withdrew as far as |

the region of the great invisible Forefather, and
of the three great triple-powers.   And because
of the great fear of their agitation, the great
Forefather, he and the three triple-powers, kept
on running hither and thither in his region,
and they could not close all their regions because
of the great fear in which they were.   And they
agitated all their æons together and all their
spheres and all their orders, fearing and being
greatly agitated because of the great light which
was about me—not of the former quality that it
was about me when I was on the earth of mankind, when the light-vesture came over me,—
for the world could not bear the light such as it
was in its truth, else would the world at once
be destroyed and all upon it,—but the light
which was about me in the twelve æons was

eight-thousand-and-seven-hundred-myriad times greater than that which was about me in the world among you.

"It came to pass then, when all those who are in the twelve æons saw the great light which was about me, that they were all thrown into agitation one over against the other, and ran hither and thither in the æons. And all æons and all heavens and their whole ordering were agitated one over against the other | on account of the great fear which was on them, for they knew not the mystery which had taken place. And Adamas, the great Tyrant, and all the tyrants in all the æons began to fight in vain against the light, and they knew not against whom they fought, because they saw nothing but the overmastering light. *CHAP. 15. Adamas and the tyrants fight against the light. 25.*

"It came to pass then, when they fought against the light, that they were weakened all together one with another, were dashed down in the æons and became as the inhabitants of the earth, dead and without breath of life.

"And I took from all a third of their power, that they should no more be active in their evil doings, and that, if the men who are in the world, invoke them in their mysteries—those which the angels who transgressed have brought down, that is their sorceries,—in order that, therefore, if they invoke them in their evil doings, they may not be able to accomplish them. *He taketh from them a third of their power.*

"And the Fate and the sphere over which they rule, I have changed and brought it to pass that they spend six months turned to the left and accomplish their influences, and that six months they face to the right and accomplish *He changeth the motion of their spheres.*

their influences. For by command of the First
Commandment and by command of the First
26.   Mystery | Yew, the Overseer of the Light, had
set them facing the left at every time and accomplishing their influences and their deeds.

CHAP. 16.   "It came to pass then, when I came into their
region, that they mutinied and fought against
the light. And I took the third of their power,
in order that they should not be able to accomplish
their evil deeds. And the Fate and the sphere,
over which they rule, I have changed, and set
them facing the left six months and accomplishing
their influences, and I have set them turned
another six months to the right and accomplishing
their influences."

CHAP. 17.   When then he had said this to his disciples,
he said unto them : " Who hath ears to hear,
let him hear."

It came to pass then, when Mary had heard
the Saviour say these words, that she gazed
fixedly into the air for the space of an hour.
She said : " My Lord, give commandment unto
me to speak in openness."

Mary
Magdalene
asketh and
receiveth
permission
to speak.
      And Jesus, the compassionate, answered and
said unto Mary : " Mary, thou blessed one,
whom I will perfect in all mysteries of those of
the height, discourse in openness, thou, whose
heart is raised to the kingdom of heaven more
than all thy brethren."

CHAP. 18.   Then said Mary to the Saviour : " My Lord,
the word which thou hast spoken unto us : ' Who
27. | hath ears to hear, let him hear,' thou sayest
in order that we may understand the word which
thou hast spoken. Hearken, therefore, my Lord,
that I may discourse in openness.

" The word which thou hast spoken: ' I Mary inter-
preteth the
discourse
from the
words of
Isaiah. have taken a third from the power of the rulers of all the æons, and changed their Fate and their sphere over which they rule, in order that, if the race of men invoke them in the mysteries— those which the angels who transgressed have taught them for the accomplishing of their evil and lawless deeds in the mystery of their sorcery,' —in order then that they may no more from this hour accomplish their lawless deeds, because thou hast taken their power from them and from their horoscope - casters and their consulters and from those who declare to the men in the world all things which shall come to pass, in order that they should no more from this hour know how to declare unto them any thing at all which will come to pass (for thou hast changed their spheres, and hast made them spend six months turned to the left and accomplishing their in- fluences, and another six months facing the right and accomplishing their influences),—concerning this word then, my Lord, the power which was in the prophet Isaiah, hath spoken thus and proclaimed aforetime in a spiritual simili- tude, discoursing on the ' Vision about Egypt ': ' Where then, O Egypt, where are thy consulters and horoscope-casters and those who cry | out 28. of the earth and those who cry out of their belly? Let them then declare unto thee from now on the deeds which the lord Sabaōth will do!'

" The power then which was in the prophet Isaiah, prophesied before thou didst come, that thou wouldst take away the power of the rulers of the æons and wouldst change their sphere and their Fate, in order that they might

know nothing from now on. For this cause it
hath said also : ' Ye shall then know not of what
the lord Sabaōth will do ' ; that is, none of the
rulers will know what thou wilt do from now on,
—for they are ' Egypt,' because they are matter.
The power then which was in Isaiah, prophesied
concerning thee aforetime, saying : ' From now
on ye shall then know not what the lord Sabaōth
will do.' Because of the light-power which thou
didst receive from Sabaōth, the Good, who is
in the region of the Right, and which is in thy
material body to-day, for this cause then,
my Lord Jesus, thou hast said unto us : ' Who
hath ears to hear, let him hear,'—in order that
thou mightest know whose heart is ardently
raised to the kingdom of heaven."

CHAP. 19.   It came to pass then, when Mary had finished
saying these words, that he said: "Well said, Mary,
for thou art blessed before all women on the earth, |
29.   because thou shalt be the fulness of all fulnesses
Jesus com-   and the perfection of all perfections."
mendeth
Mary. She   Now when Mary had heard the Saviour speak
further
questioneth   these words, she exulted greatly, and she came
him on the   before Jesus, fell down before him, adored
changing of
the spheres. his feet and said unto him : " My Lord, hearken
unto me, that I may question thee on this word,
before that thou discoursest with us about the
regions whither thou didst go."

Jesus answered and said unto Mary : " Discourse in openness and fear not ; all things on
which thou questionest, I will reveal unto thee."

CHAP. 20.   She said : " My Lord, will all the men who know
the mystery of the magic of all the rulers of all
the æons of the Fate and of those of the sphere,
in the way in which the angels who transgressed

have taught them, if they invoke them in their
mysteries, that is in their evil magic, to the
hindering of good deeds,—will they accomplish
them henceforth from now on or not ? "

Jesus answered and said unto Mary : " They Jesus explaineth
will not accomplish them as they accomplished further the
them from the beginning, because I have taken conversion
of the
away a third of their power ; but they will raise a spheres.
loan from those who know the mysteries of the
magic of the thirteenth æon. And if they invoke
the mysteries of the magic of those who are in
the thirteenth æon, | they will accomplish them 30.
well and surely, because I have not taken away
power from that region, according to the command
of the First Mystery."

And it came to pass, when Jesus had finished CHAP. 21.
saying these words, that Mary continued again
and said : " My Lord, will not then the horoscope-
casters and consulters from now on declare unto
men what will come to pass for them ? "

And Jesus answered and said unto Mary :
" If the horoscope-casters find the Fate and the
sphere turned towards the left, according to their
first extension, their words will come to pass,
and they will say what is to take place. But
if they chance on the Fate or the sphere turned to
the right, they are bound to say nothing true,
for I have changed their influences and their
squares and their triangles and their octagons ;
seeing that their influences from the beginning
onwards were continuously turned to the left
and their squares and their triangles and their
octagons. But now I have made them spend
six months turned to the left and six months
turned to the right. He who then shall find their

reckoning from the time when I changed them, setting them so as to spend six months facing towards their left and six months facing their right paths,—he who then shall observe them **31.** in this wise, | will know their influences surely and will declare all things which they will do. In like manner also the consulters, if they invoke the names of the rulers and chance on them facing the left, will tell [men] with accuracy all things concerning which they shall ask their decans. On the contrary, if the consulters invoke their names when they face to the right, they will not give ear unto them, because they are facing in another form compared with their former position in which Yew had established them; seeing that other are their names when they are turned to the left and other their names when they are turned to the right. And if they invoke them when they are turned to the right, they will not tell them the truth, but they will confound them with confusion and threaten them with threatening. Those then who do not know their path, when they are turned to the right, and their triangles and their squares and all their figures, will find nothing true, but will be confounded in great confusion and will find themselves in great delusion, because I have now changed the works which they effected aforetime in their squares, when turned to the left, and in their triangles and in their octagons, in which they were busied continuously turned to the left; and I have made them spend six months forming all their configurations turned to the right, in order that they may be confounded in **32.** confusion in their whole range. | And moreover

I have made them spend six months turned to the left and accomplishing the works of their influences and all their configurations, in order that the rulers who are in the æons and in their spheres and in their heavens and in all their regions, may be confounded in confusion and deluded in delusion, so that they may not understand their own paths."

It came to pass then, when Jesus had finished **CHAP. 22.** saying these words, while Philip sat and wrote Philip questioneth all the words that Jesus spake,—thereafter then Jesus. it came to pass that Philip came forward, fell down and adored the feet of Jesus, saying: " My Lord and Saviour, grant me authority to discourse before thee and to question thee on this word, before thou discoursest with us concerning the regions whither thou didst go because of thy ministry."

And the compassionate Saviour answered and said unto Philip : " Authority is given thee to bring forward the word which thou willest."

And Philip answered and said unto Jesus : " My Lord, on account of what mystery hast thou changed the binding of the rulers and their æons and their Fate and their sphere and all their regions, and made them confounded in confusion on their path and deluded in their course ? Hast thou then done this unto them for the salvation of the world or hast thou not ? "

And Jesus answered and said unto Philip and **CHAP. 23.** to all the disciples together : " I have | changed 33. their path for the salvation of all souls. Amēn, Why the path of the amēn, I say unto you : If I had not changed æons was changed their path, a host of souls would have been destroyed, and they would have spent a long time, if the rulers of the æons and the rulers of the Fate and of the sphere and of all their regions and all their heavens and all their æons had not been brought to naught; and the souls would have continued a long time here outside, and the completion of the number of perfect souls would have been delayed, which [souls] shall be counted in the Inheritance of the Height through the mysteries and shall be in the Treasury of the Light. For this cause then I have changed their path, that they might be deluded and fall into agitation and yield up the power which is in the matter of their world and which they fashion into souls, in order that those who shall be saved, might be quickly purified and raised on high, they and the whole power, and that those who shall not be saved, might be quickly destroyed."

CHAP. 24.
Mary ques-
tioneth him
again.

34.

It came to pass then, when Jesus had finished saying these words unto his disciples, that Mary, the fair in her discourse and the blessed one, came forward, fell at the feet of Jesus and said: " My Lord, suffer me that I speak before thee, and | be not wroth with me, if oft I give thee trouble questioning thee."

The Saviour, full of compassion, answered and said unto Mary: " Speak the word which thou willest, and I will reveal it to thee in all openness."

Mary answered and said unto Jesus: " My Lord, in what way will the souls have delayed themselves here outside, and in what type will they be quickly purified ? "

CHAP. 25.

And Jesus answered and said unto Mary: " Well said, Mary; thou questionest finely with thy excellent question, and thou throwest light on all things with surety and precision. Now, therefore, from now on will I hide nothing from you, but I will reveal unto you all things with surety and openness. Hearken then, Mary, and give ear, all ye disciples : Before I made proclamation to all the rulers of the æons and to all the rulers of the Fate and of the sphere, they were all bound in their bonds and in their spheres and in their seals, as Yew, the Overseer of the Light, had bound them from the beginning ; and every one of them remained in his order, and every one journeyed according to his course, as Yew, the Overseer of the Light, had established them. And when the time of the number of Melchisedec, the great Receiver of the Light, The coming of Melchise- came, he was wont to come into the midst of dec. the æons and of all the rulers | who are bound in 35. the sphere and in the Fate, and he carried away the purification of the light from all the rulers of the æons and from all the rulers of the Fate and from those of the sphere—for he carried away then that which brings them into agitation —and he set in motion the hastener who is over them, and made them turn their circles swiftly, and he [*sc.* the hastener] carried away their power which was in them and the breath of their mouth and the tears [*lit.* waters] of their eyes and the sweat of their bodies.

" And Melchisedec, the Receiver of the Light, Of the fashioning purifieth those powers and carrieth their light into of the souls. the Treasury of the Light, while the servitors of of men. all the rulers gather together all matter from them all ; and the servitors of all the rulers of the Fate and the servitors of the sphere which is below the æons, take it and fashion it into souls of men and cattle and reptiles and wild-beasts and birds, and send them down into the world of mankind. And further the receivers of the sun and the receivers of the moon, if they look above and see the configurations of the paths of the æons and the configurations of the Fate and those of the sphere, then they take from them the light-power; and the | receivers of the sun get it ready and deposit it, until they hand it over to the receivers of Melchisedec, the Light-purifier. And their material refuse they bring to the sphere which is below the æons, and fashion it into [souls of] men, and fashion it also into souls of reptiles and of cattle and of wild-beasts and of birds, according to the circle of the rulers of that sphere and according to all the configurations of its revolution, and they cast them into this world of mankind, and they become souls in this region, as I have just said unto you.

"This then they accomplished continuously before their power was diminished in them and they waned and became exhausted, or powerless. It came to pass then, when they became power-less, that their power began to cease in them, so that they became exhausted in their power, and their light, which was in their region, ceased and their kingdom was destroyed, and the universe became quickly raised up.

"It came to pass then, when they had perceived this at the time, and when the number of the cipher of Melchisedec, the Receiver [of the Light], happened, then had he to come out again and enter into the midst of the rulers of all the æons and into the midst of all the rulers of the Fate and of those of the sphere; and he threw them into agitation, and made them quickly abandon

36.

CHAP. 26.

their circles. And forthwith they were constrained, and cast forth the power out of themselves, out of the breath of their mouth and
the | tears of their eyes and the sweat of their 37.
bodies.

" And Melchisedec, the Receiver of the Light, The rulers
purifieth them, as he doth continually ; he carrieth matter so
their light into the Treasury of the Light. And that souls
all the rulers of the æons and the rulers of the fashioned.
Fate and those of the sphere turn to the
matter of their refuse ; they devour it and do not
let it go and become souls in the world. They
devour then their matter, so that they may not
become powerless and exhausted and their power
cease in them and their kingdom become destroyed,
but in order that they may delay and linger a
long time until the completion of the number of
the perfect souls who shall be in the Treasury of
the Light.

" It came to pass then, when the rulers of the CHAP. 27.
æons and those of the Fate and those of the
sphere continued to carry out this type,—turning
on themselves, devouring the refuse of their
matter, and not allowing souls to be born into
the world of mankind, in order that they might
delay in being rulers, and that the powers
which are in their powers, that is the souls,
might spend a long time here outside,—they
then persisted doing this continually for two
circles.

" It came to pass then, when I wished to ascend
for the ministry for the sake of which I was
called | by command of the First Mystery, that 38.
I came up into the midst of the tyrants of the
rulers of the twelve æons, with my light-vesture

about me, shining most exceedingly, and there was no measure for the light which was about me.

Adamas and the tyrants fight against the light-vesture.

" It came to pass then, when those tyrants saw the great light which was about me, that the great Adamas, the Tyrant, and all the tyrants of the twelve æons, all together began to fight against the light of my vesture, desiring to hold it fast among them, in order to delay in their rulership. This then they did, not knowing against whom they fought.

Jesus taketh from them a third of their power and changeth their course.

" When then they mutinied and fought against the light, thereon by command of the First Mystery I changed the paths and the courses of their æons and the paths of their Fate and of their sphere. I made them face six months towards the triangles on the left and towards the squares and towards those in their aspect and towards their octagons, just as they had formerly been. But their manner of turning, or facing, I changed to another order, and made them other six months face towards the works of their influences in the squares on the right and in their triangles and in those in their aspect and in their octagons. And I made them to be confounded in great confusion and deluded in great delusion |

39.

—the rulers of the æons and all the rulers of the Fate and those of the sphere ; and I set them in great agitation, and thence on they were no longer able to turn towards the refuse of their matter to devour it, in order that their regions may continue to delay and they [themselves] may spend a long time as rulers.

" But when I had taken away a third of their power, I changed their spheres, so that they spend a time facing to the left and another time

facing to the right. I have changed their whole
path and their whole course, and I have made the
path of their course to hurry, so that they may
be quickly purified and raised up quickly. And I
have shortened their circles, and made their path
more speedy, and it will be exceedingly hurried.
And they were thrown into confusion in their
path, and from then on were no more able to
devour the matter of the refuse of the purification They no
of their light. And moreover I have shortened more have
the power
their times and their periods, so that the perfect of devour-
number of souls who shall receive the mysteries ing their
matter.
and be in the Treasury of the Light, shall be
quickly completed. For had I not changed
their courses, and had I not shortened their
periods, they would not have let any soul come
into the world, because of the matter of their
refuse | which they devoured, and they would 40.
have destroyed many souls. For this cause I
said unto you aforetime: 'I have shortened the
times because of my elect; otherwise no soul
would have been able to be saved.' And I have
shortened the times and the periods because of
the perfect number of the souls who shall receive
the mysteries, that is to say, the 'elect'; and
had I not shortened their periods, no material
soul would have been saved, but they would have
perished in the fire which is in the flesh of the
rulers. This then is the word on which thou dost
question me with precision."

It came to pass then, when Jesus had finished
speaking these words unto his disciples, that they
fell down all together, adored him and said to
him: "Blessed are we before all men, for unto
us thou hast revealed these great exploits."

And Jesus continued again in his discourse and said unto his disciples : " Hearken concerning the things which befell me among the rulers of the twelve æons and all their rulers and their lords and their authorities and their angels and their archangels. When then they had seen the vesture of light which was about me, they and their unpaired, then every one of them saw the mystery

41.

of his name, that it was on my | vesture of light, which was about me. They fell down all together, adored the vesture of light which was about me, and cried out all together, saying : ' How hath the lord of the universe passed through us without our knowing it ? ' And they all sang praises together to the interiors of the interiors. And all their triple-powers and their great forefathers and their ungenerated and their self-generated and their generated and their gods and their light-sparks and their light-bearers—in a word all their great ones—saw the tyrants of their region, that their power was diminished in them. And they were in weakness and themselves fell into great and immeasurable fear. And they gazed on the mystery of their name on my vesture, and they had set out to come and adore the mystery of their name which was on my vesture, and they could not because of the great light which was about me ; but they adored a little removed from me, and they adored the light of my vesture and all cried out together, singing praises to the interiors of the interiors.

" It came to pass then, when this befell among the tyrants who are below these rulers, that they all lost power and fell down to the ground in their æons and became as the dead world-

dwellers with no breath in them, as they | be- 42.
came in the hour when I took from them their
power.

"It came to pass then thereafter, when I left
those æons, that every one of all those who were
in the twelve æons, was bound to their order all
together, and they accomplished their works as
I have established them, so that they spend six
months turned to the left and accomplishing
their works in their squares and their triangles
and in those which are in their aspect, and that
further they spend another six months facing to
the right and towards their triangles and their
squares and those which are in their aspect.
Thus then will those who are in the Fate and in
the sphere travel.

"It came to pass then thereafter that I ascended CHAP. 29.
to the veils of the thirteenth æon. It came to Jesus entereth the
pass then, when I had arrived at their veils, that thirteenth
æon and
they drew apart of their own accord and opened findeth Pis-
themselves for me. I entered in into the thir- tis Sophia.
teenth æon and found Pistis Sophia below the
thirteenth æon all alone and no one of them with
her. And she sat in that region grieving and
mourning, because she had not been admitted
into the thirteenth æon, her higher region.
And she was moreover grieving because of the
torments which Self-willed, who is one of the
three triple-powers, had inflicted on her. But
this,—when I shall come to speak with you
respecting their expansion, | I will tell you the 43.
mystery, how this befell her.

"It came to pass then, when Pistis Sophia saw Sophia and
me shining most exceedingly and with no measure her fellow-
powers be-
for the light which was about me, that she was in hold the
light.

great agitation and gazed at the light of my vesture. She saw the mystery of her name on my vesture and the whole glory of its mystery, for formerly she was in the region of the height, in the thirteenth æon,—but she was wont to sing praises to the higher light, which she had seen in the veil of the Treasury of the Light.

"It came to pass then, when she persisted in singing praises to the higher light, that all the rulers who are with the two great triple-powers, and her invisible who is paired with her, and the other two-and-twenty invisible emanations gazed [at the light],—in as much as Pistis Sophia and her pair, they and the other two-and-twenty emanations make up four-and-twenty emanations, which the great invisible Forefather and the two great triple-powers have emanated."

CHAP. 30.
Mary desireth to hear the story of Sophia.

It came to pass then, when Jesus had said this unto his disciples, that Mary came forward and said : " My Lord, I have heard thee say aforetime : ' Pistis Sophia is herself one of the four-and-twenty emanations,—how then is she not in their region ? | But thou hast said : ' I found her below the thirteenth æon.' "

44.

[THE STORY OF PISTIS SOPHIA]

Sophia desireth to enter the Light-world.

And Jesus answered and said unto his disciples : " It came to pass, when Pistis Sophia was in the thirteenth æon, in the region of all her brethren the invisibles, that is the four-and-twenty emanations of the great Invisible,—it came to pass then by command of the First Mystery that Pistis Sophia gazed into the height. She saw the light of the veil of the Treasury of the Light, and she

longed to reach to that region, and she could not
reach to that region.   But she ceased to perform
the mystery of the thirteenth æon, and sang
praises to the light of the height, which she had
seen in the light of the veil of the Treasury of the
Light.

" It came to pass then, when she sang praises The rulers
to the region of the height, that all the rulers in hate her
for ceasing
the twelve æons, who are below, hated her, because in their
mystery.
she had ceased from their mysteries, and because
she had desired to go into the height and be above
them all.   For this cause then they were enraged
against her and hated her, [as did] the great triple-
powered Self-willed, that is the third triple-power,
who is in the thirteenth æon, he who had become
disobedient, in as much as he had not emanated
the whole purification of his power in him, and
had not given the purification of his light at the
time when the rulers gave their purification, in
that he desired to rule over the whole thirteenth
æon | and those who are below it.   45.

" It came to pass then, when the rulers of the Self-willed
twelve æons were enraged against Pistis Sophia, uniteth him-
self with
who is above them, and hated her exceedingly, the rulers of
the twelve
that the great triple-powered Self-willed, of whom æons and
I have just now told you, joined himself to the emanateth
a lion-faced
rulers of the twelve æons, and also was enraged power to
plague
against Pistis Sophia and hated her exceedingly, Sophia.
because she had thought to go to the light which
is higher than her.   And he emanated out of
himself a great lion-faced power, and out of his
matter in him he emanated a host of other very
violent material emanations, and sent them into
the regions below, to the parts of the chaos, in
order that they might there lie in wait for Pistis

Sophia and take away her power out of her, because she thought to go to the height which is above them all, and moreover she had ceased to perform their mystery, and lamented continuously and sought after the light which she had seen. And the rulers who abide, or persist, in performing the mystery, hated her, and all the guards who are at the gates of the æons, hated her also.

" It came to pass then thereafter by command of the First Commandment that the great triple-powered Self-willed, who is one of the three |

46. triple-powers, pursued Sophia in the thirteenth æon, in order that she should look towards the parts below, so that she might see in that region his lion-faced light-power and long after it and go to that region, so that her light might be taken from her.

CHAP. 31.

Sophia taketh the lion-faced power of Self-willed for the true Light.

" It came to pass then thereafter that she looked below and saw his light-power in the parts below; and she knew not that it is that of the triple-powered Self-willed, but she thought that it came out of the light which she had seen from the beginning in the height, which came out of the veil of the Treasury of the Light. And she thought to herself: I will go into that region without my pair and take the light and thereout fashion for myself light-æons, so that I may go to the Light of lights, which is in the Height of heights.

" This then thinking, she went forth from her own region, the thirteenth æon, and went down to the twelve æons. The rulers of the æons pursued her and were enraged against her, because she had thought of grandeur. And she

went forth also from the twelve æons, and came
into the regions of the chaos and drew nigh to
that lion-faced light-power to devour it. But all |
the material emanations of Self-willed surrounded 47.
her, and the great lion-faced light-power devoured The emana-
all the light-powers in Sophia and cleaned out her Self-willed
light and devoured it, and her matter was thrust light-powers
into the chaos ; it became a lion-faced ruler in out of
the chaos, of which one half is fire and the other Sophia.
darkness,—that is Yaldabaōth, of whom I have
spoken unto you many times. When then this
befell, Sophia became very greatly exhausted,
and that lion-faced light-power set to work to
take away from Sophia all her light-powers, and
all the material powers of Self-willed surrounded
Sophia at the same time and pressed her sore.

" And Pistis Sophia cried out most exceedingly, CHAP. 32.
she cried to the Light of lights which she had seen
from the beginning, in which she had had faith,
and uttered this repentance, saying thus :

" ' 1. O Light of lights, in whom I have had The first
faith from the beginning, hearken now then, of Sophia.
O Light, unto my repentance. Save me, O Light,
for evil thoughts have entered into me.

" ' 2. I gazed, O Light, into the lower parts and
saw there a light, thinking : I will go to that
region, | in order that I may take that light. 48.
And I went and found myself in the darkness
which is in the chaos below, and I could no more
speed thence and go to my region,. for I was
sore pressed by all the emanations of Self-willed,
and the lion-faced power took away my light
in me.

" ' 3. And I cried for help, but my voice hath
not reached out of the darkness. And I looked

unto the height, that the Light, in which I had had faith, might help me.

" ' 4. And when I looked unto the height, I saw all the rulers of the æons, how in their numbers they looked down on me and rejoiced over me, though I had done them no ill; but they hated me without a cause. And when the emanations of Self-willed saw the rulers of the æons rejoicing over me, they knew that the rulers of the æons would not come to my aid; and those emanations which sore pressed me with violence, took courage, and the light which I had not taken from them, they have taken from me.

" ' 5. Now, therefore, O Light of Truth, thou knowest that I have done this in my innocence, thinking that the lion-faced light-power belonged to thee; and the sin which I have done is open before thee.

" ' 6. Suffer me no more to lack, O Lord, for I have had faith in thy light from the beginning; O Lord, O Light of the powers, suffer me no more to lack my light.

" ' 7. For because of thy inducement and for the sake of thy light am I fallen into this oppression, and shame hath covered me.

" ' 8. And because of | the illusion of thy light, I am become a stranger to my brethren, the invisibles, and to the great emanations of Barbēlō.

" ' 9. This hath befallen me, O Light, because I have been zealous for thy abode; and the wrath of Self-willed is come upon me—of him who had not hearkened unto thy command to emanate from the emanation of his power—because I was in his æon without performing his mystery.

" ' 10. And all the rulers of the æons mocked me.

" ' 11. And I was in that region, mourning and seeking after the light which I had seen in the height.

" ' 12. And the guards of the gates of the æons searched for me, and all who remain in their mystery mocked me.

" ' 13. But I looked up unto the height towards thee and had faith in thee. Now, therefore, O Light of lights, I am sore pressed in the darkness of chaos. If now thou wilt come to save me,— great is thy mercy,—then hear me in truth and save me.

" ' 14. Save me out of the matter of this darkness, that I may not be submerged therein, that I may be saved from the emanations of god Self-willed which press me sore, and from their evil doings.

" ' 15. Let not this darkness submerge me, and let not this lion-faced power entirely devour the whole of my power, and | let not this chaos ⁵⁰· shroud my power.

" ' 16. Hear me, O Light, for thy grace is precious, and look down upon me according to the great mercy of thy Light.

" ' 17. Turn not thy face from me, for I am exceedingly tormented.

" ' 18. Haste thee, hearken unto me and save my power.

" ' 19. Save me because of the rulers who hate me, for thou knowest my sore oppression and my torment and the torment of my power which they have taken from me. They who have set me in all this evil are before thee ; deal with them according to thy good pleasure.

" ' 20. My power looked forth from the midst

of the chaos and from the midst of the darkness, and I waited for my pair, that he should come and fight for me, and he came not, and I looked that he should come and lend me power, and I found him not.

" ' 21. And when I sought the light, they gave me darkness; and when I sought my power, they gave me matter.

" ' 22. Now, therefore, O Light of lights, may the darkness and the matter which the emanations of Self-willed have brought upon me, be unto them for a snare, and may they be ensnared therein, and recompense them and may they be made to stumble and not come into the region of their Self-willed.

" ' 23. May they remain in the darkness and not behold the light; may they behold the chaos for ever, and let them not look unto the height.

" ' 24. Bring upon them their revenge, and may thy judgment lay hold upon them.

51.　" ' 25. Let them not henceforth | come into their region to their god Self-willed, and let not his emanations henceforth come into their regions; for their god is impious and self-willed, and he thought that he had done this evil of himself, not knowing that, had I not been brought low according to thy command, he would not have had any authority over me.

" ' 26. But when thou hadst by thy command brought me low, they pursued me the more, and their emanations added pain to my humiliation.

" ' 27. And they have taken light-power from me and fallen again to pressing me sore, in order to take away all the light in me. Because of this in which they have set me, let them not ascend to the thirteenth æon, the region of Righteousness.

" ' 28. But let them not be reckoned in the lot of those who purify themselves and the light, and let them not be reckoned with those who will quickly repent, that they may quickly receive mysteries in the Light.

" ' 29. For they have taken my light from me, and my power hath begun to cease in me and I am destitute of my light.

" ' 30. Now, therefore, O Light, which is in thee and is with me, I sing praises to thy name, O Light, in glory.

" " 31. May my song of praise please thee, O Light, as an excellent mystery, which leadeth to the gates of the Light, which they who shall repent will utter, and the light of which will purify them.

" ' 32. Now, therefore, let | all matters rejoice ; 52. seek ye all the Light, that the power of the stars which is in you, may live.

" ' 33. For the Light hath heard the matters, nor will it leave any without having purified them.

" ' 34. Let the souls and the matters praise the Lord of all æons, and [let] the matters and all that is in them [praise him].

" ' 35. For God shall save their soul from all matters, and a city shall be prepared in the Light, and all the souls who are saved, will dwell in that city and will inherit it.

" ' 36. And the soul of them who shall receive mysteries will abide in that region, and they who have received mysteries in its name will abide therein.' "

It came to pass then, when Jesus had spoken CHAP. 33.

these words unto his disciples, that he said unto them : " This is the song of praise which Pistis Sophia uttered in her first repentance, repenting of her sin, and reciting all which had befallen her. Now, therefore : ' Who hath ears to hear, let him hear.' "

Mary again came forward and said : " My Lord, my indweller of light hath ears, and I hear with my light-power, and thy spirit which is with me, hath sobered me. Hearken then that I may speak. concerning the repentance which Pistis Sophia hath uttered, speaking of |

53. her sin and all that befell her. Thy light-power hath prophesied thereof aforetime through the prophet David in the sixty-eighth Psalm :

Mary inter-
preteth the
first repent-
ance from
Psalm lxviii.

" ' 1. Save me, O God, for the waters are come in even unto my soul.

" ' 2. I sank, or am submerged, in the slime of the abyss, and power was not. I have gone down into the depths of the sea ; a tempest hath submerged me.

" ' 3. I have kept on crying ; my throat is gone, my eyes faded, waiting patiently for God.

" ' 4. They who hate me without a cause are more than the hairs of my head ; mighty are my foes, who violently pursued me. They required of me that which I took not from them.

" ' 5. God, thou hast known my foolishness, and my faults are not hid from thee.

" ' 6. Let not them that wait on thee, O Lord, Lord of powers, be ashamed for my sake ; let not those who seek thee be ashamed for my sake, O Lord, God of Israel, God of powers.

" ' 7. For for thy sake have I endured shame ; shame hath covered my face.

" ' 8. I am become a stranger to my brethren, a stranger unto the sons of my mother.

" ' 9. For the zeal of thy house hath consumed me ; the revilings of them that revile thee have fallen upon me.

" ' 10. I bowed my soul with fasting, and it was turned to my reproach.

" ' 11. I put on sackcloth ; I became unto them a bye-word.

" ' 12. They who sit at the gates, chattered at me ; and they who drink wine, harped about me.

" ' 13. But I prayed with my soul unto thee, | O Lord ; the time of thy well-liking is [now], 54 O God. In the fulness of thy grace give ear unto my salvation in truth.

" ' 14. Save me out of this slime, that I sink not therein ; let me be saved from them that hate me, and from the deep of waters.

" ' 15. Let not a water-flood submerge me, let not the deep swallow me, let not a well close its mouth above me.

" ' 16. Hear me, O Lord, for thy grace is good ; according to the fulness of thy compassion look down upon me.

" ' 17. Turn not thy face away from thy servant, for I am oppressed.

" ' 18. Hear me quickly, give heed to my soul and deliver it.

" ' 19. Save me because of my foes, for thou knowest my disgrace, my shame and my dishonour ; all my oppressors are before thee.

" ' 20. My heart awaiteth disgrace and misery ; I waited for him who should sorrow with me, but I could not come at him, and for him who should comfort me, and I found him not.

" ' 21. They gave me gall for my meat; and in my thirst they gave me vinegar to drink.

" ' 22. Let their table be unto them for a trap and for a snare and for a retribution and for a stumbling-block.

" ' 23. Mayest thou bend their backs at all time.

" ' 24. Pour out thy anger upon them, and let the wrath of thy anger lay hold upon them.

" ' 25. Let their encampment be desolate, let there be no dweller in their habitations.

" ' 26. For they persecuted him whom thou hast smitten, and added to the smart of their woundings.

" ' 27. They added iniquity to their iniquities; let them not come into | thy righteousness.

55.

" ' 28. Let them be wiped out of the book of the living, and let them not be written in among the righteous.

" ' 29. I am a poor wretch who is heart-broken too; it is the salvation of thy face which hath taken me unto itself.

" ' 30. I will praise the name of God in the ode, and exalt it in the song of thanksgiving.

" ' 31. This shall please God better than a young bull which putteth forth horns and hoofs.

" ' 32. May the wretched see and make merry; seek ye God, that your souls may live.

" ' 33. For God hath heard the wretched and despiseth not the prisoners.

" ' 34. Let heaven and earth praise the Lord, the sea and all that is therein.

" ' 35. For God will save Zion, and the cities of Judæa will be built up, and they will dwell there and inherit it.

" ' 36. The seed of his servants shall possess it, and they who love his name shall dwell therein.' "

It came to pass then, when Mary had finished CHAP. 34. speaking these words unto Jesus in the midst of the disciples, that she said unto him : " My Lord, this is the solution of the mystery of the repentance of Pistis Sophia." |

It came to pass then, when Jesus had heard 56. Mary speak these words, that he said unto her : " Well said, Mary, blessed one, the fulness, or all-blessed fulness, thou who shalt be sung of as blessed in all generations."

Jesus continued again in the discourse and said : CHAP. 35. " Pistis Sophia again continued and still sang The second praises in a second repentance, saying thus : of Sophia.

" ' 1. Light of lights, in whom I have had faith, leave me not in the darkness until the end of my time.

" ' 2. Help me and save me through thy mysteries ; incline thine ear unto me and save me.

" ' 3. May the power of thy light save me and carry me to the higher æons ; for thou wilt save me and lead me into the height of thy æons.

" ' 4. Save me, O Light, from the hand of this lion-faced power and from the hands of the emanations of god Self-willed.

" ' 5. For it is thou, O Light, in whose light I have had faith and in whose light I have trusted from the beginning.

" ' 6. And I have had faith in it from the time when it emanated me, and thou thyself didst make me to emanate ; and I have had faith in thy light from the beginning.

"'7. And when I had faith in thee, the rulers of the æons mocked at me, saying: She hath ceased in her mystery. Thou art my saviour and thou art my deliverer and thou art | my mystery, O Light.

"'8. My mouth was filled with glorifying, that I may tell of the mystery of thy grandeur at all times.

"'9. Now, therefore, O Light, leave me not in the chaos for the completion of my whole time; forsake me not, O Light.

"'10. For all the emanations of Self-willed have taken from me my whole light-power and have surrounded me. They desired to take away my whole light from me utterly and have set a watch on my power,

"'11. Saying one to another together: The Light hath forsaken her, let us seize her and take away the whole light in her.

"'12. Therefore then, O Light, cease not from me; turn thee, O Light, and save me from the hands of the merciless.

"'13. May they who would take away my power, fall down and become powerless. May they who would take away my light-power from me, be enwrapped in darkness and sink into powerlessness.'

"This then is the second repentance which Pistis Sophia hath uttered, singing praises to the Light."

CHAP. 36. It came to pass then, when Jesus had finished speaking these words unto his disciples, that he said unto them: "Do ye understand in what manner I discourse with you?"

And Peter started forward and said unto Jesus:

" My Lord, we will not endure this woman, Peter com-
for she taketh the opportunity from us and hath plaineth of Mary.
let none of us speak, but she discourseth many
times."

And Jesus answered and said unto his disciples :
" Let him in whom the power of his spirit shall
seethe, so that he understandeth what I say, |
come forward and speak. But now, Peter, I 58.
see thy power in thee, that it understandeth
the solution of the mystery of the repentance
which Pistis Sophia hath uttered. Now, therefore, Peter, speak the thought of her repentance
in the midst of thy brethren."

And Peter answered and said unto Jesus : Peter inter-
" O Lord, give ear that I may speak the thought preteth the second re-
of her repentance, of which aforetime thy power pentance from Psalm
prophesied through the prophet David, uttering lxx.
her repentance in the seventieth Psalm :

" ' 1. O God, my God, I have trusted in thee,
let me no more be put to shame for ever.

" ' 2. Save me in thy righteousness and set
me free ; incline thine ear unto me and save me.

" ' 3. Be unto me a strong God and a firm
place to save me ; for thou art my strength and
my refuge.

" ' 4. My God, save me from the hand of the
sinner and from the hand of the transgressor
and from the impious [one].

" ' 5. For thou art my endurance, O Lord,
thou art my hope from my youth up.

" ' 6. I have trusted myself to thee from my
mother's womb ; thou hast brought me out of
my mother's womb. My remembrance is ever in
thee.

" ' 7. I have become as the crazy for many ; |

59.   thou art my help and my strength, thou art my deliverer, O Lord.

" ' 8. My mouth was filled with glorifying, that I may praise the glory of thy splendour the whole day long.

" ' 9. Cast me not away in the time of age; if my soul fades, forsake me not.

" ' 10. For mine enemies have spoken evil against me and they who lay in wait for my soul, have taken counsel against my soul,

" ' 11. Saying together: God hath forsaken him; pursue and seize him, for there is no saviour.

" ' 12. God, give heed to my help.

" ' 13. Let them be ashamed and destroyed who calumniate my soul. Let them be enwrapped in shame and disgrace who seek evil against me.'

" This then is the solution of the second repentance which Pistis Sophia hath uttered."

CHAP. 37.   The Saviour answered and said unto Peter:
Jesus promiseth to perfect the disciples in all things.   " Finely, Peter; this is the solution of her repentance. Blessed are ye before all men on the earth, because I have revealed unto you these mysteries. Amēn, amēn, I say unto you : |
60.   I will perfect you in all fulness from the mysteries of the interior to the mysteries of the exterior and fill you with the spirit, so that ye shall be called ' spiritual, perfected in all fulness.' And, amēn, amēn, I say unto you : I will give unto you all the mysteries of all the regions of my Father and of all the regions of the First Mystery, so that he whom ye shall admit on earth, shall be admitted into the Light of the height; and he whom ye shall expel on earth, shall be expelled from the kingdom of my Father in the heaven. But hearken, therefore, and give ear attentively

to all the repentances which Pistis Sophia hath
uttered. She continued again and uttered the
third repentance, saying :

" ' 1. O Light of powers, give heed and save me. The third

" ' 2. May they who would take away my light, of Sophia.
lack and be in the darkness. May they who
would take away my power, turn into chaos and
be put to shame.

" ' 3. May they turn quickly to darkness,
who press me sore and say : We have become
lords over her.

" ' 4. May rather all those who seek the Light,
rejoice and exult, and they who desire thy mystery,
say ever : May the mystery be exalted.

" ' 5. Save me then now, O Light, for I lacked
my light, | which they have taken away, and I 61.
needed my power, which they have taken from me.
Thou then, O Light, thou art my saviour, and
thou art my deliverer, O Light. Save me quickly
out of this chaos.' "

And it came to pass, when Jesus had finished CHAP. 38.
speaking these words unto his disciples, saying :
" This is the third repentance of Pistis Sophia,"
that he said unto them : " Let him in whom a
sensitive spirit hath arisen, come forward and
speak the thought of the repentance which
Pistis Sophia hath uttered."

It came to pass then, before Jesus had finished Martha
speaking, that Martha came forward, fell down receiveth
at his feet, kissed them, cried aloud and wept permissiom
with lamentation and in humbleness, saying :
" My Lord, have mercy upon me and have compassion with me, and let me speak the solution
of the repentance which Pistis Sophia hath
uttered."

And Jesus gave his hand unto Martha and said unto her: " Blessed is every one who humbleth himself, for on him they shall have mercy. Now, therefore, Martha, art thou blessed. But proclaim then the solution of the thought of the repentance of Pistis Sophia."

Martha interpreteth the third repentance from Psalm lxix.

62.

And Martha answered and said unto Jesus in the midst of the disciples: " Concerning the repentance which Pistis Sophia hath uttered, O | my Lord Jesus, of it thy light-power in David prophesied aforetime in the sixty-ninth Psalm, saying :

" ' 1. O Lord God, give heed to my help.

" ' 2. Let them be put to shame and confounded who seek after my soul.

" ' 3. May they turn straightway and be put to shame, who say unto me : Ha, ha.

" ' 4. May all who seek thee, be joyful and exult because of thee, and they who love thy salvation, say ever : May God be exalted.

" ' 5. But I am wretched, I am poor ; O Lord, help me. Thou art my helper and defence : O Lord, delay not.'

" This then is the solution of the third repentance which Pistis Sophia hath uttered, singing praises to the height."

CHAP. 39.

It came to pass then, when Jesus had heard Martha speak these words, that he said unto her : " Well said, Martha, and finely."

And Jesus continued again in the discourse and said unto his disciples : " Pistis Sophia again continued in the fourth repentance, reciting it before she was oppressed a second time, in 63. order that the lion-faced power and | all the material emanations with it, which Self-willed had sent into the chaos, might not take away her total light in her. She uttered then this repentance as follows :

" ' 1. O Light, in whom I have trusted, give ear to my repentance, and let my voice reach unto thy dwelling-place. The fourth repentance of Sophia.

" ' 2. Turn not away thy light-image from me, but have heed unto me, if they oppress me ; and save me quickly at the time when I shall cry unto thee.

" ' 3. For my time is vanished like a breath and I am become matter.

" ' 4. They have taken my light from me, and my power is dried up. I have forgotten my mystery which heretofore I was wont to accomplish.

" ' 5. Because of the voice of the fear and the power of Self-willed my power is vanished.

" ' 6. I am become as a demon apart, who dwelleth in matter and light is not in him, and I am become as a counterfeiting spirit, which is in a material body and light-power is not in it.

" ' 7. And I am become as a decan who is alone in the air.

" ' 8. The emanations of Self-willed have sore oppressed me, and my pair hath said unto himself :

" ' 9. Instead of with light which was in her, they have filled her with chaos. I have devoured the sweat of my own matter and the anguish of the tears from the matter of my eyes, so that they who oppress me may not take the rest.

" ' 10. All this hath befallen me, O Light, by thy | commandment and thy command, and 64. it is thy commandment that I am here.

" ' 11. Thy commandment hath brought me down, and I am descended as a power of the chaos, and my power is numbed in me.

" ' 12. But thou, O Lord, art Light eternal, and dost visit them who are for ever oppressed.

" ' 13. Now, therefore, O Light, arise and seek my power and the soul in me. Thy commandment is accomplished, which thou didst decree for me in my afflictions. My time is come, that thou shouldst seek my power and my soul, and this is the time which thou didst decree to seek me.

" ' 14. For thy saviours have sought the power which is in my soul, because the number is completed, and in order that also its matter may be saved.

" ' 15. And then at that time shall all the rulers of the material æons be in fear of thy light, and all the emanations of the thirteenth material æon shall be in fear of the mystery of thy light, so that the others may put on the purification of their light.

" ' 16. For the Lord will seek the power of your soul. He hath revealed his mystery,

" ' 17. So that he may regard the repentance of them who are in the regions below; and he hath not disregarded their repentance.

" ' 18. This is then that mystery which is become the type in respect of the race which shall be born ; and the race which shall be born will sing praises to the height.

" ' 19. For the Light hath looked down from the height of its light. It will look down on | the total matter,

" ' 20. To hear the sighing of those in chains,

to loose the power of the souls whose power is bound,—

" ' 21. So that it may lay its name in the soul and its mystery in the power.' "

It came to pass while Jesus spake these words unto his disciples, saying unto them: " This is the fourth repentance which Pistis Sophia hath uttered; now, therefore, let him who understandeth, understand,"—it came to pass then, when Jesus had spoken these words, that John came forward, adored the breast of Jesus and said unto him: " My Lord, give commandment to me also, and grant me to speak the solution of the fourth repentance which Pistis Sophia hath uttered." *CHAP. 40. John asketh and receiveth permission to speak.*

Jesus said unto John: " I give thee commandment, and I grant thee to speak the solution of the repentance which Pistis Sophia hath uttered."

John answered and said: " My Lord and Saviour, concerning this repentance which Pistis Sophia hath uttered, thy light-power which was in David, hath prophesied aforetime in the one-hundred-and-first Psalm:

" ' 1. Lord, give ear unto my supplication, and let my voice reach unto thee. *John interpreteth the repentance from Psalm ci.*

" ' 2. Turn not away thy face from me; incline thine ear unto me in the day when I am oppressed; quickly give ear to me on the day when I shall cry unto thee.

" ' 3. For | my days are vanished as smoke, 66 and my bones are parched as stone.

" ' 4. I am scorched as the grass, and my heart is dried up; for I have forgotten to eat my bread.

" ' 5. From the voice of my groaning my bones cleaved to my flesh.

" ' 6. I am become as a pelican in the desert; I am become as a screech-owl in the house.

" ' 7. I have passed the night watching; I am become as a sparrow alone on the roof.

" ' 8. My enemies have reviled me all the day long, and they who honour me, have injured me.

" ' 9. For I have eaten ashes instead of my bread and mixed my drink with tears,

" ' 10. Because of thy wrath and thy rage; for thou hast lifted me up and cast me down.

" ' 11. My days have declined as a shadow, and I am dried up as the grass,

" ' 12. But thou, O Lord, thou endurest for ever, and thy remembrance unto the generation of generation[s].

" ' 13. Arise and have mercy upon Zion, for the time is come to have mercy upon her; the proper time is come.

" ' 14. Thy servants have longed for her stones, and will take pity on her land.

" ' 15. And the nations will have fear of the name of the Lord, and the kings of the earth have fear of thy sovereignty.

" ' 16. For the Lord will build up Zion and reveal himself in his sovereignty.

" ' 17. He hath regarded the prayer of the humble and hath not despised their supplication.

" ' 18. This shall be recorded for another generation, and the people who shall be created will praise the Lord.

" ' 19. Because he hath looked down on his holy height; the Lord hath looked down from the heaven on the earth,

" ' 20. To hear the sighing | of those in chains, 67. to loose the sons of those who are slain,

" ' 21. To proclaim the name of the Lord in Zion and his praise in Jerusalem.'

" This, my Lord, is the solution of the mystery of the repentance which Pistis Sophia hath uttered."

It came to pass then, when John had finished speaking these words to Jesus in the midst of his disciples, that he said unto him: " Well said, John, the Virgin, who shalt rule in the kingdom of the Light." CHAP. 41.
Jesus commendeth John.

And Jesus continued again in the discourse and said unto his disciples: " It came to pass again thus: The emanations of Self-willed again oppressed Pistis Sophia in the chaos and desired to take from her her whole light; and not yet was her commandment accomplished, to lead her out of the chaos, and not yet had the command reached me through the First Mystery, to save her out of the chaos. It came to pass then, when all the material emanations of Self-willed oppressed her, that she cried out and uttered the fifth repentance, saying: The emanations of Self-willed again squeeze the light out of Sophia.

" ' 1. Light of my salvation, I sing praise unto thee in the region of the height and again in the chaos. The fifth repentance of Sophia.

" ' 2. I sing praise unto thee in my hymn with which I sang praise in the height and with which I sang praise unto thee when I was in the chaos. Let it come into thy presence, and give heed, O Light, to my repentance.

" ' 3. For my power is filled up with | darkness, 68. and my light hath gone down into the chaos.

" ' 4. I am myself become as the rulers of the

chaos, who are gone into the darknesses below; I am become as a material body, which hath no one in the height who will save it.

" ' 5. I am become also as matters from which their power hath been taken, when they are cast down into the chaos,—[matters] which thou hast not saved, and they are condemned utterly by thy commandment.

" ' 6. Now, therefore, have they put me into the darkness below,—in darknesses and matters which are dead and in them [is] no power.

" ' 7. Thou hast brought thy commandment upon me and all things which thou hast decreed.

" ' 8. And thy spirit hath withdrawn and abandoned me. And moreover by thy commandment the emanations of my æon have not helped me and have hated me and separated themselves from me, and yet am I not utterly destroyed.

" ' 9. And my light is diminished in me, and I have cried up to the light with all the light in me, and I have stretched forth my hands unto thee.

" ' 10. Now, therefore, O Light, wilt thou not accomplish thy commandment in the chaos, and will not the deliverers, who come according to thy commandment, arise in the darkness and come and be disciples for thee?

" ' 11. Will they not utter the mystery of thy name in the chaos ?

" ' 12. Or will they not rather utter thy name in a matter of the chaos, in which thou wilt not [thyself] purify ?

" ' 18. But I have sung praises unto thee, O Light, and my repentance will reach unto thee | in the height.

69.

" ' 14. Let thy light come upon me,

" ' 15. For they have taken my light, and I am in pain on account of the Light from the time when I was emanated. And when I had looked into the height to the Light, then I looked down below at the light-power in the chaos; I rose up and went down.

" ' 16. Thy commandment came upon me, and the terrors, which thou didst decree for me, have brought me into delusion.

" ' 17. And they have surrounded me, in numbers as water, they have laid hold on me together all my time.

" ' 18. And by thy commandment thou hast not suffered my fellow-emanations to help me, nor hast thou suffered my pair to save me out of my afflictions.'

" This then is the fifth repentance which Pistis Sophia hath uttered in the chaos, when all the material emanations of Self-willed had continued and oppressed her."

When then Jesus had spoken these words CHAP. 42. unto his disciples, he said unto them : " Who hath ears to hear, let him hear ; and let him whose spirit seetheth up in him, come forward and speak the solution of the thought of the fifth repentance of Pistis Sophia."

And when Jesus had finished saying these Philip the words, Philip started forward, held up and laid scribe complaineth. down the book in his hand,—for he is the scribe of all the discourses which Jesus spake, and of all of that which he did,—Philip then | came for- 70. ward and said unto him : " My Lord, surely then it is not on me alone that thou hast enjoined to take care for the world and write down all the discourses which we shall speak and [all we shall] do? And thou hast not suffered me to come forward to speak the solution of the mysteries of the repentance of Pistis Sophia. For my spirit hath ofttimes seethed in me and been unloosed and constrained me to come forward and speak the solution of the repentance of Pistis Sophia; and I could not come forward because I am the scribe of all the discourses."

Jesus explaineth that the appointed scribes are Philip and Thomas and Matthew.

It came to pass then, when Jesus had heard Philip, that he said unto him: "Hearken, Philip, blessed one, that I may discourse with thee; for it is thou and Thomas and Matthew on whom it is enjoined by the First Mystery to write all the discourses which I shall speak and [all which I shall] do, and all things which ye shall see. But as for thee, the number of the discourses which thou hast to write, is so far not yet completed. When it is then completed, thou art to come forward and proclaim what pleaseth thee. Now, therefore, ye three have to write down all the discourses which I shall speak and [all things which I shall] do and which ye shall see, in order that ye may bear witness to all things of the kingdom of heaven."

CHAP. 43.

When then Jesus had said this, he said unto his disciples: "Who hath ears to hear, let him hear." |

71.

Mary interpreteth the words of Jesus concerning the three witnesses.

Mary started forward again, stepped into the midst, placed herself by Philip and said unto Jesus: "My Lord, my in-dweller of light hath ears, and I am ready to hear with my power, and I have understood the word which thou hast spoken. Now, therefore, my Lord, hearken that I may discourse in openness, thou who hast said unto us : ' Who hath ears to hear, let him hear.'

" Concerning the word which thou hast spoken unto Philip : 'It is thou and Thomas and Matthew on whom it hath been enjoined— to you three by the First Mystery, to write all the discourses of the kingdom of the Light and thereto to bear witness '; hearken, therefore, that I may proclaim the solution of this word. This is what thy light-power prophesied aforetime through Moses : ' By two or three witnesses shall every matter be established.' The three witnesses are Philip and Thomas and Matthew."

It came to pass then, when Jesus had heard this word, that he said : " Well said, Mary, this is the solution of the word. Now, therefore, do thou, Philip, come forward and proclaim the solution of the fifth repentance of Pistis Sophia, and thereafter take thy seat and write all the discourses which I shall speak, until the number of thy portion which thou hast to write of the words of the kingdom of the Light is completed. Then shalt thou come forward and speak what thy spirit shall understand. But do thou then | now proclaim the solution of the fifth repentance of Pistis Sophia." *Philip is now given permission to speak.*

72.

And Philip answered and said unto Jesus : " My Lord, hearken that I may speak the solution of her repentánce. For thy power hath pro- phesied aforetime concerning it through David in the eighty-seventh Psalm, saying :

" ' 1. Lord, God of my salvation, by day and by night have I cried unto thee. *Philip in- terpreteth the fifth re- pentance from Psalm lxxxvii.*

" ' 2. Let my weeping come before thee ; incline thine ear to my supplication, O Lord.

" ' 3. For my soul is full of evil, my life hath drawn nigh to the world below.

" ' 4. I am counted among them who have gone down into the pit; I am become as a man who hath no helper.

" ' 5. The free among the dead are as the slain who are thrown away and sleep in tombs, whom thou no more rememberest, and they are destroyed through thy hands.

" ' 6. They have set me in a pit below, in darkness and shadow of death.

" ' 7. Thy wrath hath settled down upon me and all thy cares have come upon me.   (Selah.)

" ' 8. Thou hast put away mine acquaintances far from me; they have made me an abomination for them.   They have abandoned me, and I cannot go forth.

" ' 9. My eye hath become dim in my misery; I have cried unto thee, O Lord, the whole day and have stretched forth my hands unto thee.

" ' 10. Wilt thou not surely work thy wonders on the dead?   Will not surely the physicians arise and confess thee?

73. " ' 11. Will they not surely proclaim thy name in the | tombs,

" ' 12. And thy righteousness in a land which thou hast forgotten?

" ' 13. But I have cried unto thee, O Lord, and my prayer shall reach thee early in the morning.

" ' 14. Turn not thy face away from me.

" ' 15. For I am miserable, I am in sorrow from my youth up.   And when I had exalted myself, I humbled myself and arose.

" ' 16. Thy angers are come upon me and thy terrors have brought me into delusion.

" ' 17. They have surrounded me as water; they have seized upon me the whole day long.

" ' 18. My fellows hast thou kept far from me and my acquaintances from my misery.'

" This is then the solution of the mystery of the fifth repentance which Pistis Sophia hath uttered, when she was oppressed in the chaos."

It came to pass then, when Jesus had heard Philip speak these words, that he said : " Well said, Philip, well-beloved. Now, therefore, come, take thy seat and write thy portion of all the discourses which I shall speak, and [of all things which I shall] do, and of all that thou shalt see." And forthwith Philip sat down and wrote. CHAP. 44.
Philip is
commended
and con-
tinueth
writing.

It came to pass thereafter that Jesus continued again in the discourse and said unto his disciples : " Then did Pistis Sophia cry to the Light. It forgave her sin, in that she had left her region and gone down into the darkness. She uttered the sixth repentance, saying thus :

" ' 1. I have sung praises | unto thee, O Light, in the darkness below. 74.
The sixth
repentance
of Sophia.

" ' 2. Hearken unto my repentance, and may thy light give heed to the voice of my supplication.

" ' 3. O Light, if thou thinkest on my sin, I shall not be able to stand before thee, and thou wilt abandon me,

" ' 4. For thou, O Light, art my saviour; because of the light of thy name I have had faith in thee, O Light.

" ' 5. And my power hath had faith in thy mystery; and moreover my power hath trusted in the Light when it was among those of the height; and it hath trusted in it when it was in the chaos below.

"' 6. Let all the powers in me trust in the Light when I am in the darkness below, and may they again trust in the Light if they come into the region of the height.

"' 7. For it is [the Light] which hath compassion on us and delivereth us ; and a great saving mystery is in it.

"' 8. And it will save all powers out of the chaos because of my transgression. For I have left my region and am come down into the chaos.'

'" Now, therefore, whose mind is exalted, let him understand."

It came to pass then, when Jesus had finished speaking these words unto his disciples, that he said unto them : " Understand ye in what manner I discourse with you ? "

Andrew came forward and said : " My Lord, concerning the solution of the sixth repentance of Pistis Sophia, thy light-power prophesied aforetime through David in the one-hundred-and-twenty-ninth Psalm, saying : |

75.
Andrew interpreteth
the sixth
repentance
from Psalm
cxxix.

"' 1. Out of the depths I have cried unto thee, O Lord.

"' 2. Hearken unto my voice ; let thine ears give heed to the voice of my supplication.

"' 3. O Lord, if thou heedest my iniquities, who will be able to pass [the test] ?

"' 4. For pardon is in thy hands ; for the sake of thy name have I waited for thee, O Lord.

"' 5. My soul hath waited for thy word.

"' 6. My soul hath hoped in the Lord from the morning until the evening. Let Israel hope in the Lord from the morning until the evening.

"' 7. For grace standeth by the Lord and with him is great redemption.

" ' 8. And he will deliver Israel from all his iniquities.' "

Jesus said unto him : " Well said, Andrew, blessed one. This is the solution of her repentance. Amēn, amēn, I say unto you : I will perfect you in all mysteries of the Light and all gnoses from the interiors of the interiors to the exteriors of the exteriors, from the Ineffable down to the darkness of darknesses, from the Light of lights down to the .... of matter, from all the gods down to the demons, from all the lords down to the decans, from all the authorities down to the servitors, from the creation of men down to [that] of the wild-beasts, of the cattle and of the reptiles, in order that ye may be called perfect, perfected in | all fulness. Amēn, amēn, I say unto you : In the region where I shall be in the kingdom of my Father, ye will also be with me. And when the perfect number is completed, so that the Mixture shall be dissolved, I will give commandment that they bring all tyrant gods, who have not given up the purification of their light, and will give commandment to the wise fire, over which the perfect pass, to eat into those tyrants, until they give up the last purification of their light."

It came to pass then, when Jesus had finished speaking these words unto his disciples, that he said unto them : " Understand ye in what manner I speak with you ? "

Mary said : " Yea, Lord, I have understood the word which thou hast spoken. Concerning then the word which thou hast said : At the dissolution of the whole Mixture thou shalt take thy seat on a light-power and thy disciples,

Jesus commendeth Andrew.

He promiseth that the tyrants shall be judged and consumed by the wise fire.

76.

Mary interpreteth the words of Jesus.

that is ourselves, shall sit on the right of thee, and thou shalt judge the tyrant gods, who have not given up the purification of their light, and the wise fire will bite into them, until they give up the last light in them,—concerning this word then thy light-power prophesied aforetime through David, in the eighty-first Psalm, saying:

77.

"' God shall sit in the assembly (synagogue) | of the gods and try the gods.'"

Jesus said unto her: " Well said, Mary."

CHAP. 46.
The repentance of Sophia is not yet accepted. She is mocked by the æons.

Jesus continued again in the discourse and said unto his disciples: " It came to pass, when Pistis Sophia had finished uttering the sixth repentance for the forgiveness of her transgression, that she turned again to the height, to see if her sins were forgiven her, and to see whether they would lead her up out of the chaos. But by commandment of the First Mystery not yet was she hearkened to, so that her sin should be forgiven and she should be led up out of the chaos. When then she had turned to the height to see whether her repentance were accepted from her, she saw all the rulers of the twelve æons mocking at her and rejoicing over her because her repentance was not accepted from her. When then she saw that they mocked at her, she grieved exceedingly and lifted up her voice to the height in her seventh repentance, saying:

The seventh repentance of Sophia.

"' 1. O Light, I have lifted up my power unto thee, my Light.

"' 2. On thee have I had faith. Let me not be scorned; let not the rulers of the twelve æons, who hate me, rejoice over me.

"' 3. For all who have faith in thee shall not be put to shame. Let them who have taken away my power, remain in darkness; and let them not get from it any profit, but let it be taken away from them. |

" ' 4. O Light, show me thy ways, and I shall 78 be saved in them; and show me thy paths, whereby I shall be saved out of the chaos.

" ' 5. And guide me in thy light, and let me know, O Light, that thou art my saviour. On thee will I trust the whole of my time.

" ' 6. Give heed that thou save me, O Light, for thy mercy endureth for ever.

" ' 7. As to my transgression, which I have committed from the beginning in my ignorance, put it not to my account, O Light, but rather save me through thy great mystery of the forgiveness of sins because of thy goodness, O Light.

" ' 8. For good and sincere is the Light. For this cause will it grant me my way, to be saved out of my transgression;

" ' 9. And for my powers, which are diminished through the fear of the material emanations of Self-willed, will it draw near after its commandment, and will teach my powers, which are diminished because of the merciless, its gnosis.

" ' 10. For all gnoses of the Light are saving means and are mysteries for all who seek the regions of its Inheritance and its mysteries.

" ' 11. For the sake of the mystery of thy name, O Light, forgive my transgression, for it is great.

" ' 12. To every one who trusteth in the Light it will give the mystery which suiteth him;

" ' 13. And his soul will abide in the regions of the Light and his power will inherit | the Trea- 79, sury of the Light.

" ' 14. The Light giveth power to them who

have faith in it; and the name of its mystery belongeth to those who trust in it. And it will show them the region of the Inheritance, which is in the Treasury of the Light.

" ' 15. But I have ever had faith in the Light, for it will save my feet from the bonds of the darkness.

" ' 16. Give heed unto me, O Light, and save me, for they have taken away my name from me in the chaos.

" ' 17. Because of all the emanations my afflictions and my oppression have become exceedingly manifold. Save me out of my transgression and this darkness.

" ' 18. And look upon the grief of my oppression and forgive my transgression.

" ' 19. Give heed to the rulers of the twelve æons, who have hated me through jealousy.

" ' 20. Watch over my power and save me, and let me not remain in this darkness, for I have had faith in thee.

" ' 21. And they have made of me a great fool for having had faith in thee, O Light.

" ' 22. Now, therefore, O Light, save my powers from the emanations of Self-willed, by whom I am oppressed.'

" Now, therefore, who is sober, let him be sober."

When then Jesus had spoken this unto his disciples, Thomas came forward and said : " My Lord, I am sober, I am plentifully sober, and my spirit is ready in me, and I rejoice exceedingly that thou hast revealed these words unto us. But indeed I have borne with my brethren until now, so that I should not anger them ; nay rather I have borne with every one that he should come before thee and speak | the solution of the 80. repentance of Pistis Sophia. Now, therefore, my Lord, concerning the solution of the seventh repentance of Pistis Sophia thy light-power hath prophesied through the prophet David in the twenty-fourth Psalm, thus:

" ' 1. O Lord, unto thee have I lifted up my soul, O my God.

Thomas interpreteth the seventh repentance from Psalm xxiv.

" ' 2. I have abandoned myself unto thee; let me not be put to shame and let not mine enemies mock at me.

" ' 3. For all who wait upon thee shall not be put to shame; let them be put to shame who do iniquity without a cause.

" ' 4. O Lord, show me thy ways and teach me thy paths.

" ' 5. Lead me in the way of thy truth and teach me, for thou art my God and my saviour; on thee will I wait all the day long.

" ' 6. Call to remembrance thy mercies, O Lord, and the favours of thy grace, for they are from eternity.

" ' 7. Remember not the sins of my youth and those of my ignorance. Remember me according to the fulness of thy mercy because of thy goodness, O Lord.

" ' 8. The Lord is gracious and sincere; therefore will he instruct sinners in the way.

" ' 9. He will guide the tender-hearted | in the 81. judgment and will teach the tender-hearted his ways.

" ' 10. All the ways of the Lord are grace and truth for them who seek his righteousness and his testimonies.

" ' 11. For thy name's sake, O Lord, forgive me my sin, [for] it is exceedingly great.

" ' 12. Who is the man who feareth the Lord? For him will he establish laws in the way which he hath chosen.

" ' 13. His soul will abide in good things and his seed will inherit the land.

" ' 14. The Lord is the strength of them who fear him; and the name of the Lord belongeth to them who fear him, to make known unto them his covenant.

" ' 15. Mine eyes are raised ever unto the Lord, for he will draw my feet out of the snare.

" ' 16. Look down upon me and be gracious unto me, for I am an only-begotten; I am wretched.

" ' 17. The afflictions of my heart have increased; bring me out of my necessities.

" ' 18. Look upon my abasement and my woe, and forgive me all my sins.

" ' 19. Look upon mine enemies, how they have increased themselves and hated me with unjust hatred.

" ' 20. Preserve my soul and save me; let me not | be put to shame, for I have hoped on thee.

82.

" ' 21. The simple and sincere have joined themselves to me, for I have waited on thee, O Lord.

" ' 22. O God, deliver Israel from all his afflictions.' "

Jesus commendeth Thomas.

And when Jesus had heard the words of Thomas, he said unto him: " Well said, Thomas, and finely. This is the solution of the seventh repentance of Pistis Sophia. Amēn, amēn, I say unto you : All generations of the world shall bless you on earth, because I have revealed this unto you and ye have received of my spirit and have become understanding and spiritual, understanding what I say. And hereafter will I fill you full with the whole light and the whole power of the spirit, so that ye may understand from now on all which shall be said unto you and which ye shall see. Yet a little while and I will speak with you concerning the height without within and within without."

Jesus continued again in the discourse and said unto his disciples : " It came to pass then, when Pistis Sophia had uttered the seventh repentance in the chaos, that the commandment through the First Mystery had not come to me | to save her and lead her up out of the chaos. Nevertheless of myself out of compassion without commandment I led her into a somewhat spacious region in the chaos. And when the material emanations of Self-willed had noticed that she had been led into a somewhat spacious region in the chaos, they ceased a little to oppress her, for they thought that she would be led up out of the chaos altogether. When this then took place, Pistis Sophia did not know that I was her helper ; nor did she know me at all, but she continued and persisted withal singing praises to the Light of the Treasury, which she had seen aforetime and on which she had had faith, and she thought that it [sc. the Light] also was her helper and it was the same to which she had sung praises, thinking it was the Light in truth. But as indeed she had had faith in the Light which belongeth to the Treasury in truth, therefore will she be led up out

CHAP. 47.
Jesus leadeth Sophia to a less confined region, but without the commandment of the First Mystery.
83.

of the chaos and her repentance will be accepted from her. But the commandment of the First Mystery was not yet accomplished to accept her repentance from her. But hearken now in order that I may tell you all things which befell Pistis Sophia.

"It came to pass, when I had led her unto a somewhat spacious region in the chaos, that the emanations of Self-willed ceased entirely to oppress her, thinking that she would be led up out of the chaos altogether. It came to pass

then, when | the emanations of Self-willed had noticed that Pistis Sophia had not been led up out the chaos, that they turned about again all together, oppressing her vehemently. Because of this then she uttered the eighth repentance, because they had not ceased to oppress her, and had turned about to oppress her to the utmost. She uttered this repentance, saying thus:

" ' 1. On thee, O Light, have I hoped. Leave me not in the chaos ; deliver me and save me according to thy gnosis.

" ' 2. Give heed unto me and save me. Be unto me a saviour, O Light, and save me and lead me unto thy light.

" ' 3. For thou art my saviour and wilt lead me unto thee. And because of the mystery of thy name lead me and give me thy mystery.

" ' 4. And thou wilt save me from this lion-faced power, which they have laid as a snare for me, for thou art my saviour.

" ' 5. And in thy hands will I lay the purification of my light ; thou hast saved me, O Light, according to thy gnosis.

" ' 6. Thou art become wroth with them who

keep watch over me and will not be able to lay
hold of me utterly. But I have had faith in the
Light.

" ' 7. I will rejoice and will sing praises that
thou hast had mercy upon me and hast heeded
and saved me from the oppression in which I
was. And thou wilt set free my power out of
the chaos.

" ' 8. And thou hast not left me in the hand of
the lion-faced power ; but thou hast led me into
a region which is not oppressed.' "

When then Jesus had said this unto his disciples, he answered again and said unto them :
" It came to pass then, when the lion-faced
power had noticed that Pistis Sophia had not
been led up altogether out of the chaos, | that it
came again with all the other material emanations
of Self-willed, and they oppressed Pistis Sophia
again. It came to pass then, when they oppressed
her, that she cried out in the same repentance,
saying :

" ' 9. Have mercy upon me, O Light, for they
have oppressed me again. Because of thy commandment, the light in me is distracted and my
power and my understanding.

" ' 10. My power hath begun to wane whiles
I am in these afflictions, and the number of my
time whiles I am in the chaos. My light is
diminished, for they have taken away my power
from me, and all the powers in me are tossed
about.

" ' 11. I am become powerless in the presence
of all the rulers of the æons, who hate me, and
in the presence of the four-and-twenty emanations,
in whose region I was. And my brother, my

CHAP. 48.
The emana-
tions of
Self-willed
oppress her
again.

85.

She con-
tinueth her
repentance.

pair, was afraid to help me, because of that in which they have set me.

" ' 12. And all the rulers of the height have, counted me as matter in which is no light. I am become as a material power which hath fallen out of the rulers,

" ' 13. And all who are in the æons said : She hath become chaos. And thereafter all the pitiless powers encompassed me together and proposed to take away the whole light in me.

" ' 14. But I have trusted in thee, O Light, and said : Thou art my saviour.

" ' 15. And my commandment, which thou hast decreed for me, is in thy hands. Save me out of the hands of the emanations of Self-willed, which oppress me and persecute me.

" ' 16. Send thy light over me, for I am as naught before thee, | and save me according to thy compassion.

86.

" ' 17. Let me not be despised, for I have sung praises unto thee, O Light. Let chaos cover the emanations of Self-willed, let them be led down into the darkness.

" ' 18. Let the mouth of them be shut up, who would devour me with guile, who say : Let us take the whole light in her,—although I have done them no ill.' "

CHAP. 49.

And when Jesus had spoken this, Matthew came forward and said : " My Lord, thy spirit hath stirred me and thy light hath made me sober to proclaim this eighth repentance of Pistis Sophia. For thy power hath prophesied thereof aforetime through David in the thirtieth Psalm, saying :

" ' 1. On thee, O Lord, have I hoped. Let

me never be put to shame ; save me according Matthew interpreteth the eighth repentance from Psalm xxx.
to thy righteousness.

" ' 2. Incline thine ear unto me, save me
quickly. Be thou unto me a protecting God and
a house of refuge to save me.

" ' 3. For thou art my support and my refuge ;
for thy name's sake thou wilt guide me and
feed me.

" ' 4. And thou wilt draw me out of this snare,
which they have laid privily for me ; for thou
art my protection.

" ' 5. Into thy hands I will render my spirit ;
| thou hast redeemed me, O Lord, God of Truth. 87.

" ' 6. Thou hast hated them who hold to vain
emptiness ; but I have trusted.

" ' 7. And I shall rejoice because of my Lord
and make merry over thy grace. For thou hast
looked down upon my humbleness and saved my
soul out of my necessities.

" ' 8. And thou hast not shut me up in the
hands of my foes ; thou hast set my feet on a
broad space.

" ' 9. Be gracious unto me, O Lord, for I am
afflicted ; my eye is distracted in the wrath and
my soul and my body.

" ' 10. For my years have wasted away in sad-
ness and my life is wasted in sighing. My power
is enfeebled in misery and my bones are distracted.

" ' 11. I am become a mockery for all my foes
and my neighbours. | I am become a fright 88.
for my acquaintances, and they who saw me, are
fled away from me.

" ' 12. I am forgotten in their heart as a corpse,
and I have become as a ruined vessel.

" ' 13. For I have heard the scorn of many who

encompass me round about. Massing themselves together against me, they took counsel to take away my soul from me.

" ' 14. But I have trusted in thee, O Lord. I said : Thou art my God.

" ' 15. My lots are in thy hands. Save me from the hand of my foes and free me from my persecutors.

" ' 16. Reveal thy face over thy slave, and free me according to thy grace, O Lord.

" ' 17. Let me not be put to shame, for I have cried unto thee. Let the impious be put to shame and turn towards hell.

" ' 18. Let the crafty lips be struck dumb, which allege iniquity against the righteous in pride and scorn.' "

CHAP. 50.
Jesus commendeth Matthew and promiseth his disciples that they shall sit on thrones with him.
89.

And when Jesus had heard these words, he said : " Finely [said], Matthew. Now, therefore, amēn, I say unto | you : When the perfect number is completed and the universe is raised hence, I will take my seat in the Treasury of the Light, and ye yourselves will sit on twelve light-powers, until we have restored all the orders of the twelve saviours to the region of the inheritances of every one of them."

And when he had said this, he said : " Understand ye what I say ? "

Mary interpreteth the words of Jesus.

Mary came forward and said : " O Lord, concerning this matter thou hast said to us aforetime in similitude : ' Ye have awaited with me in the trials, and I will bequeath unto you a kingdom, as my Father hath bequeathed it unto me, that ye may eat and drink at my table in my kingdom ; and ye shall sit on twelve thrones and judge the twelve tribes of Israel.' "

He said unto her : " Well said, Mary."

Jesus continued again and said unto his disciples : " It came to pass then thereafter, when
the emanations of Self-willed oppressed Pistis
Sophia in the chaos, that she uttered the ninth
repentance, saying :

" ' 1. O Light, smite down them who have The ninth repentance of Sophia.
taken away my power from me, and take away
the power from them who have taken away mine
from me.

" ' 2. For I am thy power and thy light.
| Come and save me.   90.

" ' 3. Let great darkness cover my oppressors.
Say unto my power : I am he who will save
thee.

" ' 4. Let all those who would take away my
light from me utterly, lack their power. Let
them face about unto the chaos and become
powerless, who would take away my light from
me utterly.

" ' 5. Let their power be as dust, and let Yew,
thy angel, smite them.

" ' 6. And if they would go into the height,
let darkness seize upon them and let them slip
down and turn to the chaos. And let thy angel
Yew pursue them and cast them down into the
darkness below.

" ' 7. For they have set a lion-faced power as
a trap for me, although I have done them no ill,
from which its light will be taken ; and they have
oppressed the power in me, which they will not
be able to take away.

" ' 8. Now, therefore, O Light, take away the
purification from the lion-faced power without its
knowing it,—the thought which Self-willed hath

thought, to take away my light; take away his own and let the light be taken away from the lion-faced power, which set the trap for me.

" ' 9. But my power will exult in the Light and rejoice that he will save it.

" ' 10. And all the portions of my power shall say: There is no saviour but thee. For thou wilt save me out of the hand of the lion-faced power, which hath taken away my power from me, and thou savest me out of the hands of them who have taken away my power and my light from me.

" ' 11. For they have risen up against me, lying against me and saying | that I know the mystery of the Light which is in the height, [the Light] in which I have had faith. And they have constrained me, [saying:] Tell unto us the mystery of the Light in the height,—that which I know not.

" ' 12. And they have requited me with all this ill because I have had faith in the Light of the height; and they have made my power lightless.

" ' 13. But when they constrained me, I sat in the darkness, my soul bowed down in mourning.

" ' 14. And do thou, O Light—for that reason sing I praise to thee—save me. I know that thou wilt save me because I fulfilled thy will ever since I was in my æon. I fulfilled thy will, as the invisibles who are in my region, and as my pair. And I mourned, looking unceasingly and searching for the Light.

" ' 15. Now, therefore, have all the emanations of Self-willed surrounded me and rejoiced over me and sore oppressed me without my knowing

[them]. And they have fled away and ceased from me but have had no pity upon me.

" ' 16. They have returned again and made trial of me and they have oppressed me in great oppression and ground their teeth against me, desiring to take away my light from me utterly.

" ' 17. How long, therefore, O Light, dost thou suffer them, that they oppress me ? Save my power from their evil thoughts and save me from the hand of the lion-faced power ; for I alone of the invisibles am in this region.

" ' 18. I will sing praises unto thee, O Light, | in the midst of all who are gathered together 92. against me, and I will cry unto thee in the midst of all who oppress me.

" ' 19. Now, therefore, O Light, let not them who hate me and desire to take away my power from me, rejoice over me—who hate me and flash their eyes against me, though I have not done anything unto them.

" ' 20. For indeed they have fawned upon me with sweet words, asking me concerning the mysteries of the Light which I know not, and have craftily spoken against me and been enraged against me, because I have had faith in the Light in the height.

" ' 21. They have opened their chops against me and said : Well indeed, we will take from her her light.

" ' 22. Now, therefore, O Light, thou hast known their guile ; suffer them not and let not thy help be far from me.

" ' 23. Quickly, O Light, vindicate and avenge me,

" ' 24. And give judgment on me according

to thy goodness. Now, therefore, O Light of lights, let them not take away my light from me,

" ' 25. And let them not say in their heart: Our power is glutted with her light. And let them not say: We have consumed her power.

" ' 26. But rather let darkness come upon them, and let those who long to take away my light from me, become powerless, and let them be clothed with chaos and darkness, who say there: We will take away her light and her power.

" ' 27. Now, therefore, save me that I may rejoice, for I long for the thirteenth æon, the region of Righteousness, and | I shall say ever-more: May the light of thy angel Yew shine more and more.

93.

" ' 28. And my tongue will sing praises to thee in thy gnosis my whole time in the thirteenth æon.' "

CHAP. 51.

It came to pass, when Jesus had finished saying these words unto his disciples, that he said unto them: " Who is sober among you, let him pro-claim their solution."

James came forward, kissed the breast of Jesus and said: " My Lord, thy spirit hath sobered me, and I am ready to proclaim their solution. Concerning them indeed thy power hath pro-phesied aforetime through David in the thirty-fourth Psalm, saying thus concerning the ninth repentance of Pistis Sophia:

James in-
terpreteth
the ninth
repentance
from Psalm
xxxiv.

" ' 1. Give sentence, O Lord, on them who do me injustice, and fight against them who fight against me.

" ' 2. Lay hand on weapon and shield and stand up to help me.

"' 3. Draw forth a sword and conceal it [*sic*] from my oppressors. Say unto my soul: I am thy salvation.

"' 4. Let them be put to shame and abashed who strive after my soul; let them fall back and be put to shame who imagine evil against me.

"' 5. Let them be as chaff | before the wind, 94. and let the angel of the Lord pursue after them.

"' 6. Let their way be darkness and slippery, and let the angel of the Lord oppress them.

"' 7. For without cause have they hid a snare for me for their own spoiling, and they have mocked at my soul in vain.

"' 8. Let a snare come upon them which they know not, and let the net which they have hid for me, catch them, and let them fall into this snare.

"' 9. But my soul will exult in the Lord and rejoice in its salvation.

"' 10. All my bones shall say: O Lord, who can be like unto thee?—thou who settest free the wretched from the hand | of him who is 95. stronger than him; and thou savest a wretched and poor [one] from the hands of them who spoil him.

"' 11. Unjust witnesses came forward and have asked me that which I knew not.

"' 12. They have requited me evil for good and childlessness for my soul.

"' 13. But when they molested me, I clothed me in a sack and humbled my soul with fasting, and my prayer will return into my breast.

"' 14. I was pleasing unto thee, as unto my neighbour and as unto my brother; and I humbled myself as one in mourning and as one who is sad.

" ' 15. They have rejoiced over me, and they are put to shame. Scourges have gathered themselves together against me and I knew not ; they were cut off and were troubled.

" ' 16. They have brought me to trial and mocked me with mocking ; they have ground their teeth against me.

96.

" ' 17. O Lord, when wilt thou look upon me ? Restore again my soul from their evil works and save my only one from the hands of the lions.

" ' 18. I will confess to thee, O Lord, in the great assembly, and I will sing praises to thee in the midst of a countless people.

" ' 19. Let not them who unjustly treat me as a foe, rejoice over me, who hate me without a cause and wink with their eyes.

" ' 20. For indeed they discourse with me with words of peace, though they plot wrath with craft.

" ' 21. They opened their chops wide against me and said : Well indeed, our eyes have filled our sight with him.

" ' 22. Thou hast seen, O Lord. Keep not silence, O Lord, withdraw not thyself from me.

97.

" ' 23. Arise, O Lord, | and give heed to my vindication, give heed to my vengeance, my God and my Lord.

" ' 24. Judge me, O Lord, according to thy justice ; let them not rejoice over me, my God.

" ' 25. And let them not say : Well done, our soul. Let them not say : We have consumed him.

" ' 26. Let them be put to shame and be scorned, who rejoice at my mischance. Let them be clothed with shame and disgrace who speak boastingly against me.

" ' 27. Let them who desire my justification, exult and rejoice and let them who desire the peace of his slave, say : May the Lord be great and arise.

" ' 28. My tongue will exult over thy justification and over thy honour all the day long.' " |

When James then had said this, Jesus said unto him : " Well said, finely, James. This is the solution of the ninth repentance of Pistis Sophia. Amēn, amēn, I say unto you : Ye shall be the first in the kingdom of heaven before all invisibles and all gods and rulers who are in the thirteenth æon and in the twelfth æon ; and not only ye, but also every one who shall accomplish my mysteries."

And when he had said this, he said unto them : " Understand ye in what manner I discourse with you ? "

Mary started forward again and said : " Yea, O Lord, this is what thou didst say unto us aforetime : ' The last shall be first and the first shall be last.' The first then, who were created before us, are the invisibles, for indeed they arose before mankind, they and the gods and the rulers ; and the men who shall receive mysteries, will be first into the kingdom of heaven."

Jesus said unto her : "Well said, Mary."

Jesus continued again and said unto his disciples : " It came to pass then, when Pistis Sophia had proclaimed the ninth repentance, that the lion-faced power oppressed her again, desiring to take away all powers from her. She cried out again to the Light, saying : |

Marginal notes:
98.
CHAP. 52. Jesus commendeth James and promiseth the first place unto the disciples.

Mary interpreteth the words of Jesus.

The repentance of Sophia is accepted. Jesus is sent to help her.

" ' O Light, in whom I have had faith from the beginning, for whose sake I have endured these great pains, help me.'

" And in that hour her repentance was accepted from her. The First Mystery hearkened unto her, and I was sent off at his command. I came to help her, and led her up out of the chaos, because she had repented, and also because she had had faith in the Light and had endured these great pains and these great perils. She had been deluded through the god-like Self-willed, and had not been deluded through anything else, save through a light-power, because of its resemblance to the Light in which she had had faith. For this cause then was I sent forth at the command of the First Mystery to help her secretly. I did not however yet go to the region of the æons at all ; but I passed down through the midst out of them, without any single power knowing it, either those of the interior of the interior or those of the exterior of the exterior, save only the First Mystery.

" It came to pass then, when I came into the chaos to help her, that she saw me, that I was understanding and shone exceedingly and was full of compassion for her. For I was not self-willed as the lion-faced power, which had taken away the light-power from Sophia, and had also oppressed her in order to take away from her the whole light in her. Sophia then saw me, that I shone ten-thousand times more than the lion-faced power, | and that I was full of compassion for her. And she knew that I came out of the Height of heights, in whose light she had had faith from the beginning. Pistis Sophia then took courage and uttered the tenth repentance, saying :

" ' 1. I have cried unto thee, O Light of lights, in my oppression and thou hast hearkened unto me. The tenth repentance of Sophia.

" ' 2. O Light, save my power from unjust and lawless lips and from crafty traps.

" ' 3. The light which was being taken from me in crafty snaring, will not be brought unto thee.

" ' 4. For the traps of Self-willed and the nooses of the merciless [one] are spread out.

" ' 5. Woe unto me, that my dwelling was far off, and I was in the dwellings of the chaos.

" ' 6. My power was in regions which are not mine.

" ' 7. And I entreated those merciless [ones] ; and when I entreated them, they fought against me without a cause.' "

When then Jesus had said this unto his disciples, he said unto them : " Now, therefore, let him whom his spirit stirreth, come forward and speak the solution of the tenth repentance of Pistis Sophia." CHAP. 53.

Peter answered and said : " O Lord, concerning this thy light-power prophesied aforetime through David in the one-hundred-and-nineteenth Psalm, saying :

" ' 1. I cried unto thee, O Lord, in my oppression, and thou hearkenest unto me. Peter interpreteth the tenth repentance from Psalm cxix.

" ' 2. O Lord, save | my soul from unjust lips and from crafty tongues.

" ' 3. What will be given unto thee or what [101] will be added unto thee with a crafty tongue ?

" ' 4. The arrows of the strong [one] are made sharp with the coal of the desert.

" ' 5. Woe unto me, that my dwelling is far off, and I dwelt in the tents of Kedar.

" ' 6. My soul hath dwelt in many regions as a guest.

" ' 7. I was peaceful with them who hate peace ; if I spake unto them, they fought against me without a cause.'

" This is now, therefore, O Lord, the solution of the tenth repentance of Pistis Sophia, which she hath uttered when the material emanations of Self-willed oppressed her, they and his lion-faced power, and when they oppressed her exceedingly."

Jesus said unto him : " Well said, Peter, and finely. This is the solution of the tenth repentance of Pistis Sophia."

Jesus continued again in the discourse and said unto his disciples : " It came to pass then, when this lion-faced power saw me, how I drew nigh unto Pistis Sophia, shining very exceedingly, that it grew still more furious and emanated from itself a multitude of exceedingly violent emanations. When this then befell, Pistis Sophia uttered the eleventh repentance, saying :

" ' 1. Why hath the mighty power raised itself in evil ?

" ' 2. Its plotting taketh away the light from me all the time, and as sharp iron have they

taken away power | from me.

" ' 3. I chose to descend into the chaos rather than to abide in the thirteenth æon, the region of Righteousness.

" ' 4. And they desired to lead me craftily, in order to consume my whole light.

" ' 5. For this cause then will the Light take

away their whole light, and also their whole matter will be made naught. And it will take away their light and not suffer them to abide in the thirteenth æon, their dwelling-place, and will not have their name in the region of those who shall live.

" ' 6. And the four-and-twenty emanations will see what hath befallen thee, O lion-faced power, and will be afraid and not be disobedient, but give the purification of their light.

" ' 7. And they will see thee and will rejoice over thee and say : Lo, an emanation which hath not given the purification of its light, so that it may be saved, but boasted itself in the abundance of the light of its power, because it did not emanate from the power in it, and hath said : I will take away the light from Pistis Sophia, which will now be taken from it.'

" Now, therefore, let him in whom his power is raised, come forward and proclaim the solution of the eleventh repentance of Pistis Sophia."

Then Salome came forward and said : " My Lord, concerning this thy light-power prophesied aforetime through David in the fifty-first Psalm, saying :

" ' 1. Why doth the mighty [one] boast himself in | his wickedness ?

" ' 2. Thy tongue hath studied unrighteousness all the day long ; as a sharp razor hast thou practised craft.

" ' 3. Thou lovedst wickedness more than goodness ; thou lovedst to speak unrighteousness more than righteousness.

" ' 4. Thou lovedst all words of submerging and a crafty tongue.

" ' 5. Wherefor will God bring thee to naught

103.

Salome interpreteth the repentance from Psalm li.

utterly, and will uproot thee and drag thee out from thy dwelling-place, and will root out thy root and cast it away from the living. (Selah.)

" ' 6. The righteous will see and be afraid, and they will mock at him and say:

" ' 7. Lo, a man who made not God for his helper, but trusted to his great riches and was mighty in his vanity.

104.

" ' 8. But I am as a | fruit-bearing olive-tree in the house of God. I have trusted in the grace of God from all eternity.

" ' 9. And I will confess unto thee, for thou hast dealt faithfully with me; and I will wait on thy name, for it is auspicious in the presence of thy holy [ones].'

" This then is now, therefore, my Lord, the solution of the eleventh repentance of Pistis Sophia. While thy light-power hath roused me, I have spoken it according to thy desire."

Jesus commendeth Salome.

It came to pass then, when Jesus had heard these words which Salome spake, that he said: " Well said, Salome. Amēn, amēn, I say unto you: I will perfect you in all mysteries of the kingdom of the Light."

CHAP. 55.
Self-willed aideth his emanations and they again oppress Sophia.

And Jesus continued again in the discourse and said unto his disciples: " It came to pass then thereafter, that I drew near unto the chaos, shining very exceedingly, to take away the light from that lion-faced power. As I shone exceedingly, it was in fear and cried out to its self-willed god, that he should help it. And forthwith the self-willed god looked out of the thirteenth æon, and looked down into the chaos, exceedingly

105.

wrathful | and desiring to help his lion-faced power. And forthwith the lion-faced power, it and all its emanations, surrounded Pistis Sophia, desiring to take away the whole light in Sophia. It came to pass then, when they oppressed Sophia, that she cried to the height, crying unto me that I should help her. It came to pass then, when she looked to the height, that she saw Self-willed exceedingly wrathful, and she was in fear, and uttered the twelfth repentance because of Self-willed and his emanations. She cried on high unto me, saying :

" ' 1. O Light, forget not my praise-singing.

" ' 2. For Self-willed and his lion-faced power have opened their chops against me and have acted craftily against me.

" ' 3. They have surrounded me, desiring to take away my power, and have hated me, because I have sung praises unto thee.

" ' 4. Instead of loving me they slandered me. But I sang praises.

" ' 5. They plotted a plot to take away my power, because I have sung to thee praises, O Light ; and hated me, because I have loved thee.

" ' 6. Let the darkness come over Self-willed, and let the ruler of the outermost darkness abide at his right hand.

" ' 7. And when thou passest sentence, take from him his power ; and the deed which he hath plotted, to take from me my light,—mayest thou take his from him.

" ' 8. And may all his powers of his light in him finish, and let | another of the three triple-powers receive his sovereignty.

" ' 9. May all the powers of his emanations be lightless and may his matter be without any light in it.

The twelfth repentance of Sophia.

106.

" ' 10. May his emanations remain in the chaos and not dare to go to their region. May their light in them die away and let them not go to the thirteenth æon, their region.

" ' 11. May the Receiver, the Purifier of the lights, purify all the lights which are in Self-willed, and take them from them.

" ' 12. May the rulers of the lower darkness rule over his emanations, and let no one give them shelter in his region ; and let no one hearken to the power of his emanations in the chaos.

" ' 13. Let them take away the light in his emanations and blot out their name from the thirteenth æon, yea rather take his name for ever out of that region.

" ' 14. And on the lion-faced power let them bring the sin of him who emanated it, before the Light, and not wipe out the iniquity of the matter which hath brought him [*sc.* Self-willed] forth.

" ' 15. And may their sin be altogether before the Light eternally, and may they let them not look beyond [the chaos] and take their names out of all regions ;

" ' 16. Because they have not spared me and have oppressed him whose light and | whose power they have taken away, and also conformably with those who set me therein, they desired to take away my whole light from me.

" ' 17. They loved to descend to the chaos ; so let them abide therein, and they shall not be brought up [therefrom] from now on. They desired not the region of Righteousness for dwelling-place, and they shall not be taken thither from now on.

" ' 18. He put on darkness as a garment, and it entered into him as water, and it entered in into all his powers as oil.

" ' 19. Let him wrap himself into the chaos as into a garment, and gird himself with the darkness as with a leathern girdle for ever.

" ' 20. Let this befall them who have brought this upon me for the Light's sake and have said : Let us take away her whole power.

" ' 21. But do thou, O Light, have mercy upon me for the sake of the mystery of thy name, and save me in the goodness of thy grace.

" ' 22. For they have taken away my light and my power ; and my power hath inwardly tottered, and I could not stand upright in their midst.

" ' 23. I am become as matter which is fallen ; I am tossed hither and thither as a demon in the air.

" ' 24. My power hath perished, because I possess no mystery ; and my matter hath become dwindled because of my light, for they have taken it away.

" ' 25. And they mocked me ; they looked at me, nodding at me.

" ' 26. Help me according to thy mercy.' |

" Now, therefore, let him whose spirit is ready, 10a. come forward and utter the solution of the twelfth repentance of Pistis Sophia."

And Andrew came forward and said : " My CHAP. 56. Lord and Saviour, thy light-power hath prophesied aforetime through David concerning this repentance which Pistis Sophia hath uttered, and said in the one-hundred-and-eighth Psalm :

" ' 1. God, keep not silent at my praise-singing.

90   PISTIS SOPHIA

Andrew in-
terpreteth
the twelfth
repentance
from Psalm
cviii.

" ' 2. For the mouths of the sinner and crafty have opened their chops against me and with crafty deceitful tongue have talked behind me.

" ' 3. And they have surrounded me with words of hate and have fought against me without a cause.

" ' 4. Instead of loving me they have slandered me. But I prayed.

" ' 5. They showed evil against me for good and hate for my love.

" ' 6. Set a sinner over him, and let. the slanderer stand at his right hand.

" ' 7. When sentence is passed upon him, may he go forth condemned and his prayer become sin.

" ' 8. May his days be shortened and another receive his overseership.

" ' 9. May his children become orphans and his wife a widow.

" ' 10. May his children be carried away and be driven forth and beg ; may they be thrown out of their houses.

" ' 11. May the money-lender sift out all that 109. he hath, | and may strangers plunder all his best efforts.

" ' 12. Let there be no man to back him, and no one to take pity on his orphans.

" ' 13. May his children be exterminated and his name blotted out in a single generation.

" ' 14. Let the sin of his fathers be remembered before the Lord, and the sin of his mother be not blotted out.

" ' 15. Let them be ever present to the Lord and his memory be rooted out from the earth ;

" ' 16. In that he hath not thought of using

mercy and hath persecuted a poor and wretched
man and hath persecuted a sorry creature to
slay him.

" ' 17. He loved cursing,—and it shall come
unto him. He desired not blessing,—it shall
stay far from him.

" ' 18. He clothed himself with cursing as with
a vesture, and it entered into his bowels as water,
and it was as oil in his bones.

" ' 19. May it be for him as a garment in which
he shall be wrapped, and as a girdle with which
he shall ever be girded.

" ' 20. This is the work of them who slander
[me] before the Lord, and speak unlawfully
against my soul.

" ' 21. But do thou, O Lord God, be gracious
unto me ; for thy name's sake save me.

" ' 22. For I am poor and I am wretched ;
my heart is tumult within me. |

" ' 23. I am carried away in the midst as a 110.
shadow which hath sunk down, and I am shaken
out as grass-hoppers.

" ' 24. My knees have become weak from fasting, and my flesh is altered from [lack of] oil.

" ' 25. But I have become a mock unto them ;
they saw me and wagged their heads.

" ' 26. Help, O Lord God, and save me according to thy grace.

" ' 27. May they know that this is thy hand,
and that thou, O Lord, hast fashioned them.'

" This is then the solution of the twelfth
repentance which Pistis Sophia uttered, when
she was in the chaos."

And Jesus continued again in the discourse CHAP. 57.
and said unto his disciples : " It came to pass

again thereafter that Pistis Sophia cried unto me, saying :

" ' O Light of lights, I have transgressed in the twelve æons, and have descended from them ; wherefor have I uttered the twelve repentances, [one] for each æon. Now, therefore, O Light of lights, forgive me my transgression, for it is exceedingly great, because I have abandoned the regions of the height and have come to dwell in the regions of the chaos.'

" When then Pistis Sophia had said this, she continued again in the thirteenth repentance, saying :

The thirteenth repentance of Sophia.

" ' 1. Hearken unto me singing praises unto thee, O Light of lights. Hearken unto me uttering the repentance for the thirteenth æon, the region out of which I have come down, in order that the thirteenth repentance of the thirteenth æon may be accomplished,—those [æons] | which I have overstepped and out of which I have come down.

111.

" ' 2. Now, therefore, O Light of lights, hearken unto me singing praises unto thee in the thirteenth æon, my region out of which I have come down.

" ' 3. Save me, O Light, in thy great mystery and forgive my transgression in thy forgiveness.

" ' 4. And give unto me the baptism and forgive my sins and purify me from my transgression.

" ' 5. And my transgression is the lion-faced power, which will never be hidden from thee ; for because of it have I gone down.

" ' 6. And I alone among the invisibles, in whose regions I was, have transgressed, and have gone down into the chaos. Moreover I have transgressed, that thy commandment may be accomplished.'

" This then Pistis Sophia said. Now, therefore, let him whom his spirit urgeth to understand her words, come forward and proclaim her thought."

Martha came forward and said : " My Lord, my spirit urgeth me to proclaim the solution of that which Pistis Sophia hath spoken ; thy power hath prophesied aforetime concerning it through David in the fiftieth Psalm, saying thus :

" ' 1. Be gracious unto me, O God, according to thy | great grace ; according to the fulness of thy mercy blot out my sin.

" ' 2. Wash me throughly from my iniquity.

" ' 3. And may my sin be ever present to thee,

" ' 4. That thou mayest be justified in thy words and prevail when thou judgest me.'

" This is then the solution of the words which Pistis Sophia hath uttered."

· Jesus said unto her : " Well said, finely, Martha, blessed [one]."

And Jesus continued again in the discourse and said unto his disciples : " It came to pass then, when Pistis Sophia had said these words, that the time was fulfilled that she should be led out of the chaos. And of myself, without the First Mystery, I despatched out of myself a light-power, and I sent it down to the chaos, so that it might lead Pistis Sophia forth from the deep regions of the chaos, and lead [her] to the higher regions of the chaos, until the command should come from the First Mystery that she should be led entirely forth out of the chaos. And my light-power led Pistis Sophia up to the higher regions

Martha interpreteth the thirteenth repentance from Psalm l. 112.

CHAP. 58. *Jesus sendeth forth a light-power to help Sophia.*

of the chaos. It came to pass then, when the emanations of Self-willed had noticed that Pistis Sophia was led forth into the higher regions of the chaos, that they also sped after her upwards, desiring to bring her again into the lower regions of the chaos. And my light-power, which I had sent to lead up Sophia out of the chaos, shone exceedingly. It came to pass then, when the

emanations of Self-willed pursued Sophia, | when she had been led into the higher regions of the chaos, that she again sang praises and cried out unto me, saying :

" ' 1. I will sing praises unto thee, O Light, for I desired to come unto thee. I will sing thee praises, O Light, for thou art my deliverer.

" ' 2. Leave me not in the chaos. Save me, O Light of the Height, for it is thou that I have praised.

" ' 3. Thou has sent me thy light through thyself and hast saved me. Thou hast led me to the higher regions of the chaos.

" ' 4. May the emanations of Self-willed which pursue me, sink down into the lower regions of the chaos, and let them not come to the higher regions to see me.

" ' 5. And may great darkness cover them and darker gloom come over them. And let them not see me in the light of thy power, which thou hast sent unto me to save me, so that they may not again get dominion over me.

" ' 6. And let not their resolution which they have formed, to take away my power, take effect for them. And as they have spoken against me, to take from me my light, take rather from them theirs instead of mine.

" ' 7. And they have proposed to take away my whole light and have not been able to take it, for thy light-power was with me.

" ' 8. Because they have taken counsel without thy commandment, O Light, therefore have they not been able to take away my light.

" ' 9. Because I | have had faith in the Light, 114. I shall not be afraid ; and the Light is my deliverer and I shall not fear.'

" Now, therefore, let him whose power is exalted, speak the solution of the words which Pistis Sophia hath uttered."

And it came to pass, when Jesus had finished speaking these words unto his disciples, that Salome came forward and said : " My Lord, my power constraineth me to speak the solution of the words which Pistis Sophia hath uttered. Thy power hath prophesied aforetime through Solomon, saying :

" ' 1. I will give thanks unto thee, O Lord, for thou art my God.

" ' 2. Abandon me not, O Lord, for thou art my hope.

" ' 3. Thou hast given me thy vindication for naught, and I am saved through thee.

" ' 4. Let them who pursue me, fall down and let them not see me.

" ' 5. May a smoke-cloud cover their eyes and an air-mist darken them, and let them not see the day, so that they may not seize me.

" ' 6. May their resolution be impotent, and may what they concoct come upon them.

" ' 7. They have devised a resolution, and it hath not taken effect for them.

" ' 8. And they are vanquished, although they

Salome interpreteth the song of Sophia from the Odes of Solomon.

be mighty, and what they have wickedly prepared is fallen upon them.

" ' 9. My hope is in the Lord, and I shall not
be afraid, for thou art my God; my Saviour.' "

It came to pass then, when Salome had finished
saying these words, that Jesus said unto her:

115. "Well said, | Salome; and finely. This is the
solution of the words which Pistis Sophia hath
uttered."

CHAP. 59. And Jesus continued again in the discourse
The power and said unto his disciples: "It came to pass
sent by then, when Pistis Sophia had finished saying
Jesus form-
eth a light- these words in the chaos, that I made the light-
wreath on power, which I had sent to save her, become a
Sophia's light-wreath on her head, so that from now on
head. the emanations of Self-willed could not have
dominion over her. And when it had become
a light-wreath round her head, all the evil matters
in her were shaken and all were purified in her.
They perished and remained in the chaos, while
the emanations of Self-willed gazed upon them
and rejoiced. And the purification of the pure
light which was in Pistis Sophia, gave power to
the light of my light-power, which had become a
wreath round her head.

" It came to pass then moreover, when it
surrounded the pure light in Sophia, and her
pure light did not depart from the wreath of
the power of the light-flame, so that the emanations of Self-willed should not rob it from it,—
when then this befell her, the pure light-power
in Sophia began to sing praises. And she praised
my light-power, which was a wreath round her
head, and she sang praises, saying:

" ' 1. The Light hath become a wreath round

my head; and I shall not depart from it, so that the Sophia uttereth another song of praise. 116.
emanations of Self-willed may not rob it from me.

" ' 2. And though all the matters be shaken, yet shall I not be shaken.

" ' 3. And though all my matters perish and remain in the chaos,—those which the emanations of Self-willed see,—yet shall I not perish.

" ' 4. For the Light is with me, and I myself am with the Light.'

" These words then Pistis Sophia uttered. Now, therefore, let him who understandeth the thought of these words, come forward and proclaim their solution."

Then Mary, the mother of Jesus, came forward Mary, his mother, asketh and receiveth permission to speak. and said : " My son according to the world, my God and Saviour according to the height, bid me proclaim the solution of the words which Pistis Sophia hath uttered."

And Jesus answered and said : " Thou also, Mary, hast received form which is in Barbēlō, according to matter, and hast received likeness which is in the Virgin of Light, according to light, thou and the other Mary, the blessed one ; and on thy account the darkness hath arisen, and moreover out of thee did come forth the material body in which I am, which I have purified and refined,—now, therefore, I bid thee proclaim the solution of the words which Pistis Sophia hath uttered."

And Mary, the mother of Jesus, answered and said : " My Lord, thy light-power hath prophesied aforetime concerning these words through Solomon in the nineteenth Ode and said :

" ' 1. The Lord is on my head as a wreath, and I shall not depart from him.

117.

Mary, his mother, interpreteth the song of Sophia from the xixth Ode of Solomon.

" ' 2. The wreath in truth | is woven for me; and it hath caused thy twigs to sprout in me.

" ' 8. For it is not like unto a wreath withered that sprouteth not. But thou art alive on my head and thou hast sprouted upon me.

" ' 4. Thy fruits are full and perfect, filled with thy salvation.' "

Jesus commendeth his mother.

It came to pass then, when Jesus had heard his mother Mary say these words, that he said unto her : " Well saïd, finely. Amĕn, amĕn, I say unto thee : They shall proclaim thee blessed from one end of the earth to the other ; for the pledge of the First Mystery hath taken up its abode with thee, and through that pledge shall all from the earth and all from the height be saved, and that pledge is the beginning and the end."

CHAP. 60.

The commandment of the First Mystery is fulfilled for taking Sophia entirely out of the chaos.

And Jesus continued again in the discourse and said unto his disciples : " It came to pass when Pistis Sophia had uttered the thirteenth repentance,—in that hour was fulfilled the commandment of all the tribulations which were decreed for Pistis Sophia for the fulfilment of the First Mystery, which was from the beginning, and the time had come to save her out of the chaos and lead her out from all the darknesses. For her repentance was accepted from her through the First Mystery ; and that mystery sent me a great light-power out of the height, that I might

118.

The First Mystery and Jesus sent forth two light-powers to help Sophia.

help Pistis Sophia | and lead her up out of the chaos. So I looked towards the æons into the height and saw that light-power which the First Mystery had sent me, that I might save Pistis Sophia out of the chaos. It came to pass, therefore, when I had seen it, coming forth from the æons and hastening down to me,—I was above

the chaos,—that another light-power went forth
out of me, that it too might help Pistis Sophia.
And the light-power which had come from the
height through the First Mystery, came down
upon the light-power which had gone out of me ;
and they met together and became a great stream
of light."

When then Jesus had said this unto his disciples,
he said : " Understand ye in what manner I
discourse with you ? "

Mary started forward again and said : "My
Lord, I understand what thou sayest. Concerning
the solution of this word thy light-power hath
prophesied aforetime through David in the eighty-
fourth Psalm, saying : *Mary Mag-
dalene inter-
preteth the
mystery from
Psalm lxxxiv.*

" ' 10. Grace and truth met together, and
righteousness and peace kissed each other.

" ' 11. Truth sprouted forth out of the earth,
and righteousness looked down from heaven.'

" ' Grace ' then is the light-power which hath
come down through the First Mystery ; for the
First Mystery hath hearkened unto Pistis Sophia
and hath had | mercy on her in all her tribulations. 119.
' Truth ' on the other hand is the power which
hath gone forth out of thee, for that thou hast
fulfilled the truth, in order to save her out of the
chaos. And ' righteousness ' again is the power
which hath come forth through the First Mystery,
which will guide Pistis Sophia. And ' peace '
again is the power which hath gone forth out of
thee, so that it should enter into the emanations
of Self-willed and take from them the lights
which they have taken away from Pistis Sophia,—
that is, so that thou mayest gather them together
into Pistis Sophia and make them at peace with

her power. 'Truth' on the other hand is the power which went forth out of thee, when thou wast in the lower regions of the chaos. For this cause thy power hath said through David: 'Truth sprouted out of the earth,' because thou wert in the lower regions of the chaos. 'Righteousness' on the other hand which hath 'looked down from heaven,'—it is the power which hath come down from the height through the First Mystery and hath entered into Pistis Sophia."

CHAP. 61. It came to pass then, when Jesus had heard these words, that he said: " Well said, Mary, blessed one, who shalt inherit the whole Light-kingdom."

Thereon Mary, the mother of Jesus, also came forward and said: " My Lord and my Saviour, give commandment unto me also that I repeat this word."

Jesus said: " Whose spirit is understanding, him I do not prevent, but I urge him on still more to speak the thought which hath moved him. | Now, therefore, Mary, my mother according to matter, thou in whom I have sojourned, I bid thee that thou also speak the thought of the discourse."

120.

Mary, the mother, further interpreteth the scripture.

And Mary answered and said: " My Lord, concerning the word which thy power hath prophesied through David: 'Grace and truth met together, righteousness and peace kissed each other. Truth sprouted forth out of the earth, and righteousness looked down from heaven,'—thus hath thy power prophesied this word aforetime about thee.

" When thou wert little, before the spirit had

come upon thee, whilst thou wert in a vineyard ^{The story}
with Joseph, the spirit came out of the height ^{of the} ^{phantom}
and came to me in my house, like unto thee; ^{spirit.}
and I had not known him, but I thought that
thou wast he. And the spirit said unto me :
'·Where is Jesus, my brother, that I meet with
him ? ' And when he had said this unto me,
I was at a loss and thought it was a phantom to
try me. So I seized him and bound him to the
foot of the bed in my house, until I went forth
to you, to thee and Joseph in the field, and I
found you on the vineyard, Joseph propping
up the vineyard. It came to pass, therefore,
when thou didst hear me speak the word unto
Joseph, that thou didst understand the word,
wert joyful and saidest : ' Where is he, that I
may see him ; else I await him in this place.'
And it came to pass, when Joseph had heard
thee say these words, that he was startled. And
we went down | together, entered the house and 121.
found the spirit bound to the bed. And we
looked on thee and him and found thee like unto
him. And he who was bound to the bed was
unloosed ; he took thee in his arms and kissed
thee, and thou also didst kiss him. Ye became
one.

" This then is the word and its solution.
' Grace ' is the spirit which hath come down out
of the height through the First Mystery, for it
hath had mercy on the race of men and sent its
spirit that he should forgive the sins of the whole
world, and they should receive the mysteries
and inherit the Light-kingdom. ' Truth ' on
the other hand is the power which hath sojourned
with me. When it had come forth out of Barbēlō,

it became material body for thee, and hath made
proclamation concerning the region of Truth.
' Righteousness ' is thy spirit, who hath brought
the mysteries out of the height to give them to
the race of men. ' Peace ' on the other hand
is the power which hath sojourned in thy material
body according to the world, which hath baptized
the race of men, until it should make it stranger
unto sin and make it at peace with thy spirit, so
that they may be at peace with the emanations
of the Light ; that is, ' Grace and truth kissed each
other.' As it saith : ' Truth sprouted forth out
of the earth,'—' truth ' is thy material body |
122.   which sprouted forth out of me according to the
world of men, and hath made proclamation concerning the region of Truth. And again as it
saith : 'Righteousness [looked down] from heaven'
—' righteousness ' is the power which looked out
of the height, which will give the mysteries of
the Light to the race of men, so that they will
become righteous and good, and inherit the Light-
kingdom."

It came to pass then, when Jesus had heard
these words which his mother Mary spake, that
he said : " Well said, finely, Mary."

CHAP. 62.   The other Mary came forward and said : " My
Lord, bear with me and be not wroth with me.
Yea, from the moment when thy mother spake
with thee concerning the solution of these words,
my power disquieted me to come forward and like-
wise to speak the solution of these words."

Jesus said unto her : " I bid thee speak their
solution."

Mary said : " My Lord, ' Grace and truth
met together,'—' grace ' then is the spirit who hath

come upon thee, when thou didst receive the baptism from John. ' Grace ' then is the godly spirit who hath come upon thee ; he hath had mercy on the race of men, hath come down and hath met with the power of Sabaōth, the Good, which is in thee and which hath made proclamation concerning the regions of Truth. It hath said again : ' Righteousness and peace kissed each other,'—' righteousness ' then is the spirit of the Light, which did come upon thee and hath brought the mysteries of the height, | to 123. give them unto the race of men. ' Peace ' on the other hand is the power of Sabaōth, the Good, which is in thee,—he who hath baptized and hath forgiven the race of men,—and it hath made them at peace with the sons of the Light. And moreover as thy power hath said through David : ' Truth sprouted forth out of the earth,'—that is the power of Sabaōth, the Good, which sprouted forth out of Mary, thy mother, the dweller on earth. ' Righteousness,' which ' looked down from heaven,' on the other hand is the spirit in the height who hath brought all mysteries of the height and given them to the race of men ; and they have become righteous and good, and have inherited the Light-kingdom."

And it came to pass, when Jesus had heard Mary speak these words, that he said : " Well said, Mary, inheritress of the Light."

And Mary, the mother of Jesus, again came forward, fell down at his feet, kissed them and said : " My Lord, my son and my Saviour, be not wroth with me, but pardon me, that I may once more speak the solution of these words. ' Grace and truth met together,'—it is I, Mary,

The other Mary further interpreteth the same scripture from the baptism of Jesus.

Mary, the mother, again further interpreteth the same scripture from the meeting of herself with Elizabeth, mother of John the Baptizer. 124.

thy mother, and Elizabeth, mother of John, whom I have met. | 'Grace' then is the power of Sabaôth in me, which went forth out of me, which thou art. Thou hast had mercy on the whole race of men. 'Truth' on the other hand is the power in Elizabeth, which is John, who did come and hath made proclamation concerning the way of Truth, which thou art,—who hath made proclamation before thee. And again, 'Grace and truth met together,'—that is thou, my Lord, thou who didst meet John on the day when thou hadst to receive the baptism. And again thou and John are 'Righteousness and peace kissed

Of the incarnation of Jesus.

each other.'—'Truth hath sprouted forth out of the earth, and righteousness looked down from heaven,'—this is, during the time when thou didst minister unto thyself, thou didst have the form of Gabriël, thou didst look down upon me from heaven and speak with me. And when thou hadst spoken with me, thou didst sprout up in me,—that is the 'truth,' that is the power of Sabaôth, the Good, which is in thy material body, that is the 'truth' which 'sprouted up out of the earth.'"

It came to pass then, when Jesus had heard his mother Mary speak these words, that he said: "Well said, and finely. This is the solution of all the words concerning which my light-power hath prophesied aforetime through the prophet David."

[THE NOTE OF A SCRIBE]

(Now these are the names which I will give 125.
from the Boundless onward. Write them with a A note by
a later hand,
sign, that the Sons of God may be revealed copied from
another
from here on.   scripture.

This is the name of the Immortal: *aaa, ōōō*;
and this is the name of the Voice, for the sake
of which the Perfect Man hath set himself in
motion: *iii*. And these are the interpretations
of the names of these mysteries: the first [name],
which is *aaa*, its interpretation is *fff*; the second,
which is *mmm* or *ōōō*, its interpretation is *aaa*;
the third, which is *pspsps*, its interpretation is *ooo*;
the fourth, which is *fff*, its interpretation is *nnn*;
the fifth, which is *ddd*, its interpretation is *aaa*.
He on the throne is *aaa*. This is the interpretation of the second: *aaaa, aaaa, aaaa*; this is the
interpretation of the whole name.)

THE SECOND BOOK OF
PISTIS SOPHIA

JOHN also came forward and said : " O Lord, bid me also speak the solution of the words which thy light-power hath prophesied aforetime through David."

And Jesus answered and said unto John : " To thee too, John, I give commandment to speak the solution of the words which my light-power hath prophesied through David :

" ' 10. Grace and truth met together, and righteousness and peace kissed each other.

" ' 11. Truth hath sprouted forth out of the earth, and righteousness looked down from heaven.' "

And John answered and said : " This is the word which thou hast said unto us aforetime : ' I have come out of the Height and entered into Sabaôth, the Good, and embraced the light-power in him.' Now, therefore, ' Grace and truth ' which ' met together,'—thou art 'grace,' thou who art sent out of the regions of the Height through thy Father, the First Mystery which

looketh within, in that he hath sent thee, | that thou mayest have mercy on the whole world. ' Truth ' on the other hand is the power of

Sabaôth, the Good, which bound itself in thee
and which thou hast cast forth to the Left,—thou
the First Mystery which looketh without. And
the little Sabaôth, the Good, took it and cast it *Of Sabaôth,*
forth into the matter of Barbêlô, and he made *Yabraôth*
proclamation concerning the regions of Truth *and the*
to all the regions of those of the Left. That *light-vesture.*
matter of Barbêlô then it is which is body for
thee to-day.

"And 'righteousness and peace' which
'kissed each other,'—'righteousness' then art
thou who didst bring all the mysteries through
thy Father, the First Mystery which looketh
within, and hast baptized this power of Sabaôth,
the Good ; and thou didst go to the region of the
rulers and didst give unto them the mysteries
of the Height ; they became righteous and good.

" 'Peace' on the other hand is the power
of Sabaôth, that is thy soul, which did enter into
the matter of Barbêlô, and all the rulers of the
six æons of Yabraôth have made peace with the
mystery of the Light.

"And 'truth' which 'sprouted forth out of
the earth,'—it is the power of Sabaôth, the Good,
which came out of the region of the Right, which
lieth outside the Treasury of the Light, and which
hath come into the region of those of the Left ; |
it hath entered into the matter of Barbêlô, and 12a.
hath made proclamation concerning the mysteries
of the region of Truth.

" 'Righteousness' on the other hand which
'looked down from heaven,' is thou the First
Mystery which looketh down without, as thou
didst come out of the spaces of the Height with
the mysteries of the Light-kingdom ; and thou

didst come down upon the light-vesture which thou didst receive from the hand of Barbēlō, which [vesture] is Jesus, our Saviour, in that thou didst come down upon him as a dove."

It came to pass then, when John had brought forward these words, that the First Mystery which looketh without, said unto him : " Well said, John, beloved brother."

CHAP. 64. The First Mystery again continued and said :

Gabriël and Michaël are summoned to help Pistis Sophia.

" It came to pass, therefore, that the power which had come out of the Height, that is I, in that my Father sent me to save Pistis Sophia out of the chaos, [that] I, therefore, and also the power which did go from me, and the soul which I had received from Sabaōth, the Good,—they drew towards one another and become a single light-stream, which shone very exceedingly. I called down Gabriël and Michaël out of the æons, at the command of my Father, the First Mystery which looketh within, and I gave unto them the light-stream and let them go down into the chaos |

129.

to help Pistis Sophia and to take the light-powers, which the emanations of Self-willed had taken from her, from them and give them to Pistis Sophia.

" And straightway, when they had brought down the light-stream into the chaos, it shone most exceedingly in the whole of the chaos, and spread itself over all their regions. And when the emanations of Self-willed had seen the great light of that stream, they were terror-stricken one with the other. And that stream drew forth out of them all the light-powers which they had taken from Pistis Sophia, and the emanations of Self-willed could not dare to lay hold of that light-

stream in the dark chaos ; nor could they lay
hold of it with the art of Self-willed, who ruleth
over the emanations.

" And Gabriēl and Michaēl led the light-stream The light-
over the body of the matter of Pistis Sophia and stream re-storeth the
poured into her all the light-powers which they light-powers to Sophia.
had taken from her. And the body of her matter
became shining throughout, and all the powers
also in her, whose light they had taken away,
took light and ceased to lack their light, for they
got their light which had been taken from them,
because the light was given them through me.
And Michaēl and Gabriēl, who ministered and
had brought the light-stream | into the chaos, 130.
will give them the mysteries of the Light ; it is
they to whom the light-stream was entrusted,
which I have given unto them and brought into
the chaos. And Michaēl and Gabriēl have taken
no light for themselves from the lights of Sophia,
which they had taken from the emanations of
Self-willed.

" It came to pass then, when the light-stream
had ingathered into Pistis Sophia all her light-
powers, which it had taken from the emanations
of Self-willed, that she became shining throughout ; and the light-powers also in Pistis Sophia,
which the emanations of Self-willed had not taken,
became joyful again and filled themselves with
light. And the lights which were poured into
Pistis Sophia, quickened the body of her matter,
in which no light was present, and which was
on the point of perishing or perished. And they
raised up all her powers which were on the point
of being dissolved. And they took unto themselves a light-power and became again as they

were before, and they increased again in their sense of the Light. And all the light-powers of Sophia knew themselves mutually through my light-stream and were saved through the light of that stream. And my light-stream, when it had taken away the lights from the emanations of Self-willed, which they had taken away from Pistis Sophia, poured them into | Pistis Sophia, and turned itself about and went up out of the chaos."

The light-stream, having accomplished its purpose, departeth from Sophia. 131.

When then the First Mystery said this to the disciples, that it had befallen Pistis Sophia in the chaos, he answered and said unto them : "Understand ye in what manner I discourse with you ? "

CHAP. 65.

Peter came forward and said : " My Lord, concerning the solution of the words which thou hast spoken, thus hath thy light-power prophesied aforetime through Solomon in his Odes :

Peter interpreteth the narrative from the Odes of Solomon.

" ' 1. A stream came forth and became a great wide flood.

" ' 2. It tore away all to itself and turned itself against the temple.

" ' 3. Dams and buildings could not hold it, nor could the art of them who hold the waters.

" ' 4. It was led over the whole land and laid hold of all.

" ' 5. They who were on the dry sand, drank ; their thirst was quieted and quenched, when the draught from the hand of the Highest was given.

" ' 6. Blessed are the ministers of that draught, to whom the water of the Lord is entrusted.

" ' 7. They have refreshed parched lips ; they whose power was taken away, have gotten joy of heart and they have laid hold of souls, having poured in the breath, so that they should not die.

" ' 8. They have raised up limbs which were fallen ; they have given power to their openness and light unto their eyes.

" ' 9. For they all have known themselves in the Lord and are saved through the water of Life eternal.'

" Hearken, therefore, my Lord, that I may set forth the word in openness. As thy | power 132. hath prophesied through Solomon : ' A stream came forth and became a great wide flood,'— this is : The light-stream hath spread itself out in the chaos over all the regions of the emanations of Self-willed.

" And again the word which thy power hath spoken through Solomon : ' It tore away all to itself and led it over the temple,'—that is : It drew all the light-powers out of the emanations of Self-willed, which they had taken from Pistis Sophia, and poured them anew into Pistis Sophia.

" And again the word thy power hath spoken : ' The dams and buildings could not hold it,'— that is : The emanations of Self-willed could not hold the light-stream within the walls of the darkness of the chaos.

" And again the word which it hath spoken : ' It was led over the whole land and filled all,' —that is : When Gabriël and Michaël had led it over the body of Pistis Sophia, they poured into her all the lights which the emanations of Self-willed had taken from her, and the body of her matter shone.

" And the word which it hath spoken : ' They who were in the dry sand, drank,'—that is :

All in Pistis Sophia whose light had before been taken away, got light.

"And the word which it hath spoken: ' Their thirst was quieted | and quenched,'—that is: Her powers ceased to lack the light, because their light, which had been taken from them, was given them [again].

"And again as thy power hath spoken: ' The draught through the Highest was given them,'—that is: The light was given unto them through the light-stream, which came forth out of thee, the First Mystery."

"And as thy power hath spoken: ' Blessed are the ministers of that draught,'—this is the word which thou hast spoken: ' Michaël and Gabriël, who have ministered, have brought the light-stream into the chaos and also led it forth again. They will give them the mysteries of the Light of the Height, they to whom the light-stream is entrusted.'

"And again as thy power hath spoken: ' They have refreshed parched lips,'—that is: Gabriël and Michaël have not taken for themselves from the lights of Pistis Sophia, which they had spoiled from the emanations of Self-willed, but they have poured them into Pistis Sophia.

"And again the word which it hath spoken: ' They whose power was taken away, have gotten joy of heart,'—that is: All the other powers of Pistis Sophia, which the emanations of Self-willed have not taken, are become exceedingly merry and have filled themselves with light from their light-fellows, for these have poured it into them. |

"And the word which thy power hath spoken: ' They have quickened souls, having poured in

the breath, so that they should not die,'—that is :
When they had poured the lights into Pistis
Sophia, they quickened the body of her matter,
from which they had before taken its lights, and
which was on the point of perishing.

" And again the word which thy power hath
spoken : ' They have raised up limbs which were
fallen, or that they should not fall,'—that is :
When they poured into her her lights, they raised
up all her powers which were on the point of being
dissolved.

" And again as thy light-power hath spoken :
' They have received again their light and have
become as they were before'; and again the
word which it hath spoken : ' They have given
light unto their eyes,'—that is : They have
received sense in the Light and known the light-
stream, that it belongeth to the Height.

" And again the word which it hath spoken :
' They all have known themselves in the Lord,'—
that is : All the powers of Pistis Sophia have
known one another through the light-stream.

" And again the word which it hath spoken :
' They are saved through water of Life eternal,'—
that is : They are saved through the whole light-
stream.

" And again the word which it hath spoken :
' The light-stream tore all to itself and drew it over
the temple,'—that is : When the light-stream had
taken all the light-powers of Pistis Sophia | and 135.
had spoiled them from the emanations of Self-
willed, it poured them into Pistis Sophia and
turned itself about and went out of the chaos
and came over thee,—thou who art the temple.

" This is the solution of all the words which

thy light-power hath spoken through the Ode of Solomon."

It came to pass then, when the First Mystery had heard Peter speak these words, that he said unto him: "Well said, blessed Peter. This is the solution of the words which have been spoken."

CHAP. 66.
The emana-
tions of
Self-willed
cry aloud
to him for
help.

And the First Mystery continued again in the discourse and said: "It came to pass then, before I had led forth Pistis Sophia out of the chaos. because it was not yet commanded me through my Father, the First Mystery which looketh within,—at that time then, after the emanations of Self-willed had perceived that my light-stream had taken from them the light-powers which they had taken from Pistis Sophia, and had poured them into Pistis Sophia, and when they again had seen Pistis Sophia, that she shone as she had done from the beginning, that they were enraged against Pistis Sophia and cried out again to their Self-willed, that he should come and help them, so that they might take away the powers in Pistis Sophia anew.

He sendeth
forth an-
other more
violent power
like unto a
flying arrow.
136.

"And Self-willed sent out of the height, out of the thirteenth æon, and sent another great light-power. It came down into the chaos | as a flying arrow, that he might help his emanations, so that they might take away the lights from Pistis Sophia anew. · And when that light-power had come down, the emanations of Self-willed which were in the chaos and oppressed Pistis Sophia, took great courage and again pursued Pistis Sophia with great terror and great alarm. And some of the emanations of Self-willed oppressed her. One of them changed itself into

the form of a great serpent; another again The fashioning of the serpent-, basilisk- and dragon-powers.
changed itself also into the form of a seven-headed
basilisk; another again changed itself into the
form of a dragon. And moreover the first power
of Self-willed, the lion-faced, and all his other very
numerous emanations, they came together and
oppressed Pistis Sophia and led her again into the
lower regions of the chaos and alarmed her again
exceedingly.

" It came to pass then that there looked down The demon-power of Adamas dasheth Sophia down.
out of the twelve æons, Adamas, the Tyrant,
who also was wroth with Pistis Sophia, because
she desired to go to the | Light of lights, which 137.
was above them all; therefore was he wroth with
her. It came to pass then, when Adamas, the
Tyrant, had looked down out of the twelve
æons, that he saw the emanations of Self-willed
oppressing Pistis Sophia, until they should take
from her all her lights. It came to pass then,
when the power of Adamas had come down into
the chaos unto all the emanations of Self-willed,—
it came to pass then, when that demon came down
into the chaos, that it dashed down Pistis Sophia.
And the lion-faced power and the serpent-form
and the basilisk-form and the dragon-form and
all the other very numerous emanations of Self-
willed surrounded Pistis Sophia all together,
desiring to take from her anew her powers in
her, and they oppressed Pistis Sophia exceedingly
and threatened her. It came to pass then, when
they oppressed her and alarmed her exceedingly,
that she cried again to the Light and sang praises,
saying:

" ' 1. O Light, it is thou who hast helped me;
let thy light come over me.

" ' 2. For thou art my protector, and I come hence unto thee, O Light, having faith in thee, O Light.

" ' 3. For thou art my saviour from the emanations of Self-willed and of Adamas, the Tyrant, and thou shalt save me from all his violent threats.'

Gabriël and
Michaël
and the
light-stream
again go to
her aid.
138.
" And when Pistis Sophia had said this, then at the commandment | of my Father, the First Mystery which looketh within, I sent again Gabriël and Michaël and the great light-stream, that they should help Pistis Sophia. And I gave commandment unto Gabriël and Michaël to bear Pistis Sophia in their hands, so that her feet should not touch the darkness below; and I gave them commandment moreover to guide her in the regions of the chaos, out of which she was to be led.

" It came to pass then, when the angels had come down into the chaos, they and the light-stream, and moreover [when] all the emanations of Self-willed and the emanations of Adamas had seen the light-stream, how it shone very exceedingly and there was no measure for the light about it, that they became terror-stricken and quitted Pistis Sophia. And the great light-stream surrounded Pistis Sophia on all sides of her, on her left and on her right and on all her sides, and it became a light-wreath round her head.

" It came to pass then, when the light-stream had surrounded Pistis Sophia, that she took great courage, and it ceased not to surround her on all her sides; and she was no longer in fear of the emanations of Self-willed which are in the

chaos, nor was she any more in fear of the other
new power of Self-willed which he had cast down
into the chaos | as a flying arrow, nor did she any 139.
more tremble at the demon power of Adamas
which had come out of the æons.

"And moreover by commandment of myself, The trans-
the First Mystery which looketh without, the Sophia.
light-stream which surrounded Pistis Sophia on
all her sides, shone most exceedingly, and Pistis
Sophia abode in the midst of the light, a great
light being on her left and on her right, and on
all her sides, forming a wreath round her head.
And all the emanations of Self-willed [could] not
change their face again, nor could they bear the
shock of the great light of the stream, which
was a wreath round her head. And all the emanations of Self-willed,—many of them fell at her
right, because she shone most exceedingly, and
many others fell at her left, and were not able
at all to draw nigh unto Pistis Sophia because of
the great light ; but they fell all one on another,
or they all came near one another, and they could
not inflict any ill on Pistis Sophia, because she
had trusted in the Light.

"And at the commandment of my Father, Jesus, the
the First Mystery which looketh within, I myself tery looking
went down into the chaos, shining most exceed- without,
causeth
ingly, | and approached the lion-faced power, Sophia to
which shone exceedingly, and took its whole light triumph.
in it and held fast all the emanations of Self-
willed, so that from now on they went not into
their region, that is the thirteenth æon. And I
took away the power of all the emanations of
Self-willed, and they all fell down in the chaos
powerless. And I led forth Pistis Sophia, she

being on the right of Gabriël and Michaël. And
the great light-stream entered again into her.
And Pistis Sophia beheld with her eyes her foes,
that I had taken their light-power from them.
And I led Pistis Sophia forth from the chaos,
she treading under foot the serpent-faced emanation of Self-willed, and moreover treading under
foot the seven-faced-basilisk emanation, and treading under foot the lion- and dragon-faced power.
I made Pistis Sophia continue to stand upon the
seven-headed-basilisk emanation of Self-willed;
and it was more mighty than them all in its
evil doings. And I, the First Mystery, stood by
it and took all the powers in it, and made to
perish its whole matter, so that no seed should
arise from it from now on." |

141.
CHAP. 67.
And when the First Mystery said this unto his
disciples, he answered and said: "Understand
ye in what manner I discourse with you?"

James came forward and said: "My Lord,
concerning then the solution of the words which
thou hast said, thus hath thy light-power prophesied thereon aforetime through David in the
ninetieth Psalm:

James in-
terpreteth
the narrative
from Psalm
xc.
"'1. Whoso then dwelleth under the help of
the Most High, will abide under the shadow of
the God of heaven.

"'2. He will say unto the Lord: Thou art
my succour and my place of refuge, my God, in
whom I trust.

"'3. For he will save me out of the snare
of the hunters and from mighty word.

"'4. He will shade thee with his breast, and
thou shalt have trust beneath his wings; his
truth shall surround thee as a shield.

" ' 5. Thou wilt not be afraid of terror by night nor of an arrow which flieth by day,

" ' 6. Of a thing which slinketh in the darkness, of a mischance and a demon at mid-day.

" ' 7. A thousand will fall on | thy left, and ten 142 thousand at thy right hand ; but they shall not come nigh thee.

" ' 8. Nay rather with thine eyes wilt thou behold, thou wilt see the requital of the sinners.

" ' 9. For thou, O Lord, art my hope. Thou hast established the Most High for thyself as refuge.

" ' 10. Harm will not come nigh unto thee ; scourge will not come nigh thy dwelling.

" ' 11. For he will give commandment to his angels on thy behalf that they guard thee on all thy ways,

" ' 12. And bear thee on their hands, that thou mayest never strike with thy foot against a stone.

" ' 13. Thou wilt stride over the serpent and basilisk and tread on lion and dragon.

" ' 14. Because he hath trusted in me, I will save him ; I will overshadow him, because he hath known my name.

" ' 15. He will cry unto me and I shall hearken unto him ; I am at his side in his tribulation and will save him and honour him,

" ' 16. And increase him with many days and show him my salvation.'

" This, my Lord, is the solution of the words which thou hast said. Hearken therefore, that I may say it in openness.

" The word then which thy power hath spoken through David : ' Whoso then dwelleth under the help of the Most High, will abide under the shadow of the God of heaven,'—that is : When Sophia had trusted in the Light, she abode under the light of the light-stream, which through thee came out of the Height.

" And the word which thy power hath spoken through David : ' I will say unto the Lord : Thou art my succour and my refuge, my God, in whom I trust,'—it is the word with which Pistis Sophia hath sung praises : | ' Thou art my succour, and I come unto thee.'

143.

" And again the word which thy power hath spoken : ' My God, in whom I trust, thou wilt save me out of the snare of the hunters and from mighty word,'—it is what Pistis Sophia hath said : ' O Light, I have faith in thee, for thou wilt save me from the emanations of Self-willed and from those of Adamas, the Tyrant, and thou wilt save me also from all their mighty threats.'

" And again the word which thy power hath spoken through David : ' He will shade thee with his breast, and thou wilt have trust beneath his wings,'—that is : Pistis Sophia hath been in the light of the light-stream, which hath come from thee, and hath continued in firm trust in the light, that on her left and that on her right, which are the wings of the light-stream.

" And the word which thy light-power hath prophesied through David : ' Truth will surround thee as a shield,'—it is the light of the light-stream which hath surrounded Pistis Sophia on all her sides as a shield.

" And the word which thy power hath spoken : ' He will not be afraid of terror by night,'—that is : Pistis Sophia hath not been afraid of the terrors and alarms into which she had been planted in the chaos, which is the 'night.'

" And the word which thy power hath spoken : | ' He will not be afraid of an arrow which flieth by 144. day,'—that is : Pistis Sophia hath not been afraid of the power which Self-willed hath sent last of all out of the height, and which hath come into the chaos as it were a flying arrow. Thy light-power therefore hath said : ' Thou wilt not be afraid of an arrow which flieth by day,'—for that power hath come out of the thirteenth æon, it being that which is lord over the twelve æons, and which giveth light unto all the æons ; wherefor hath he [David] said ' day.'

" And again the word which thy power hath spoken : ' He will not be afraid of a thing which slinketh in the darkness,'—that is : Sophia hath not been afraid of the lion-faced emanation, which caused fear for Pistis Sophia in the chaos, which is the ' darkness.'

" And the word which thy power hath spoken : ' He will not be afraid of a mischance and of a demon at mid-day,'—that is : Pistis Sophia hath not been afraid of the demon emanation of Tyrant Adamas, which hath cast Pistis Sophia to the ground in a great mischance, and which hath come forth out of Adamas out of the twelfth æon ; wherefor then hath thy power said : ' He will not be afraid of | the demon mischance at 145. mid-day,'—' mid-day,' because it hath come out of the twelve æons, which is ' mid-day '; and again [' night,' because] it hath come out of the chaos, which is the ' night,' and because it hath come out of the twelfth æon which is in the midst between both ; therefore hath thy light-power said ' mid-day,' because the twelve æons lie in the midst between the thirteenth æon and the chaos.

" And again the word which thy light-power hath spoken through David : ' A thousand will fall on his left, and ten thousand at his right hand, but they shall not come nigh him,'—that is : When the emanations of Self-willed, which are exceedingly numerous, could not bear the great light of the light-stream, many of them fell on the left hand of Pistis Sophia and many at her right, and they could not come nigh her, to do her [harm].

" And the word which thy light-power hath spoken through David : ' Nay rather with thine eyes wilt thou behold, and wilt see the requital of the sinners, for thou, O Lord, art my hope,'—that is the word : Pistis Sophia hath with her eyes beheld her foes, that is the emanations of Self-willed, who all | have fallen one on another ; not only hath she with her eyes beheld this, but thou also thyself, my Lord, the First Mystery, hast taken the light-power which is in the lion-faced power, and hast moreover taken the power of all the emanations of Self-willed and moreover thou hast imprisoned them in that chaos, [so that] from henceforth they have not gone forth to their own region. Therefore then hath Pistis Sophia with her eyes beheld her foes, that is the emanations of Self-willed, in all which David hath prophesied concerning Pistis Sophia, saying : ' Nay rather with thine eyes wilt thou behold, and thou wilt see the requital of the sinners.' Not only hath she with her eyes beheld, how they fall one on another in the chaos, but she hath also seen the requital with which it was requited them. Just as the emanations of Self-willed have thought

146.

to take away the light of Sophia from her, so hast thou requited them and repaid them in full, and hast taken the light-power in them instead of the lights of Sophia, who hath had faith in the Light of the Height.

" And as thy light-power hath spoken through David: ' Thou hast established the Most High for thyself as refuge; harm will not come nigh unto thee, scourge will not come nigh thy dwelling,' —that is: When Pistis Sophia had had faith in the Light and was afflicted, she sang praises unto it, and the emanations of Self-willed could not inflict on her any harm, | nor could they [injure] 147. her, nor could they at all come nigh her.

" And the word which thy light-power hath spoken through David : ' He will give command- ment to his angels on thy behalf, that they guard thee on all thy ways and bear thee on their hands, that thou mayest never strike with thy foot against a stone,'—it is again thy word : Thou hast given commandment to Gabriël and Michaël, that they guide Pistis Sophia in all the regions of the chaos, until they lead her forth and that they up- lift her on their hands, so that her feet do not touch the darkness beneath, and [that] on the other hand they of the lower darkness do not seize hold of her.

" And the word which thy light-power hath spoken through David : ' Thou wilt tread on serpent and basilisk and tread on lion and dragon ; because he hath trusted in me, I will save him and I will overshadow him, because he hath known my name,'—that is the word : When Pistis Sophia was on the point of coming forth out of the chaos, she trod on the emanations of Self-willed, and she trod on the serpent-faced ones and on the basilisk-faced ones, which have seven heads ; and she trod on the lion-faced power and on the dragon-faced one. Because she had had faith in the Light, is she saved from all of them.

"This, my Lord, is the solution of the words which thou hast spoken."

CHAP. 68.

It came to pass then, when the First Mystery had heard these words; that he said : " Well said,

148.

James, | beloved one."

And the First Mystery continued again in the discourse and said unto his disciples : " It came to pass, when I had led Pistis Sophia out of the chaos, that she cried out again and said :

Sophia sing-eth a song of praise.

" ' 1. I am saved out of the chaos and loosed from the bonds of the darkness. I am come unto thee, O Light.

" ' 2. For thou wert light on all sides of me, saving me and helping me.

" ' 3. And the emanations of Self-willed, which fought against me, thou hast hindered through thy light, and they could not come nigh me ; for thy light was with me and saved me through thy light-stream.

" ' 4. Because in sooth the emanations of Self-willed constrained me, they took from me my power and cast me out into the chaos with no light in me. So I became as heavy-weighing matter in comparison with them.

" ' 5. And thereafter came a light-stream unto me through thee which saved me ; it shone on my left and on my right and surrounded me on all sides of me, so that no part of me was without light.

" ' 6. And thou hast covered me with the light

of thy stream and purged from me all my evil matters ; and I shall be relieved of all my matters because of thy light.

" ' 7. And it is thy light-stream which hath raised me up and taken from me the emanations of Self-willed which constrained me.

" ' 8. And I | have become sure-trusting in 149. thy light and purified light in thy stream.

" ' 9. And the emanations of Self-willed which constrained me, have withdrawn themselves from me ; and I shone in thy great power, for thou savest for ever.'

" This is the repentance which Pistis Sophia hath uttered, when she came forth out of the chaos and was freed from the bonds of the chaos. Now, therefore, who hath ears to hear, let him hear."

It came to pass then, when the First Mystery CHAP. 69. had finished saying these words unto his disciples, that Thomas came forward, and said : " My Lord, my light-dweller hath ears and my mind hath understood the words which thou hast said. Now, therefore, give commandment unto me to set forth clearly the solution of the words."

And the First Mystery answered and said unto Thomas : " I give thee commandment to set forth the solution of the song which Pistis Sophia sang unto me."

Thomas answered and said : " My Lord, con- Thomas in-cerning the song which Pistis Sophia hath uttered, terpreteth the song of because she was saved out of the chaos, thy Sophia from light-power prophesied aforetime thereon through the Odes of Solomon, the son of David, in his Odes : Solomon.

" ' 1. I am saved | from the bonds and am fled 150. unto thee, O Lord.

" ' 2. For thou hast been on my right hand, saving me and helping me.

" ' 3. Thou hast hindered my adversaries and they have not been revealed, because thy face was with me, saving me in thy grace.

" ' 4. I was despised in the sight of many and cast out ; I have become as lead in their sight.

" ' 5. Through thee I have gotten a power which helped me ; for thou hast set lamps on my right and on my left, so that no side of me may be without light.

" ' 6. Thou hast overshadowed me with the shadow of thy grace, and I was relieved of the coats of skin.

" ' 7. It is thy right hand which hath raised me up, and thou hast taken the sickness from me.

" ' 8. I have become powerful in thy truth and purified in thy righteousness.

" ' 9. My adversaries have withdrawn themselves from me, and I am justified by thy goodness, for thy rest endureth unto all eternity.'

" This then, my Lord, is the solution of the repentance which Pistis Sophia hath uttered, when she was saved out of the chaos. Hearken, therefore, that I may say it in openness.

" The word then which thy light-power hath spoken through Solomon : ' I am saved from the bonds and am fled unto thee, O Lord,'—it is the word which Pistis Sophia hath spoken: ' I am loosed from the bonds of the darkness and am come unto thee, O Light.'

" And the word which thy power hath spoken :
151. ' Thou wert on my right hand, saving | and helping me,'—it is again the word which Pistis Sophia

hath spoken : ' Thou art become a light on all
sides of me, [saving me] and helping me.'

" And the word which thy light-power hath
spoken : ' Thou hast hindered my adversaries
and they have not been revealed,'—it is the word
which Pistis Sophia hath spoken : ' And the
emanations of Self-willed which fought against
me, thou hast hindered through thy light, and
they could not come nigh me.'

" And the word which thy power hath spoken :
' Thy face was with me, saving me in thy grace,'—
it is the word which Pistis Sophia hath spoken :
' Thy light was with me, saving me in thy light-
stream.'

" And the word which thy power hath spoken :
' I was despised in the sight of many and cast out,'
—it is the word which Pistis Sophia hath spoken :
' The emanations of Self-willed constrained me
and took my power from me, and I have been
despised before them and cast out into the chaos,
with no light in me.'

" And the word which thy power hath spoken :
' I have become as lead in their sight,'—it is the
word which Pistis Sophia hath spoken : ' When
they had taken my light from me, I became as
heavy-weighing matter before them.'

" And moreover the word which thy power
hath spoken : ' Through thee | I have gotten a 152.
power for me which helped me,'—it is again the
word which Pistis Sophia hath spoken : ' And
thereafter came a light-power unto me through
thee which saved me.'

" And the word which thy power hath spoken :
' Thou hast set lamps on my right and on my left,
so that no side of me may be without light,'—it

is the word which Pistis Sophia hath spoken: 'Thy power shone on my right and on my left and surrounded me on all sides of me, so that no part of me was without light.'

"And the word which thy power hath spoken: 'Thou hast overshadowed me with the shadow of thy grace,'—it is again the word which Pistis Sophia hath spoken: 'And thou hast covered me with the light of the stream.'

"And the word which thy power hath spoken: 'I was relieved of the coats of skin,'—it is again the word which Pistis Sophia hath spoken: 'And they have purified me of all my evil matters, and I raised myself above them in thy light.'

"And the word which thy power hath spoken through Solomon: 'It is thy right hand which hath raised me up, and hath taken the sickness from me,'—it is the word which Pistis Sophia hath spoken: 'And it is thy light-stream which hath raised me up in thy light and hath taken from me the emanations of Self-willed which constrained me.' |

153.

"And the word which thy power hath spoken: 'I have become powerful in thy truth and purified in thy righteousness,'—it is the word which Pistis Sophia hath spoken: 'I have become powerful in thy light and purified light in thy stream.'

And the word which thy power hath spoken: 'My adversaries have withdrawn themselves from me,'—it is the word which Pistis Sophia hath spoken: 'The emanations of Self-willed which constrained me, have withdrawn themselves from me.'

"And the word which thy power hath spoken through Solomon: 'And I am justified in thy

goodness, for thy rest endureth unto all eternity,'
—it is the word which Pistis Sophia hath spoken :
' I am saved in thy goodness ; for thou savest
every one.'

"This then, O my Lord, is the whole solution
of the repentance which Pistis Sophia hath uttered,
when she was saved out of the chaos and loosed
from the bonds of the darkness."

It came to pass then when the First Mystery **CHAP. 70.**
had heard Thomas say these words, that he said
unto him : "Well said, finely, Thomas, blessed
one. This is the solution of the song which
Pistis Sophia hath uttered."

And the First Mystery continued again and said
unto the disciples : "And Pistis Sophia continued
and sang praises unto me, saying :

" ' 1. I sing a song unto thee ; | through thy 154.
commandment hast thou led me down out of the Sophia
singeth an-
higher æon which is above, and hast led me up to other song
of praise.
the regions which are below.

" ' 2. And again through thy commandment
thou hast saved me out of the regions which are
below, and through thee hast thou taken there
the matter in my light-powers, and I have seen it.

" ' 3. And thou hast scattered far from me the
emanations of Self-willed which constrained me
and were hostile to me, and hast bestowed power
on me to loose myself from the bonds of the emanations of Adamas.

" ' 4. And thou hast smitten the basilisk with
the seven heads and cast it out with my hands
and hast set me above its matter. Thou hast
destroyed it, so that its seed may not raise itself
up from now on.

" ' 5. And thou wert with me, giving me power

in all this, and thy light surrounded me in all regions, and through thee hast thou made all the emanations of Self-willed powerless.

" ' 6. For thou hast taken the power of their light from them and made straight my way to lead me out of the chaos.

" ' 7. And thou hast removed me from the material darknesses and taken from them all my powers, from which the light had been taken.

155.

" ' 8. Thou hast put into them purified light and unto all my limbs, | in which was no light, thou hast given purified light from the Light of the Height.

" ' 9. And thou hast made straight the way for them [sc. my limbs], and the light of thy face hath become for me life indestructible.

" ' 10. Thou hast led me forth above the chaos, the region of chaos and extermination, in order that all the matters in it which are in that region, might be unloosed and all my powers be renewed in thy light, and thy light be in them all.

" ' 11. Thou hast deposited the light of thy stream in me and I am become purified light.'

" This again is the second song which Pistis Sophia hath uttered. Who then hath understood this repentance, let him come forward and speak it."

CHAP. 71.   It came to pass then, when the First Mystery had finished saying these words, that Matthew came forward and said : " I have understood the solution of the song which Pistis Sophia hath uttered. Now, therefore, give commandment unto me, that I speak it in openness."

And the First Mystery answered and said : " I give commandment unto thee, Matthew, to set forth the interpretation of the song which Pistis Sophia hath uttered."

And Matthew answered and said : " Concerning the interpretation of the song which Pistis Sophia hath uttered, thus thy light-power prophesied aforetime thereon through the Ode of Solomon :

" ' 1. He who hath led me down out of the higher regions which are above, hath led me up out of | the regions which are in the bottom below.

" ' 2. Who hath there taken those in the midst, he hath taught me concerning them.

" ' 3. Who hath scattered my foes and my adversaries, he hath bestowed power on me over the bonds, to unloose them.

" ' 4. Who hath smitten the serpent with the seven heads with my hands, he hath set me up above its root, that I may extinguish its seed.

" ' 5. And thou wert with me, helping me ; in all regions thy name surrounded me.

" ' 6. Thy right hand hath destroyed the venom of the slanderer ; thy hand hath cleared the way for thy faithful.

" ' 7. Thou hast freed them out of the tombs and hast removed them from the midst of the corpses.

" ' 8. Thou hast taken dead bones and hast clothed them with a body and to them who stirred not, hast thou given the activity of life.

" ' 9. Thy way is become indestructibleness and thy face [also].

" ' 10. Thou hast led thy æon above decay, so that they all may be loosed and renewed and thy light become a foundation for them all.

" ' 11. Thou hast piled thy riches upon them and they have become a holy dwelling-place.'

Matthew interpreteth the song of Sophia from the Odes of Solomon.
156.

" This then, my Lord, is the solution of the song
which Pistis Sophia hath uttered. Hearken,
therefore, that I may say it in openness.

" The word which thy power hath spoken
through Solomon : ' Who hath led me down out
of the higher regions which are above, he hath also
led me up out of the regions which are in the
bottom below,'—it is the word | which Pistis Sophia
hath spoken : ' I sing praises unto thee ; through
thy commandment hast thou led me down out of
this higher æon which is above, and hast led me to
the regions below.   And again through thy commandment thou hast saved me and led me up out
of the regions which are below.'

" And the word which thy power hath spoken
through Solomon : ' Who hath there taken those
in the midst and hath taught me concerning them,'
—it is the word which Pistis Sophis hath spoken :
' And again through thy commandment hast thou
caused the matter in the midst of my power to be
purified, and I have seen it.'

" And moreover the word which thy power hath
spoken through Solomon : ' Who hath scattered
my foes and my adversaries,'—it is the word which
Pistis Sophia hath spoken : ' Thou hast scattered
far from me all the emanations of Self-willed
which constrained me and were hostile to me.'

" And the word which thy power hath spoken :
'Who hath bestowed on me wisdom over the bonds,
to unloose them,'—it is the word which Pistis
Sophia hath spoken : ' And he hath bestowed on
me wisdom to loose myself from the bonds of
those emanations.'

" And the word which thy power hath spoken :
' Who hath smitten | the serpent with the seven

157.

158.

heads with my hands, he hath set me up above its root, that I may extinguish its seed,'—it is the word which Pistis Sophia hath spoken: 'And thou hast smitten the serpent with the seven heads through my hands and set me up above its matter. Thou hast destroyed it, so that its seed may not raise itself up from now on.'

" And the word which thy power hath spoken : ' And thou wert with me, helping me,'—it is the word which Pistis Sophia hath spoken : ' And thou wert with me, giving me power in all this.'

" And the word which thy power hath spoken : ' And thy name surrounded me in all regions,'— it is the word which Pistis Sophia hath spoken : ' And thy light surrounded me in all their regions.'

" And the word which thy power hath spoken : ' And thy right hand hath destroyed the venom of the slanderers,'—it is the word which Pistis Sophia hath spoken : ' And through thee the emanations of Self-willed became powerless, for thou hast taken from them the light of their power.'

" And the word which thy power hath spoken : ' Thy hand hath cleared the way for thy faithful,'—it is the word which Pistis Sophia hath spoken : ' Thou hast made straight my way to lead me out of the chaos, because I have had faith in thee.'

" And the word which thy power hath spoken : ' Thou hast freed them out of the tombs and hast removed them from the midst of the corpses,' —it is the word which Pistis Sophia hath spoken ; ' Thou hast freed me out of the chaos and removed me out of the material darknesses, that is | out 159. of the dark emanations which are in the chaos, from which thou hast taken their light.'

" And the word which thy power hath spoken : ' Thou hast taken dead bones and hast clothed them with a body, and to them who stirred not, thou hast given activity of life,'—it is the word which Pistis Sophia hath spoken : ' And thou hast taken all my powers in which was no light, and hast bestowed on them within purified light, and unto all my limbs, in which no light stirred, thou hast given life-light out of thy Height.'

" And the word which thy power hath spoken : ' Thy way is become indestructibleness, and thy face [also],'—it is the word which Pistis Sophia hath spoken : ' And thou hast made straight thy way for me, and' the light of thy face hath become for me life indestructible.'

" And the word which thy power hath spoken : ' Thou hast led thy æon above decay, so that all might be loosed and renewed,'—it is the word which Pistis Sophia hath spoken : ' Thou hast led me, thy power, up above the chaos and above decay, that all the matters in that region may be loosed and all my powers renewed in the Light.'

" And the word which thy power hath spoken : ' And thy light hath [become] foundation for them all,'—it is the word which Pistis Sophia hath spoken : ' And thy light hath been in them all.' |

160.   " And the word which thy light-power hath spoken through Solomon : ' Thou hast put thy riches over him, and he hath become a holy dwelling-place,'—it is the word which Pistis. Sophia hath spoken : ' Thou hast stayed the light of thy stream over me, and I have become a purified light.'

" This then, my Lord, is the solution of the song which Pistis Sophia hath uttered."

It came to pass then, when the First Mystery CHAP. 72. had heard Matthew speak these words, that he said: " Well said, Matthew, and finely, beloved. This is the solution of the song which Pistis Sophia hath uttered."

And the First Mystery continued again and said: Sophia continueth to sing. " ' 1. I will declare : Thou art the higher Light, for that hast saved me and led me unto thee, and thou hast not let the emanations of Self-willed, which are hostile unto me, take my light.

" ' 2. O Light of lights, I sing praises unto thee ; thou hast saved me.

" ' 3. O Light, thou hast led up my power out of the chaos ; thou hast saved me from them which have gone down into the darkness.'

" These words again hath Pistis Sophia uttered. Now, therefore, whose mind hath become understanding, comprehending the words which Pistis Sophia hath uttered, let him come forward and set forth their solution."

It came to pass then, when the First Mystery Mary is afraid of Peter. had finished speaking these words unto the disciples, that Mary came forward and said : " My Lord, my | mind is ever understanding, at 161. every time to come forward and set forth the solution of the words which she hath uttered ; but I am afraid of Peter, because he threatened me and hateth our sex."

And when she had said this, the First Mystery said unto her : " Every one who shall be filled with the spirit of light to come forward and set forth the solution of what I say,—no one shall be able to prevent him. Now, therefore, O Mary, set forth then the solution of the words which Pistis Sophia hath uttered."

Then Mary answered and said unto the First Mystery in the midst of the disciples: "My Lord, concerning the solution of the words which Pistis Sophia hath uttered, thus hath thy light-power prophesied aforetime through David:

Mary interpreteth the song of Sophia from Psalm xxix.

" ' 1. I will exalt thee, O Lord, for thou hast received me, and thou hast not made glad my foes over me.

" ' 2. O Lord, my God, I cried up unto thee, and thou hast healed me.

" ' 8. O Lord, thou hast led up my soul out of hell ; thou hast saved me from them which have gone down into the pit.' "

CHAP. 73.

And when Mary had said this, the First Mystery said unto her, " Well said, finely, Mary, blessed one."

162.

And he continued again | in the discourse and said unto the disciples : " Sophia again continued in this song and said :

Sophia continueth her song.

" ' 1. The Light hath become my saviour.

" ' 2. And it hath changed my darkness into light, and it has rent the chaos which surrounded me and girded me with light.' "

It came to pass then, when the First Mystery had finished saying these words, that Martha came forward and said : " My Lord, thy power hath prophesied aforetime through David concerning these words :

Martha interpreteth from Psalm xxix.

" ' 10. The Lord hath become my helper.

" ' 11. He hath changed my lamentation into joy ; he hath rent my mourning-robe and girded me with joy.' "

And it came to pass when the First Mystery had heard Martha speak these words, that he said : " Well said, and finely, Martha."

And the First Mystery continued again and said unto the disciples : " Pistis Sophia again continued in the song and said :

" ' 1. My power, sing praises to the Light and forget not all the powers of the Light which it hath given unto thee. Sophia con-tinueth her song.

" ' 2. And the powers which are in thee, sing praises to the name of his holy mystery ;

" ' 3. Who forgiveth all thy transgression, who saveth thee from all the afflictions with which the emanations of Self-willed have constrained thee ;

" ' 4. Who hath saved thy light | from the emanations of Self-willed which belong to destruction ; who hath wreathed thee with light in his compassion, until he saved thee ; 163.

" ' 5. Who hath filled thee with purified light ; and thy beginning will renew itself as an invisible of the Height.'

" With these words Pistis Sophia sang praises, because she was saved and remembered all things which I had done unto her."

It came to pass then, when the First Mystery had finished setting forth these words unto the disciples, that he said unto them : " Who hath understood the solution of these words, let him come forward and say it in openness." CHAP. 74.

Mary again came forward and said : " My Lord, concerning these words with which Pistis Sophia hath sung praises, thus thy light-power prophesied them through David :

" ' 1. My soul, praise the Lord, let all that is in me praise his holy name. Mary interpreteth from Psalm cii.

" ' 2. My soul, praise the Lord and forget not all his requitals.

" ' 3. Who forgiveth all thy iniquities ; who healeth all thy sicknesses ;

" ' 4. Who redeemeth thy life from decay ; who wreatheth thee with grace and compassion ;

" ' 5. Who satisfieth thy longing with good things ; thy youth will renew itself as an eagle's.'

" That is : Sophia will be as the invisibles who are in the Height ; he hath, therefore, said ' as an eagle,' because the dwelling-place of the eagle is in the height, and the | invisibles also are in the Height ; that is : Pistis Sophia will shine as the invisibles, as she was from her beginning."

164.

It came to pass then, when the First Mystery had heard Mary say these words, that he said : " Well said, Mary, blessed one."

Sophia is led to a region below the thirteenth æon and given a new mystery.

It came to pass then thereafter, that the First Mystery continued again in the discourse and said unto the disciples : " I took Pistis Sophia and led her up to a region which is below the thirteenth æon, and gave unto her a new mystery of the Light which is not that of her æon, the region of the invisibles. And moreover I gave her a song of the Light, so that from now on the rulers of the æons could not [prevail] against her. And I removed her to that region until I should come after her and bring her to her higher region.

" It came to pass then, when I had removed her to that region, that she again uttered this song thus :

She continueth to sing.

" ' 1. In faith have I had faith in the Light ; and it remembered me and hearkened to my song.

" ' 2. It hath led my power up out of the chaos and the nether darkness of the whole matter and it hath led me up. It hath removed me to a higher

and surer æon, lofty and firm; it hath changed
my place on the way which leadeth to my region.

" ' 3. And it hath given unto me a new mystery,
which is not that of my æon, and given unto me a
song of the Light. Now, therefore, O Light, all
the rulers will see what thou hast done unto me,
and | be afraid and have faith in the Light.'   165.

" This song then Pistis Sophia uttered, rejoicing
that she had been led up out of the chaos and
brought to regions which are below the thirteenth
æon. Now, therefore, let him whom his mind
stirreth, so that he understandeth the solution of
the thought of the song which Pistis Sophia hath
uttered, come forward and say it."

Andrew came forward and said : " My Lord,
this is concerning what thy light-power hath prophesied aforetime through David :

" ' 1. In patience I tarried for the Lord; he Andrew in-
hath given heed unto me and ear unto my terpreteth
                                            from Psalm
weeping.   xxxix.

" ' 2. He hath led up my soul out of the pit of
misery and out of the filthy mire ; he hath set my
feet on a rock and made straight my steps.

" ' 3. He hath put in my mouth a new song, a
song of praise for our God. Many will see and
be afraid and hope in the Lord.' "

It came to pass then, when Andrew had set
forth the thought of Pistis Sophia, that the First
Mystery said unto him : " Well said, Andrew,
blessed one."

And he continued again in the discourse and CHAP. 75.
said unto the disciples : " These are all adven-
tures which have befallen Pistis Sophia. | It 166.
came to pass then, when I had led her to the
region which is below the thirteenth æon, and was

about to go unto the Light and depart from her, that she said unto me:

The conversation of Sophia and the Light.

" ' O Light of lights, thou wilt go to the Light and depart from me. And Tyrant Adamas will know that thou hast departed from me and will know that my saviour is not at hand. And he will come again to this region, he and all his rulers who hate me, and Self-willed also will bestow power unto his lion-faced emanation, so that they all will come and constrain me all together and take my whole light from me, in order that I may become powerless and again without light. Now, therefore, O Light and my Light, take from them the power of their light, so that they may not be able to constrain me from now on.'

The Light promiseth to seal the regions of Self-willed.

" It came to pass then, when I heard these words which Pistis Sophia had spoken unto me, that I answered her, saying: ' My Father, who hath emanated me, hath not yet given me commandment to take their light from them; but I will seal the regions of Self-willed and of all his rulers who hate thee because thou hast had faith in the Light. And I will also seal the regions of Adamas and of his rulers, so that none of them may be able to fight with thee, until their time is completed and the season cometh that my Father give me commandment to take their light from them.'

CHAP. 76. 167.

" And thereafter I said again unto her: ' Hearken that I | may speak with thee about their time, when this which I have said unto thee, will come to pass. It will come to pass when [the] three times are completed.'

" Pistis Sophia answered and said unto me:

' O Light, by what shall I know when the three times will take place, so that I may be glad and rejoice that the time is near for thee to bring me to my region, and moreover rejoice therein that the time is come when thou wilt take the light-power from all them which hate me, because I have had faith in thy light ? '

" And I answered and said unto her : ' If thou seest the gate of the Treasury of the Great Light which is opened after the thirteenth æon, and that is the left [one],—when that gate is opened, then are the three times completed.' *How Sophia will know that the time of her final deliverance hath come.*

" Pistis Sophia again answered and said : ' O Light, by what shall I know,—for I am in this region,—that that gate is opened ? '

" And I answered and said unto her : ' When that gate is opened, they who are in all the æons will know because of the Great Light which will obtain in all their regions. But see, I have now settled that they shall venture no ill against thee, until the three times are completed. And thou wilt have the power of going down into their twelve æons, | when it pleaseth thee, and also of returning and going into thy region, which is below the thirteenth æon, and in which thou now art. But thou wilt not have the power of passing through the gate of the Height which is in the thirteenth æon, so as to enter into thy region whence thou didst come down. Moreover, if then the three times are completed, Self-willed and all his rulers will again constrain thee, to take thy light from thee, being enraged against thee and thinking that thou hast imprisoned his power in the chaos, and thinking that thou hast taken its light from it. He will then be embittered *What will come to pass at that time.* 168.

against thee, to take from thee thy light, in order that he may send it down into the chaos and it may get down to that emanation of his, so that it may be able to come up out of the chaos and go to his region. Adamas will attempt this. But I will take all thy powers from him and give them unto thee, and I will come to take them. Now, therefore, if they constrain thee at that time, then sing praises to the Light, and I will not delay to help thee. And I will quickly come unto thee to the regions which are below thee. And I will come down to their regions to take their light from them. And I will come to this region whither I have removed thee, and which is below 169. the thirteenth | æon, until I bring thee to thy region whence thou art come.'

" It came to pass then, when Pistis Sophia had heard me say these words unto her, that she rejoiced with great joy. But I removed her to the region which is below the thirteenth æon. I went to the Light and departed from her."

And all these adventures the First Mystery told to the disciples, that they should come to pass for Pistis Sophia. And he sat on the Mount of Olives, narrating all these adventures in the midst of the disciples. And he continued again and said unto them : " And ·it came to pass again after this, while I was in the world of men and sat in the way, that is in this region which is the Mount of Olives, before my vesture was sent unto me, which I had deposited in the four-and-twentieth mystery from the interior, but the first from the exterior, which is the Great Uncontainable, in which I am enwrapped, and before I had gone to the Height to receive my second vesture,—

The time for the final deliverance of Sophia is completed.

while I sat with you in this region, which is the
Mount of Olives, that the time was completed
of which I had said to Pistis Sophia: ' Adamas
and all his rulers will constrain thee.'

" It came to pass then, when that time came on,— CHAP. 77.
and I was in the world of men, | sitting with you 170.
in this region, which is the Mount of Olives,—
that Adamas looked down out of the twelve æons
and looked down at the regions of the chaos and
saw his demon power which is in the chaos, that
no light at all was in it, because I had taken its
light from it ; and he saw it, that it was dark and Adamas
could not go to his region, that is to the twelve forth two
æons.   Thereon Adamas again remembered Pistis of darkness
Sophia and became most exceedingly wroth to plague
against her, thinking that it was she who had im- Sophia.
prisoned his power in the chaos, and thinking that
it was she who had taken its light from it.   And
he was exceedingly embittered ; he piled wrath on
wrath and emanated out of himself a dark emanation and another, chaotic and evil, the violent
[one], so as through them to harass Pistis Sophia.
And he made a dark region in his region, so as to
constrain Sophia therein.   And he took many of
his rulers ; they pursued after Sophia, in order
that the two dark emanations which Adamas had
emanated, might lead her into the dark chaos
which he had made, and constrain her in that
region and harass her, until they should take her
whole light from her, and Adamas should take
the light from Pistis Sophia and give it to the
two dark violent emanations, and they should
carry it to the great chaos which is below and
dark, | and cast it into his dark power which is 171.
chaotic, if perchance it might be able to come to his

region, because it had become exceedingly dark, for I had taken its light-power from it.

" It came to pass then, when they pursued after Pistis Sophia, that she cried out again and sang praises to the Light, since I had said unto her : ' If thou shalt be constrained and singest praises unto me, I will come quickly and help thee.' It came to pass then, when she was constrained,—and I sat with you in this region, that is on the Mount of Olives,—that she sang praises to the Light, saying :

Sophia again singeth a song to the Light. " ' 1. O Light of lights, I have had faith in thee. Save me from all these rulers who pursue after me, and help me,

" ' 2. That in sooth they may never take from me my light, as the lion-faced power [did]. For thy light is not with me and thy light-stream to save me. Nay, Adamas is the more enraged against me, saying unto me : Thou hast imprisoned my power in the chaos.

" ' 3. Now, therefore, O Light of lights, if I have done this and have imprisoned it, if I have done any injustice at all to that power,

" ' 4. Or if I have constrained it, as it hath constrained me, then let all these rulers who pursue after me, take my light from me and leave me empty ;

" ' 5. And let foe Adamas pursue after my power and seize upon it and take my light from me and cast it into his dark power which is in the chaos, and keep my power | in the chaos.

172.

" ' 6. Now, therefore, O Light, lay hold on me in thy wrath and lift up thy power above my foes who have lifted themselves up against me to the very end.

" ' 7. Quicken me quickly, as thou hast said unto me : I will help thee.' "

It came to pass then, when the First Mystery had finished saying these words unto the disciples, that he said : " Who hath understood the words which I have spoken, let him come forward and set forth their solution." CHAP. 78.

James came forward and said : " My Lord, concerning this song which Pistis Sophia hath sung, thus thy light-power hath prophesied afore-time through David in the seventh Psalm :

" ' 1. O Lord, my God, in thee have I hoped. Free me from my pursuers and save me,

" ' 2. That in sooth he may never steal away my soul as a lion, without any one to deliver and save. James interpreteth the song from Psalm vii.

" ' 3. O Lord, my God, if I have done this, if injustice is on my hands,

" ' 4. If I have requited those who requite me with evil, then let me fall down empty through my foes.

" ' 5. And let the foe pursue after my soul and seize it, and trample my life to the ground and lay my honour in the dust. (Selah.)

" ' 6. Arise, O Lord, in thy wrath, raise thyself up for the end of my foes.

" ' 7. Arise according to the commandment which thou hast commanded.' " |

It came to pass then, when the First Mystery had heard James speak these words, that he said : " Well said, James, beloved." 173.

And the First Mystery continued again and said unto the disciples : " It came to pass then, when Pistis Sophia had finished uttering the words of this song, that she turned herself back CHAP. 79.

to see whether Adamas and his rulers had turned back to go to their æon. And she saw them, how they pursued after her. Then she turned unto them and said unto them :

" ' 1. Why pursue ye after me and say: I should not have help, that it [*sc.* the Light] should save me from you ?

" ' 2. Now, therefore, my vindicator is the Light and a strong [one]; but it is long-suffering until the time of which it hath said unto me : I will come and help thee. And it will not bring its wrath upon you always. But this is the time of which he hath spoken unto me.

" ' 3. Now, therefore, if ye turn not back and cease not to pursue after me, then will the Light make ready its power, and it will make itself ready in all its powers.

" ' 4. And in its power hath it made itself ready, so that it may take your lights which are in you, and ye may become dark ; and its power hath brought it to pass, so that it may take your power from you and ye go to ground.'

" And when Pistis Sophia had said this, she looked at the region of Adamas and saw the dark and chaotic region | which he had made, and saw also the two dark exceedingly violent emanations which Adamas had emanated, in order that they might seize Pistis Sophia and cast her down into the chaos which he had made, and constrain and harass her in that region, until they should take her light from her. It came to pass then, when Pistis Sophia had seen those two dark emanations and the dark region which Adamas had made, that she feared and cried unto the Light, saying :

" ' 1. O Light, lo ! Adamas, the doer of violence, is wrathful ; he hath made a dark emanation,

" ' 2. And he hath also emanated another chaos and hath made another dark and chaotic [one] and made it ready.

" ' 3. Now, therefore, O Light, the chaos which he hath made, in order to cast me down therein and take from me my light-power, take then from him his own.

" ' 4. And the plan which he hath devised, to take my light,—they are to take his own from him ; and the injustice which he hath spoken, to take my lights from me,—take then all of his.'

" These are the words which Pistis Sophia hath uttered in her song. Now, therefore, who is sober in spirit, let him come forward and set forth the solution of the words which Pistis Sophia [hath uttered] in her song."

Martha again came forward and said : " My Lord, | I am sober in my spirit and understand the words which thou sayest. Now, therefore, give me commandment to set forth their solution in openness."

And the First Mystery answered and said unto Martha : " I give thee commandment, Martha, to set forth the solution of the words which Pistis Sophia hath uttered in her song."

And Martha answered and said : " My Lord, these are the words which thy light-power hath prophesied aforetime through David in the seventh Psalm, saying :

" ' 12. God is a righteous vindicator and strong and long-suffering, who bringeth not on his wrath every day.

" ' 13. If ye turn not, he will whet his sword; he hath bent his bow and made it ready.

" ' 14. And he hath made ready for him instruments of death; he hath made his arrows for those who will be burnt up.

" ' 15. Behold, injustice hath been in labour, hath conceived wrong and brought forth iniquity.

" ' 16. It hath digged a pit and hollowed it out. It will fall into the hole which it hath made.

" ' 17. Its wrong will return on its own head, and its injustice will come down on its pate.' "

When Martha had said this, the First Mystery which looketh without, said unto her: " Well said, finely, Martha, blessed [one]."

It came to pass then, when Jesus had finished telling his disciples all the adventures which had befallen Pistis Sophia when she was in the chaos, and the way | she had sung praises to the Light, that it should save her and lead her out of the chaos, and lead her into the twelve æons, and also the way it had saved her out of all her afflictions with which the rulers of the chaos had constrained her, because she longed to go to the Light, that Jesus continued again in the discourse and said unto his disciples: " It came to pass then after all this, that I took Pistis Sophia and led her into the thirteenth æon, shining most exceedingly, there being no measure for the light which was about me. I entered into the region of the four-and-twenty invisibles, shining most exceedingly. And they fell into great commotion; they looked and saw Sophia, who was with me. Her they knew, but me they knew not, who I was, but held me for some sort of emanation of the Light-land.

" It came to pass then, when Pistis Sophia saw her fellows, the invisibles, that she rejoiced in great joy and exulted exceedingly and desired to proclaim the wonders which I had wrought on her below in the earth of mankind, until I saved her. She came into the midst of the | in- 177. visibles, and in their midst sang praises unto me, saying :

" ' 1. I will give thanks unto thee, O Light, for thou art a saviour; thou art a deliverer for all time.

" ' 2. I will utter this song to the Light, for it hath saved me and saved me out of the hand of the rulers, my foes.

Sophia singeth the praises of the Light to her fellow-invisibles

" ' 3. And thou hast preserved me in all the regions, thou hast saved me out of the height and the depth of the chaos and out of the æons of the rulers of the sphere.

" ' 4. And when I was come out of the Height, I wandered round in regions in which is no light, and I could not return to the thirteenth æon, my dwelling-place.

" ' 5. For there was no light in me nor power. My power was utterly weakened (?).

" ' 6. And the Light saved me in all my afflictions. I sang praises unto the Light, and it hearkened unto me, when I was constrained.

" ' 7. It guided - me in the creation of the æons to lead me up into the thirteenth æon, my dwelling-place.

" ' 8. I will give thanks unto thee, O Light, that thou hast saved me, and for thy wondrous works unto the race of men.

" ' 9. When I failed of my power, thou hast given me power ; and when I failed of my light, thou didst fill me with purified light.

" ' 10. I was in the darkness and in the shadow of the chaos, bound with the mighty fetters of the chaos, and no light was in me.

" ' 11. For I have provoked the commandment of the Light and have transgressed, and I have made wroth the commandment of the Light, because I had gone out of my region.

178.   " ' 12. And when I | had gone down, I failed of my light and became without light, and no one had helped me.

" ' 13. And in my affliction I sang praises unto the Light, and it saved me out of my afflictions.

" ' 14. And it hath also broken asunder all my bonds and led me up out of the darkness and the affliction of the chaos.

" ' 15. I will give thanks unto thee, O Light, that thou hast saved me and that thy wondrous works have been wrought in the race of men.

" ' 16. And thou hast shattered the upper gates of the darkness and the mighty bolts of the chaos.

" ' 17. And thou didst let me depart out of the region in which I had transgressed, and my light was taken, because I have transgressed.

" ' 18. And I ceased from my mysteries and went down to the gates of the chaos.

" ' 19. And when I was constrained, I sang praises to the Light. It saved me out of all my afflictions.

" ' 20. Thou sentest thy stream; it gave me power and saved me out of all my afflictions.

" ' 21. I will give thanks unto thee, O Light, that thou hast saved me, and for thy wondrous works in the race of men.'

" This then is the song which Pistis Sophia

hath uttered in the midst of the four-and-twenty invisibles, desiring that they should know all the wondrous works which I had done for her, and desiring that they should know that I have gone to the world of men and have given them the mysteries of the Height. Now, therefore, who is exalted in his thought, let him come forward and say the solution of the song which Pistis Sophia hath uttered."

It came to pass then, when Jesus | had finished CHAP. 82. saying these words, that Philip came forward and 179. said : " Jesus, my Lord, my thought is exalted, and I have understood the solution of the song which Pistis Sophia hath uttered. The prophet David hath prophesied concerning it aforetime in the one-hundred-and-sixth Psalm, saying :

" ' 1. Give ye thanks unto the Lord, for he is Philip in-terpreteth good, for his grace is eternal. the song

" ' 2. Let the delivered of the Lord say this, from Psalm for it is he who hath delivered them out of the cvi. hand of their foes.

" ' 3. He hath gathered them together out of their lands, from the east and from the west and from the north and from the sea.

" ' 4. They wandered round in the desert, in a waterless country ; they found not the way to the city of their dwelling-place.

" ' 5. Hungry and thirsty, their soul fainted in them.

" ' 6. He saved them out of their necessities. They cried unto the Lord and he hearkened unto them in their affliction.

" ' 7. He led them on a straight way, that they might go to the region of their dwelling-place.

" ' 8. Let them give thanks unto the Lord for

his graciousness and his wondrous works unto the children of men.

" ' 9. For he hath satisfied a hungering soul; he hath filled a hungering soul with good things,

" ' 10. Them who sat in darkness and the shadow of death, who were fettered in misery and iron.

180.

" ' 11. For | they had provoked the word of God and made wroth the determination of the Most High.

" ' 12. Their heart was humbled in their miseries; they become weak and no one helped them.

" ' 13. They cried unto the Lord in their affliction; he saved them out of their necessities.

" ' 14. And he led them out of the darkness and the shadow of death and brake their bonds asunder.

" ' 15. Let them give thanks unto the Lord for his graciousness and his wondrous works unto the children of men.

" ' 16. For he hath shattered the gates of brass and burst the bolts of iron asunder.

" ' 17. He hath taken them unto himself out of the way of their iniquity. For they were brought low because of their iniquities.

" ' 18. Their heart abhorred all manner of meat and they were near unto the gates of death.

" ' 19. They cried unto the Lord in their affliction and he saved them out of their necessities.

" ' 20. He sent his word and healed them and freed them from their miseries.

" ' 21. Let them give thanks unto the Lord for

his graciousness and his wondrous works unto
the children of men.'

" This then, my Lord, is the solution of the song
which Pistis Sophia hath uttered. Hearken,
therefore, my Lord, that I may say it clearly.
The word in sooth which David hath spoken :
' Give ye thanks unto the Lord, for he is good,
for his grace is eternal,'—it is the word which
Pistis Sophia hath spoken: 'I will give thanks
unto thee, O Light, for thou art a saviour and
thou art a deliverer for all time.'

" And the word which hath David spoken : |
' Let the delivered of the Lord say this, for he 181.
hath delivered them out of the hand of their
foes,'—it is the word which Pistis Sophia hath
spoken : ' I will utter this song to the Light, for
it hath saved me and saved me out of the hand
of the rulers, my foes.'   And the rest of the Psalm.

" This then, my Lord, is the solution of the
song which Pistis Sophia hath uttered in the
midst of the four-and-twenty invisibles, desiring
that they should know all the wondrous works
which thou hast done for her, and desiring that
they should know that thou hast given thy
mysteries to the race of men."

It came to pass then, when Jesus had heard
Philip say these words, that he said : " Well said,
blessed Philip. This is the solution of the song
which Pistis Sophia hath uttered."

[END OF THE STORY OF PISTIS SOPHIA]

It came to pass then again, after all this, that CHAP. 83.
Mary came forward, adored the feet of Jesus and Mary ques-
said : " My Lord, be not wroth with me, if I tioneth
Jesus.

question thee, because we question concerning everything with precision and certainty. For thou hast said unto us aforetime : ' Seek that ye may find, and knock that it may be opened unto you. For every one who seeketh shall find, and to every one who knocketh it shall be opened.' Now, therefore, my Lord, who is it whom I shall seek, or who is it at whom we shall knock ? Or who rather is able to give us the decision upon the words concerning which we shall question thee ? Or | who rather knoweth the power of the words concerning which we shall question ? Because thou in the mind hast given us mind of the Light and hast given us sense and an exceedingly exalted thought ; for which cause, therefore, no one existeth in the world of men nor any one in the height of the æons, who can give the decision on the words concerning which we question, save thee alone, who knoweth [*sic*] the universe, who is perfected in the universe ; because we do not question in the manner in which the men of the world question, but because we question in the gnosis of the Height which thou hast given unto us, and we question moreover in the type of the excellent questioning which thou hast taught us, that we may question therein. Now, therefore, my Lord, be not wroth with me, but reveal unto me the matter concerning which I shall question thee."

It came to pass, when Jesus had heard Mary Magdalene say these words, that he answered and said unto her : " Question concerning what thou desirest to question, and I will reveal it unto thee with precision and certainty. Amēn, amēn, I say unto you : Rejoice in great joy and exult

182.

most exceedingly.   If ye question concerning
all with precision, then shall I exult most exceedingly, because ye question concerning all with
precision and question in the manner in which it
beseemeth to question.   Now, therefore, question
concerning what thou wouldst question, | and I 183.
will reveal it unto thee with joy."

It came to pass then, when Mary had heard
the Saviour say these words, that she rejoiced
in great joy and exulted most exceedingly and
said unto Jesus : " My Lord and Saviour, of
what manner then are the four-and-twenty invisibles and of what type, or rather of what
quality are they, or of what quality is then their
light ? "

And Jesus answered and said unto Mary : CHAP. 84.
" What is there in this world which is like unto Of the glory
of the four-
them, or rather what region is there in this world and-twenty
which is comparable to them ?   Now, therefore, invisibles.
to what am I to liken them, or rather what am I
to say concerning them ?   For nothing existeth in
this world to which I shall be able to liken them,
and no form existeth in it which is able to be like
them.   Now, therefore, nothing existeth in this
world which is of the quality of the heaven.   [But]
amēn, I say unto you : Every one of the invisibles
is nine times greater than the heaven and the
sphere above it and the twelve æons all together,
as I have already said unto you at another time.
And no light existeth in this world which is more
excellent than the light of the sun.   Amēn, amēn,
I say unto you : The four-and-twenty invisibles
shine ten-thousand times more than the light of
the sun which is in this world, as I have already |
said unto you at another time.   For the light 184.

of the sun in its shape in truth is not in this world, for its light pierceth through many veils and regions. But the light of the sun in its shape in truth, which is in the region of the Virgin of Light, shineth ten-thousand times more than the four-and-twenty invisibles and the great invisible forefather and also the great triple-powered god, as I have already said unto you at another time.

" Now, therefore, Mary, there is no form in this world, nor any light, nor any shape, which is comparable to the four-and-twenty invisibles, so that I may liken it to them. But yet a little while and I will lead thee and thy brethren and fellow-disciples into all the regions of the Height and will lead you into the three spaces of the First Mystery, save only the regions of the space of the Ineffable, and ye shall see all their shapes in truth without similitude.

" And if I lead you into the height and ye shall see the glory of them of the height, then will ye be in very great amazement.

Of the glory of the Fate.

" And if I lead you into the region of the rulers of the Fate, then will ye see the glory in which they are, and because of their overtowering great glory ye will deem this world before you as 185. darkness of darknesses, and | ye will look at the whole world of men, how it will have the condition of a speck of dust for you because of the great distance it is far distant from it, and because of the great condition it is considerably greater than it.

Of the glory of the twelve æons.

" And if I lead you into the twelve æons, then will ye see the glory in which they are ; and because of the great glory the region of the rulers of the Fate will count for you as the dark-

ness of darknesses, and it will have for you the
condition of a speck of dust because of the great
distance it is far distant from it and because of
the great condition it is considerably greater
than them, as I have already said unto you at
another time.

" And if I lead you moreover into the thirteenth Of the glory
æon, then will ye see the glory in which they are ; of the thir-
the twelve æons will count for you as the darkness teenth æon.
of darknesses, and ye shall look at the twelve
æons, how it [sc. their region] will have for you
the likeness of a speck of dust because of the
great distance it is far distant from it, and because of the great condition it is considerably
greater than the former.

" And if I lead you into the region of those Of the glory
of the Midst, then will ye see the glory in which of the Midst.
they are ; the thirteen æons will count for you as
the darkness of darknesses. And again ye will
look at the twelve æons | and upon the whole 186.
Fate and the whole ordering and all the spheres
and all the others in which they are ; they will
have for you the condition of a speck of dust
because of the great distance it [sc. their region]
is distant from it and because of the great condition it is considerably greater than the former.

" And if I lead you into the region of those Of the glory
of the Right, then will ye see the glory in which of the
they are ; the region of those of the Midst will Right.
count for you as the night which is in the world
of men. And if ye look at the Midst, it will
have for you the condition of a speck of dust
because of the great distance the region of those
of the Right is considerably distant from it.

" And if I lead you into the Light-land, that

Of the glory
of the Trea-
sury.

is into the Treasury of the Light, and ye see the glory in which they are, then will the region of those of the Right count for you as the light at mid-day in the world of men, when the sun is not out ; and if ye look at the region of those of the Right, it will have for you the condition of a speck of dust because of the great distance the Treasury of the Light is distant from it.

Of the glory
of the In-
heritance.

"And if I lead you into the region of those who have received the inheritances and have received the mysteries of the Light, and ye see the glory of the Light in which they are, then the Light-land will count for you as the light of the sun which is in the world of men.   And if ye look

upon the Light-land, | then will it count for you as a speck of dust because of the great distance the Light-land is distant from it, and because of the greatness [by which] it is considerably greater than the former."

It came to pass then, when Jesus had finished speaking these words unto his disciples, that Mary Magdalene started forward and said : " My Lord, be not wroth with me if I question thee, because we question thee concerning all with precision."

And Jesus answered and said unto Mary : " Question concerning what thou desirest to question, and I will reveal it unto thee in openness without similitude, and all concerning which thou questionest, I will say unto thee with precision and certainty.   I will perfect you in all power and all fulnesses, from the interior of the interiors to the exterior of the exteriors, from that Ineffable to the darkness of darknesses, so that ye shall be called ' the fulnesses perfected

in all gnoses.' Now, therefore, Mary, question
concerning what thou mayest question, and I
will reveal it to thee with great joy and great
exultation."

It came to pass then, when Mary had heard Mary again
the Saviour say these words, that she rejoiced in Jesus.
exceedingly great joy and exulted, and said :
" My Lord, will then the men of the world who
have received the mysteries of the Light, | be 188.
superior to the emanations of the Treasury in
thy kingdom ? For I have heard thee say :
' If I lead you into the region of those who have
received the mysteries of the Light, then will the
region of the [emanations of the] Light-land
count for you as a speck of dust because of the
great distance in which it is distant from it, and
because of the great light in which it is,'—that
is the Light-land is the Treasury, the region of the
emanations,—will therefore then, my Lord, the
men who have received the mysteries, be superior
to the Light-land and superior to those [emana-
tions] in the kingdom of the Light ? "

And Jesus answered and said unto Mary : CHAP. 86.
" Finely indeed dost thou question concerning
all with precision and certainty. But hearken,
Mary, that I may speak with thee about the
consummation of the æon and the ascension of
the universe. It will not yet take place ; but I
have said unto you : ' If I lead you into the region
of the inheritances of those who shall receive the
mystery of the Light, | then will the Treasury of 189.
the Light, the region of the emanations, count
for you as a speck of dust only and as the light of
the sun by day.'

" I have therefore said : ' This will take place

at the time of the consummation [and] of the
ascension of the universe.' The twelve saviours
of the Treasury and the twelve orders of every
one of them, which are the emanations of the
seven Voices and of the five Trees, they will be
with me in the region of the inheritances of the
Light; being kings with me in my kingdom,
and every one of them being king over his emanations, and moreover every one of them being king
according to his glory, the great according to
his greatness and the little according to his
littleness.

" And the saviour of the emanations of the
first Voice will be in the region of the souls of
those who have received the first mystery of the
First Mystery in my kingdom.

" And the saviour of the emanations of the
second Voice will be in the region of the souls of
those who have received the second mystery of
the First Mystery.

" In like manner also will the saviour of the
emanations of the third Voice be in the region
of the souls of those who have received the third
mystery of the First Mystery in the | inheritances
of the Light.

190.

" And the saviour of the emanations of the
fourth Voice of the Treasury of the Light will be
in the region of the souls of those who have
received the fourth mystery of the First Mystery
in the inheritances of the Light.

" And the fifth saviour of the fifth Voice of
the Treasury of the Light will be in the region of
the souls of those who have received the fifth
mystery of the First Mystery in the inheritances
of the Light.

" And the sixth saviour of the emanations of the sixth Voice of the Treasury of the Light will be in the region of the souls of those who have received the sixth mystery of the First Mystery.

" And the seventh saviour of the emanations of the seventh Voice of the Treasury of the Light will be in the region of the souls of those who have received the seventh mystery of the First Mystery in the Treasury [sic] of the Light.

" And the eighth saviour, that is the saviour of the emanations of the first Tree of the Treasury of the Light, will be in the region of the souls of those who have received the | eighth mystery of 191. the First Mystery in the inheritances of the Light.

" And the ninth saviour, that is the saviour of the emanations of the second Tree of the Treasury of the Light, will be in the region of the souls of those who have received the ninth mystery of the First Mystery in the inheritances of the Light.

" And the tenth saviour, that is the saviour of the emanations of the third Tree of the Treasury of the Light, will be in the region of the souls of those who have received the tenth mystery of the First Mystery in the inheritances of the Light.

" In like manner also the eleventh saviour, that is the saviour of the fourth Tree of the Treasury of the Light, will be in the region of the souls of those who have received the eleventh mystery of the First Mystery in the inheritances of the Light.

" And the twelfth saviour, that is the saviour of the emanations of the fifth Tree of the Treasury of the Light, will be in the region of the souls of those who have received the twelfth mystery of the First Mystery in the inheritances of the Light.

192.

Of the ascension of those of the Treasury into the Inheritance.

" And the seven | Amēns and the five Trees and the three Amēns will be on my right, being kings in the inheritances of the Light. And the Twin-saviours, that is the Child of the Child, and the nine guards will bide also at my left, being kings in the inheritances of the Light.

Of their respective ranks in the kingdom.

" And every one of the saviours will rule over the orders of his emanations in the inheritances of the Light as they did also in the Treasury of the Light.

" And the nine guards of the Treasury of the Light will be superior to the saviours in the inheritances of the Light. And the Twin-saviours will be superior to the nine guards in the kingdom. And the three Amēns will be superior to the Twin-saviours in the kingdom. And the five Trees will be superior to the three Amēns in the inheritances of the Light.

Of the powers of the Right, and their emanation and ascension.

" And Yew and the guard of the veil of the Great Light, and the receiver of Light and the two great guides and the great Sabaōth, the Good, will be kings in the first saviour of the first Voice of the Treasury of the Light, [the saviour] who

193.

will be in | the region of those who have received the first mystery of the First Mystery. For in sooth Yew and the guard of the region of those of the Right and Melchisedec, the great receiver of the Light, and the two great guides have come forth out of the purified and utterly pure light of the first Tree up to the fifth.

" Yew in sooth is the overseer of the Light, who hath come forth first out of the pure light of the first Tree ; on the other hand the guard of the veil of those of the Right hath come forth out of the second Tree ; and the two guides again

have come forth out of the pure and utterly
purified light of the third and fourth Trees of
the Treasury of the Light ; Melchisedec again
hath come forth out of the fifth Tree ; on the
other hand Sabaōth, the Good, whom I have
called my father, hath come forth out of Yew,
the overseer of the Light.

" These six then by command of the First
Mystery the last Helper hath caused to be in the
region of those of the Right, for the economy of
the ingathering of the upper light out of the æons
of the rulers and out of the worlds and all races
in them,—of every one of whom I will tell you
the employment over which he hath been set in
the expansion of the universe. Because, therefore, of the importance of the employment over
which they have been set, | they will be fellow- 194.
kings in the first [saviour] of the first Voice of the
Treasury of the Light, whó will be in the region
of the souls of those who have received the first
mystery of the First Mystery.

" And the Virgin of Light and the great guide Of the
of the Midst, whom the rulers of the æons are powers of
the Midst
wont to call the Great Yew after the name of a and their
ascension.
great ruler who is in their region,—he and the
Virgin of Light and his twelve ministers, from
whom ye have received your shape and from whom
ye have received the power, they all will be kings
with the first saviour of the first Voice in the
region of the souls of those who will receive the
first mystery of the First Mystery in the inheritances of the Light.

" And the fifteen helpers of the seven virgins
of the Light who are in the Midst, they will expand
themselves in the regions of the twelve saviours,

and the rest of the angels of the Midst, every one of them according to his glory, will rule with me in the inheritances of the Light. And I shall rule over them all in the inheritances of the Light.

"All this then which I have said unto you, will not take place at this time, but it will take place at the consummation of the æon, that is at the ascension of the universe ; that is at the dissolution of the universe and at the total ascension of the numbering | of the perfect souls of the inheritances of the Light.

"Before the consummation, therefore, this which I have said unto you, will not take place, but every one will be in his own region, into which he hath been set from the beginning, until the numbering of the ingathering of the perfect souls is completed.

"The seven Voices and the five Trees and the three Amēns and the Twin-saviours and the nine guards and the twelve saviours and those of the region of the Right and those of the region of the Midst, every one will abide in the region in which they have been set, until the numbering of the perfect souls of the inheritances of the Light shall be raised up all together.

"And also all the rulers who have repented, they also will abide in the region into which they have been set, until the numbering of the souls of the Light shall be raised up all together.

"[The souls] will all come, every one at the time when he will receive the mysteries ; and all the rulers who have repented, will pass through and come into the region of the Midst. And those of the Midst will baptize them and give unto them the spiritual unction and seal them with the

seals of their mysteries. And they will pass
through those of all the regions of the Midst, and
they will pass through the region of the Right
and the interior of the region of the nine guards
and the interior of the region of the Twin-
saviours and the interior of the region of the
three | Amēns and of the twelve saviours and the 196.
interior of the five Trees and of the seven Voices.
Every one giveth unto them his seal of his mystery, and they pass into the interior of them all
and go to the region of the inheritances of the
Light ; and every one bideth in the region up to
which he hath received mysteries in the inheritances of the Light.

"In a word, all the souls of men who shall Of the rank
receive the mysteries of the Light, will precede of the souls
all the rulers who have repented, and they will fect.
precede all those of the region of the Midst and
those of the whole region of the Right, and they
will precede those of the whole region of the
Treasury of the Light. In a word, they will
precede all those of the region [of the Treasury],
and they will precede all those of the regions of
the first Commandment, and they will pass into
the interior of them all and go into the Inheritance
of the Light up to the region of their mystery ; and
every one abideth in the region up to which he
hath received mysteries. And those of the region
of the Midst and of the Right and those of the
whole region of the Treasury, every one abideth in
the region of the order into which he hath been
set from the beginning on, until the universe shall
be raised up. And every one of them accomplisheth his economy to which he hath been set,
in respect of the ingathering of the souls who

have received the mysteries, in respect of this economy, so that they may seal | all the souls who will receive the mysteries and who will pass through their interior towards the Inheritance of the Light.

"Now, therefore, Mary, this is the word concerning which thou dost question me with precision and certainty. For the rest now then, who hath ears to hear, let him hear."

CHAP. 87.

"It came to pass then, when Jesus had finished speaking these words, that Mary Magdalene started forward and said :

Mary interpreteth the discourse from the scriptures.

"My Lord, my indweller of light hath ears and I comprehend every word which thou sayest. Now, therefore, my Lord, on account of the word which thou hast spoken : ' All the souls of the race of men who shall receive the mysteries of the Light, will go into the Inheritance of the Light before all the rulers who will repent, and before those of the whole region of the Right and before the whole region of the Treasury of the Light,'—on account of this word, my Lord, thou hast said unto us aforetime : ' The first will be last and the last will be first,'—that is, the ' last ' are the whole race of men which will enter into the Light-kingdom sooner than all those of the region of the Height, who are the ' first.' On this account, therefore, my Lord, hast thou said unto us : ' Who hath ears to hear, let him hear,'—that is thou desirest to know whether we | comprehend every word which thou speakest. This, therefore, is the word, my Lord."

It came to pass then, when Mary had finished saying these words, that the Saviour was greatly astonished at the definitions of the words which she spake, for she had become pure spirit utterly. Jesus answered again and said unto her : " Well said, spiritual and pure Mary. This is the solution of the word."

It came to pass then again after all these words, that Jesus continued in the discourse and said unto his disciples : " Hearken, that I may discourse with you concerning the glory of those of the Height, how they are, according to the manner in which I discoursed with you unto this day.

" Now, therefore, if I lead you into the region of the last Helper, who surroundeth the Treasury of the Light, and if I lead you into the region of that last Helper and ye see the glory in which he is, then will the region of the Inheritance of the Light count for you only for the size of a city of the world, because of the greatness in which the last Helper is, and because of the great light in which he is.

" And thereafter I will discourse with you also concerning the glory of the Helper who is above the little Helper. But I shall not be able to discourse with you concerning the regions of those who are above all Helpers ; | for there existeth no type in this world, to describe them, for there existeth in this world no likeness which is like unto them, that I may compare them therewith, nor greatness nor light which is like unto them, not only in this world, but they also have no likeness with those of the Height of Righteousness from their region upwards. On this account, therefore, there existeth in fact no manner of describing them in this world because of the great glory of those of the Height and because of the

CHAP. 88.

Of the last Helper.

That the regions beyond the Helpers are indescribable.

199.

great immeasurable greatness. On this account, therefore, there existeth no manner to describe it in this world."

It came to pass then, when Jesus had finished speaking these words unto his disciples, that Mary Magdalene came forward and said unto Jesus : " My Lord, be not wroth with me if I question thee, because I trouble repeatedly. Now, therefore, my Lord, be not wroth with me if I question thee concerning all with precision and certainty. For my brethren will herald it among the race of men, so that they may hear and repent and be saved from the violent judgments of the evil rulers and go to the Height and inherit the Light-kingdom ; because, my Lord, we are compassionate not only towards ourselves, but compassionate towards the whole race of men, so that they may be saved from all the violent judgments. Now, therefore, my Lord, on this account we question concerning all with certainty ; for my brethren herald it to the whole race of men, | in order that they may escape the violent rulers of the darkness and be saved out of the hands of the violent receivers of the outermost darkness."

200.

It came to pass, when Jesus had heard Mary say these words, that the Saviour answered in great compassion towards her and said unto her : " Question concerning what thou desirest to question, and I will reveal it unto thee with precision and certainty and without similitude."

CHAP. 89.
Mary further questioneth Jesus.

It came to pass then, when Mary had heard the Saviour say these words, that she rejoiced with great joy and exulted exceedingly and said unto Jesus : " My Lord, by how much

greatness then is the second Helper greater than
the first Helper ?   By how much distance is he
distant from him, or rather how many times more
does he shine than the latter ? "

Jesus answered and said unto Mary in the Of the second Helper.
midst of the disciples : " Amēn, amēn, I say unto
you : The second Helper is distant from the first
Helper in great immeasurable distance in regard
to the height above and the depth below and the
length and the breadth.   For he is exceedingly
distant from him in great immeasurable distance
through the angels and all the archangels and
through the gods and all the invisibles.   And he
is very considerably greater than the latter in
an incalculable measure | through the angels and 201.
archangels and through the gods and all the
invisibles.   And he shineth more than the latter
in an utterly immeasurable measure, there being
no measure for the light in which he is, and no
measure for him through angels and archangels
and through the gods and all the invisibles, as
I have already said unto you at another time.

" In like manner also the third Helper and Of the third, fourth, and fifth Helpers.
fourth and fifth Helper,—one is greater than the
other . . . and shineth more than the latter and
is distant from him in a great immeasurable
distance through the angels and archangels and
the gods and all the invisibles, as I have already
said unto you at another time.   And I will tell
unto you also the type of every one [of them]
at their expansion."

It came to pass then, when Jesus had finished CHAP. 90. Mary again questioneth Jesus.
saying these words unto his disciples, that Mary
Magdalene came forward again, continued and
said unto Jesus : " My Lord, in what type will

be those who have received the mystery of the Light, in the midst of the last Helper ? "

And Jesus answered and said unto Mary in the midst of the disciples : " They who have received the mystery of the Light, if they come out of | the body of the matter of the rulers, then will every one be in his order according to the mystery which he hath received. Those who have received the higher mysteries, will abide in the higher order ; those who have received the lower mysteries will be in the lower orders. In a word, up to what region every one hath received mysteries, there will he abide in his order in the Inheritance of the Light. For which cause I have said unto you aforetime : ' Where your heart is, there will your treasure be,'—that is up to what region every one hath received mysteries, there shall he be."

It came to pass, when Jesus had finished saying these words unto his disciples, that John came forward and said unto Jesus : " My Lord and my Saviour, give me also commandment that I discourse before thee, and be not wroth with me if I question concerning all with precision and certainty ; for thou, my Lord, hast promised me in a promise to make revelation unto us of all concerning which I shall question thee. Now, therefore, my Lord, hide nothing from us at all in the matter on which we shall question thee."

And Jesus answered in great compassion and said unto John : " To thee also, blessed John, and beloved, I give commandment to speak the word which pleaseth thee, and I will reveal it unto thee face to face without similitude, and I

will say unto thee | all on which thou wilt question 203.
me with precision and certainty."

And John answered and said unto Jesus: John ques-
"My Lord, will then every one abide in the region Jesus.
up to which he hath received the mysteries, and
hath he no power to go into other orders which
are above him ; and hath he no power to go into
the orders which are below him ? "

And Jesus answered and said unto John: CHAP. 91.
"Finely indeed do ye question on all with precision and certainty. But now, therefore, John,
hearken that I may discourse with thee. Every
one who hath received mysteries of the Light,
will abide in the region up to which every one hath
received mysteries, and he hath not the power
to go into the height into the orders which are
above him.

"So that he who hath received mysteries in Of the first
the first Commandment, hath the power to go ment.
Command-
into the orders which are below him, that is into
all the orders of the third [?] space ; but he hath
not the power to go into the height to the orders
which are above him.

"And he who shall receive the mysteries of Of the first
the First Mystery, which is the four-and-twen- space.
tieth mystery from without and the head of the
first space which is without,—he hath the power
to go into all the orders which are without
him ; but he hath not the power to go into the
regions which are above him or to pass through
them.

"And of those who have received the mysteries Of the
in the orders of the four-and-twenty mysteries, | space.
second
every one will go into the region in which he 204.
hath received mysteries, and he will have the

power to pass through all the orders and spaces
which are without him; but he hath not the power
to go into the higher orders which are above him
or to pass through them.

Of the third
space.

" And he who hath received mysteries in the
orders of the First Mystery which is in the third
space, hath the power to go into all the lower
orders which are below him and to pass through
all; but on the other hand he hath not the power
to go into the regions which are above him or to
pass through them.

Of the
Thrice-spirit-
uals.

" And he who hath received mysteries of the
first Thrice-spiritual, which ruleth over the four-
and-twenty mysteries all together which rule
over the space of the First Mystery, of whose
region at the expansion of the universe I will tell
you—he, therefore, who shall receive the mystery
of that Thrice-spiritual, hath the power to go
down into all orders which are below him; but
he hath not the power to go into the height into
the orders which are above him, that is into all
the orders of the space of the Ineffable.

" And he who hath received the mystery of the
second Thrice-spiritual, hath the power to go
into all the orders of the first Thrice-spiritual |

205.

and to pass through them all and all their orders
which are in them; but he hath not the power
to go into the higher orders of the third Thrice-
spiritual.

" And he who hath received the mystery of
the third Thrice-spiritual, which ruleth over the
three Thrice-spirituals and the three spaces of
the First Mystery all together, [hath the power
to go into all the orders which are below him];
but he hath not the power to go into the height

into the orders which are above him, that is
into the orders of the space of the Ineffable.

" And he who hath received the master- Of the master-mys-tery.
mystery of the First Mystery of the Ineffable,
that is the twelve mysteries of the First Mystery
all together, which rule over all the spaces of the
First Mystery,—he, therefore, who shall receive
that mystery, hath the power to pass through all
the orders of the spaces of the three Thrice-
spirituals and the three spaces of the First Mystery and all their orders, and hath the power to
pass through all the orders of the inheritances
of the Light, to pass through them from without
within and from within without and from above
below and from below | above and from the height 206.
to the depth and from the depth to the height and
from the length to the breadth and from the
breadth to the length ; in a word, he hath the
power to pass through all the regions of the inheritances of the Light, and he hath the power to
bide in the region where he pleaseth, in the
Inheritance of the Light-kingdom.

" And amēn, I say unto you : That man will
at the dissolution of the world be king over all
the orders of the Inheritance of the Light. And he
who shall receive that mystery of the Ineffable
which I am,—

" That mystery knoweth why the darkness Of the gnosis of the master-mys-tery.
hath arisen and why the light hath arisen.

" And that mystery knoweth why the darkness
of the darknesses hath arisen and why the light
of the lights hath arisen.

" And that mystery knoweth why the chaos
hath arisen and why the treasury of the light
hath arisen.

" And that mystery knoweth why the judgments have arisen and why the light-land and the region of the inheritances of the light have arisen.

" And that mystery knoweth why the chastisements of the sinners have arisen and why the rest of the kingdom of the light hath arisen.

207.   " And that mystery knoweth | why the sinners have arisen and why the inheritances of the light have arisen.

" And that mystery knoweth why the impious have arisen and why the good have arisen.

" And that mystery knoweth why the chastisements and judgments have arisen and why all the emanations of the light have arisen.

" And that mystery knoweth why the sins have arisen and why the baptisms and the mysteries of the light have arisen.

" And that mystery knoweth why the fire of chastisement hath arisen and why the seals of the light, so that the fire should not harm them, have arisen.

" And that mystery knoweth why wrath hath arisen and why peace hath arisen.

" And that mystery knoweth why slander hath arisen and why songs of the light have arisen.

" And that mystery knoweth why the prayers of the light have arisen.

" And that mystery knoweth why cursing hath arisen and why blessing hath arisen.

" And that mystery knoweth why knavery hath arisen and why deceit hath arisen.

208.   " And that mystery | knoweth why the slaying hath arisen and why the quickening of the souls hath arisen.

" And that mystery knoweth why adultery

and fornication have arisen and why purity hath arisen.

" And that mystery knoweth why intercourse hath arisen and why continence hath arisen.

" And that mystery knoweth why insolence and boasting have arisen and why humbleness and meekness have arisen.

" And that mystery knoweth why tears have arisen and why laughter hath arisen.

" And that mystery knoweth why slander hath arisen and why good report hath arisen.

" And that mystery knoweth why appreciation hath arisen and why disdain of men hath arisen.

" And that mystery knoweth why murmuring hath arisen and why innocence and humbleness have arisen.

" And that mystery knoweth why sin hath arisen and why purity hath arisen.

" And that mystery knoweth why strength hath arisen and why weakness hath arisen.

" And that mystery knoweth why | motion of 209. body hath arisen and why its utility hath arisen.

" And that mystery knoweth why poverty hath arisen and why wealth hath arisen.

" And that mystery knoweth why the freedom [?] of the world hath arisen and why slavery hath arisen.

" And that mystery knoweth why death hath arisen and why life hath arisen."

It came to pass then, when Jesus had finished **CHAP. 92.** saying these words unto his disciples, that they rejoiced in great joy and exulted when they heard Jesus say these words.

And Jesus continued again in the discourse and said unto them : " Hearken, therefore, now still further, O my disciples, so that I discourse with you concerning the whole gnosis of the mystery of the Ineffable.

" That mystery of the Ineffable knoweth why unmercifulness hath arisen and why mercifulness hath arisen.

" And that mystery knoweth why ruin hath arisen and why everlasting eternity hath arisen.

" And that mystery knoweth why the reptiles have arisen and why they will be destroyed.

" And that mystery knoweth why the wild beasts have arisen | and why they will be destroyed.

" And that mystery knoweth why the cattle have arisen and why the birds have arisen.

" And that mystery knoweth why the mountains have arisen and why the precious stones therein have arisen.

" And that mystery knoweth why the matter of gold hath arisen and why the matter of silver hath arisen.

" And that mystery knoweth why the matter of copper hath arisen and why the matter of iron and of stone hath arisen.

" And that mystery knoweth why the matter of lead hath arisen.

" And that mystery knoweth why the matter of glass hath arisen and why the matter of wax hath arisen.

" And that mystery knoweth why herbs, that is the vegetables, have arisen and why all matters have arisen.

" And the mystery knoweth why the waters of the earth and all things in them have arisen and why also the earth hath arisen.

" And that mystery knoweth why the seas |
and the waters have arisen and why the wild 211.
beasts in the seas have arisen.

" And that mystery knoweth why the matter
of the world hath arisen and why it [the world]
will be utterly destroyed."

Jesus continued again and said unto his dis- CHAP. 93.
ciples : " Yet further, O my disciples and companions and brethren, let every one be sober in
the spirit which is in him, let him understand and
comprehend all the words which I shall say
unto you ; for from now on will I begin to discourse with you concerning all the gnoses of that
Ineffable.

" That mystery knoweth why the west hath
arisen and why the east hath arisen.

" And that mystery knoweth why the south
hath arisen and why the north hath arisen.

" Yet further, O my disciples, hearken and continue to be sober and hearken to the total gnosis
of the mystery of the Ineffable.

" That mystery knoweth why the demons have
arisen and why mankind hath arisen.

" And that mystery knoweth why the heat
hath arisen and why the pleasant air hath
arisen.

" And that mystery knoweth why the stars
have arisen and why the clouds have arisen. |

" And that mystery knoweth why the earth 212.
became deep and why the water came thereon.

" And that mystery knoweth why the earth
became dry and why the water came thereon.

" And that mystery knoweth why famine hath
arisen and why superfluity hath arisen.

" And that mystery knoweth why the hoarfrost hath arisen and why the healthful dew hath arisen.

" And that mystery knoweth why the dust hath arisen and why the delightsome freshness hath arisen.

" And that mystery knoweth why the hail hath arisen and why the pleasant snow hath arisen.

" And that mystery knoweth why the west wind hath arisen and why the east wind hath arisen.

(" And that mystery knoweth why the fire of the height hath arisen and why the waters have arisen.

" And that mystery knoweth why the east wind hath arisen. [? miscopied.])

" And that mystery knoweth why the south wind hath arisen and why the north wind hath arisen.

" And that mystery knoweth why the stars of the heaven and the | disks of the light-givers have arisen and why the firmament with all its veils hath arisen.

213.

" And that mystery knoweth why the rulers of the spheres have arisen and why the sphere with all its regions hath arisen.

" And that mystery knoweth why the rulers of the æons have arisen and why the æons with their veils have arisen.

" And that mystery knoweth why the tyrant rulers of the æons have arisen and why the rulers who have repented have arisen.

" And that mystery knoweth why the servitors have arisen and why the decans have arisen.

" And that mystery knoweth why the angels have arisen and why the archangels have arisen.

" And that mystery knoweth why the lords have arisen and why the gods have arisen.

" And that mystery knoweth why the jealousy in the height hath arisen and why concord hath arisen.

" And that mystery knoweth why hate hath arisen and why love hath arisen.

" And that mystery knoweth why discord hath arisen and why concord hath arisen.

" And that mystery knoweth why avarice | hath 214. arisen and why renunciation of all hath arisen and love of possessions hath arisen.

" And that mystery knoweth why love of the belly hath arisen and why satiety hath arisen.

" And that mystery knoweth why the paired have arisen and why the unpaired have arisen.

" And that mystery knoweth why impiety hath arisen and why fear of God hath arisen.

" And that mystery knoweth why the light-givers have arisen and why the sparks have arisen.

" And that mystery knoweth why the thrice-powerful have arisen and why the invisibles have arisen.

" And that mystery knoweth why the fore-fathers have arisen and why the purities have arisen.

" And that mystery knoweth why the great self-willed hath arisen and why his faithful have arisen.

" And that mystery knoweth why the great triple-powerful hath arisen and why the great invisible forefather hath arisen.

" And that mystery knoweth why the thir-teenth æon hath arisen and why the region | of 215. those of the Midst hath arisen.

" And that mystery knoweth why receivers of the Midst have arisen and why the virgins of the light have arisen.

" And that mystery knoweth why the ministers of the Midst have arisen and why the angels of the Midst have arisen.

" And that mystery knoweth why the light-land hath arisen and why the great receiver of the light hath arisen.

" And that mystery knoweth why the guards of the region of the Right have arisen and why the leaders of them have arisen.

" And that mystery knoweth why the gate of life hath arisen and why Sabaōth, the Good, hath arisen.

" And that mystery knoweth why the region of the Right hath arisen and why the light-land, which is the treasury of the light, hath arisen.

" And that mystery knoweth why the emanations of the light have arisen and why the twelve saviours have arisen.

" And that mystery knoweth why the three gates of the treasury of the light have arisen and why the nine guards have arisen.

216. " And | that mystery knoweth why the twin-saviours have arisen and why the three Amēns have arisen.

" And that mystery knoweth why the five Trees have arisen and why the seven Amēns have arisen.

" And that mystery knoweth why the Mixture which existeth not, hath arisen and why it is purified."

CHAP. 94. And Jesus continued again and said unto his disciples : " Still further, O my disciples, be

sober and let every one of you bring hither the
power of sensing the Light before him, that ye
may sense with sureness. For from now on I
will discourse with you concerning the whole
region in truth of the Ineffable and concerning
the manner, how it is."

It came to pass then, when the disciples had The dis-
heard Jesus utter these words, that they gave ciples lose
way and let go entirely.

Then Mary Magdalene came forward, threw herself at the feet of Jesus, kissed them and wept aloud
and said : " Have mercy upon me, my Lord,
for my brethren have heard and let go of the words
which thou saidest unto them. Now, therefore,
my Lord, concerning the gnosis of all the things
which thou hast said, that they are in the mys-
tery | of the Ineffable ; but I have heard thee 217.
say unto me : ' From now on I will begin to discourse with you concerning the total gnosis of the
mystery of the Ineffable,'—this word, therefore,
which thou saidest, thou hast not gone forward
to complete the word. For this cause, therefore,
my brethren have heard and have let go and
ceased to sense in what manner thou discoursest
with them. Concerning the word which thou
saidest unto them, now, therefore, my Lord, if
the gnosis of all.this is in that mystery, where is
the man who is in the world, who hath the ability
to understand that mystery with all its gnoses
and the type of all these words which thou hast
spoken concerning it ? "

It came to pass then, when Jesus had heard CHAP. 95.
Mary say these words and knew that the disciples
had heard and had begun to let go, that he en-
couraged them and said unto them : " Grieve

no more, my disciples, concerning the mystery of the Ineffable, thinking that ye will not understand it. Amēn, I say unto you : That mystery is yours, and every one's who will give ear unto you, so that they renounce this whole world and the whole matter therein and renounce all the evil thoughts therein and renounce all the cares of this æon.

218.

Jesus explaineth that that mystery is really simpler than all mysteries.

" Now, therefore, I say unto you : | For every one who will renounce the whole world and all therein and will submit himself to the godhead, that mystery is far easier than all the mysteries of the Light-kingdom and it is sooner to understand than them all and it is easier [?] than them all. He who reacheth unto the gnosis of that mystery, renounceth this whole world and all the cares therein.

" For this cause have I said to you aforetime : ' All ye who are heavy under your burden, come hither unto me, and I will quicken you. For my burden is easy and my yoke is soft.' Now, therefore, he who will receive that mystery, renounceth the whole world and the cares of all the matter therein. For this cause, therefore, my disciples, grieve not, thinking that ye will not understand that mystery. Amēn, I say unto you : That mystery is far sooner to understand than all mysteries. And amēn, I say unto you : That mystery is yours and every one's who will renounce the whole world and the whole matter therein.

" Now, therefore, hearken, my disciples and my companions and my brethren, that I may urge you on to the gnosis of the mystery of the

219.

Ineffable | concerning which I discourse with you,

because I have in sooth gotten as far as to tell
you the whole gnosis at the expansion of the
universe ; for the expansion of the universe is its
gnosis.

" But now then hearken that I may discourse
with you progressively concerning the gnosis of
that mystery.

" That mystery knoweth wherefor the five Of the rend-
Helpers have rent themselves asunder and where- ing asunder
and emana-
for they have come forth from the Fatherless [pl.]. tion of the
powers of
" And that mystery knoweth wherefor the the universe.
great Light of lights hath rent itself asunder and
wherefor it hath come forth from the Fatherless.

" And that mystery knoweth wherefor the
first Commandment hath rent itself asunder and
wherefor it hath divided itself into the seven
mysteries and wherefor it is named the first
Commandment and wherefor it hath come forth
from the Fatherless.

" And that mystery knoweth wherefor the
Great Light of the Impressions of the Light hath
rent itself asunder and wherefor it hath set itself
up without emanations and wherefor it hath
come forth from the Fatherless.

" And that mystery knoweth wherefor the
First Mystery, that is the four-and-twentieth
mystery from without, hath rent itself asunder
and wherefor it imitated in itself the twelve
mysteries according to the number of the
numbering of the Uncontainables | and Bound- 220.
less and wherefor it hath come forth from the
Fatherless.

" And that mystery knoweth wherefor the Of those of
twelve Immoveables have rent themselves asunder the second
space of the
and wherefor they have set themselves with all Ineffable.

their orders and wherefor they have come forth
from the Fatherless.

" And that mystery knoweth wherefor the
Unwaverables have rent themselves asunder and
wherefor they have set themselves up, divided
into twelve orders, and wherefor they have come
forth from the Fatherless, which belong to the
orders of the space of the Ineffable.

" And that mystery knoweth wherefor the
Incomprehensibles, which pertain to the second
space of the Ineffable, have rent themselves
asunder and wherefor they have come forth from
the Fatherless.

" And that mystery knoweth wherefor the
twelve Undesignatables have rent themselves
asunder and wherefor they have set themselves
up after all the orders of the Unindicatables,
themselves being uncontainable and boundless,
and wherefor they have come forth from the
Fatherless.

" And that mystery knoweth wherefor these
Unindicatables have rent themselves asunder,—
[they] who have not indicated themselves nor
brought themselves into publicity according to
the economy of the One and Only, the Ineffable,
and wherefor they have come forth | from the
Fatherless.

221.

" And that mystery knoweth wherefor the
Super-deeps have rent themselves asunder and
wherefor they have distributed themselves, being
a single order, and wherefor they have come
forth from the Fatherless.

" And that mystery knoweth wherefor the
twelve orders of the Unspeakables have rent
themselves asunder and wherefor they have

divided themselves, being three portions, and wherefor they have come forth from the Fatherless.

" And that mystery knoweth wherefor all the Imperishables, being their twelve orders, have rent themselves asunder and wherefor they have settled themselves, being expanded in a single order, and wherefor they have divided themselves and formed different orders, being uncontainable and boundless, and wherefor they have come forth from the Fatherless.

" And that mystery knoweth wherefor the Impassables have rent themselves asunder and wherefor they have set, themselves up, being twelve boundless spaces, and have settled themselves, being three orders of spaces, according to the economy of the One and Only, the Ineffable, and wherefor they have come forth from the Fatherless.

" And that mystery knoweth wherefor the twelve Uncontainables, which belong to the orders | of the One and Only, the Ineffable, have 222. rent themselves asunder and wherefor they have come forth from the Fatherless, until they were brought to the space of the First Mystery, which is the second space.

" And that mystery knoweth wherefor the four-and-twenty myriads of Praise-singers have rent themselves asunder and wherefor they have extended themselves outside the veil of the First Mystery, which is the twin-mystery, that which looketh within and without, of the One and Only, the Ineffable, and wherefor they have come forth from the Fatherless.

" And that mystery knoweth wherefor all the

Uncontainables have rent themselves asunder—
[those], which I have just named, which are in the
regions of the second space of the Ineffable, which
is the space of the First Mystery, and wherefor
those Uncontainables and Boundless have come
forth from the Fatherless.

Of those of
the first
space of the
Ineffable.
" And that mystery knoweth wherefor the
four-and-twenty mysteries of the first Thrice-
spiritual have rent themselves asunder and wherefor they are called the four-and-twenty spaces
of the first Thrice-spiritual and wherefor they
have come forth from the second Thrice-
spiritual.

223.
" And that mystery knoweth wherefor the
four-and-twenty mysteries of the | second Thrice-
spiritual have rent themselves asunder and
wherefor they have come forth from the third
Thrice-spiritual.

" And that mystery knoweth why the four-
and-twenty mysteries of the third Thrice-spiritual
—that is the four-and-twenty spaces of the third
Thrice-spiritual—have rent themselves asunder
and wherefor they have come forth from the
Fatherless.

" And that mystery knoweth wherefor the
five Trees of the first Thrice-spiritual have rent
themselves asunder and wherefor they have
extended themselves, standing one behind the
the other and moreover bound one to the other
with all their orders, and wherefor they have
come forth from the Fatherless.

" And that mystery knoweth wherefor the
five Trees of the second Thrice-spiritual have
rent themselves asunder and wherefor they have
come forth from the Fatherless.

" And that mystery knoweth wherefor the five Trees of the third Thrice-spiritual have rent themselves asunder and wherefor they have come forth from the Fatherless.

" And that mystery knoweth why the Fore-uncontainables of the first Thrice-spiritual have rent themselves asunder and wherefor they have come forth from the Fatherless.

" And that mystery knoweth wherefor the Fore-uncontainables of the second Trispiritual have rent themselves asunder and wherefor | they have come forth from the Fatherless. 224.

" And that mystery knoweth wherefor all the Fore-uncontainables of the third Thrice-spiritual have rent themselves asunder and wherefor they have come forth from the Fatherless.

" And that mystery knoweth wherefor the first Thrice-spiritual from below—those who belong to the orders of the One and Only, the Ineffable—hath rent itself asunder and wherefor it hath come forth from the second Thrice-spiritual.

" And that mystery knoweth wherefor the third Thrice-spiritual—that is the first Thrice-spiritual from above—hath rent itself asunder and wherefor it hath come forth from the twelfth Pro-thrice-spiritual, which is in the last region of the Fatherless.

" And that mystery knoweth wherefor all the the regions which are in the space of the Ineffable, and all those in them, have expanded themselves, and wherefor they have come forth from the last Limb of the Ineffable.

" And that mystery knoweth itself, wherefor it hath rent itself asunder to come forth from the Ineffable,—that is from That which ruleth them

all and which expanded them all according to |
their orders.

225.

CHAP. 96.
Jesus pro-
miseth to
explain fur-
ther all in
detail.

" Of all these then will I speak unto you
at the expansion of the universe—in a word,
all those whom I have spoken of unto you :
those who will arise and those who will come,
those who emanate, and those who come forth,
and those who are without over them, and those
who are implanted in them, those who will contain the region of the First Mystery and those
who are in the space of the Ineffable—of these
will I speak unto you, because I will reveal them
unto you, and I will speak of them unto you
according to every region and according to every
order, at the expansion of the universe. And I
will reveal unto you all their mysteries which
rule over them all, and their Pro-thrice-spirituals
and their Super-thrice-spirituals which rule over
their mysteries and their orders.

" Now, therefore, the mystery of the Ineffable
knoweth wherefor all these have arisen of whom
I have spoken unto you in openness, and through
which all these have arisen. It is the mystery
which is in them all ; and it is the out-going of
them all, and it is the up-going of them all, and
it is the setting-up of them all.

" And the mystery of the Ineffable is the
mystery which is in all these of whom I have
spoken unto you, and of whom I will speak unto
you at the expansion of the universe. And it is
the mystery which is in them all, and it is the
one only mystery of the Ineffable and the gnosis

of all these | of whom I have spoken unto you,
and of whom I will speak unto you, and of whom
I have not spoken. Of these will I speak unto

you at the expansion of the universe and of their total gnosis one with another, wherefor they have arisen. It is the one and only word of the Ineffable.

"And I will tell you the expansion of all mysteries and the types of every one of them and the manner of their completion in all their figures. And I will tell you the mystery of the One and Only, the Ineffable, and all its types, all its figures and its whole economy, wherefor it hath come forth from the last Limb of the Ineffable. For that mystery is the setting-up of them all.

"And that mystery of the Ineffable is more-over also a one and only word, which existeth in the speech of the Ineffable, and it is the economy of the solution of all the words which I have spoken unto you. *Of the one and only word of the Ineffable.*

"And he who will receive the one and only word of that mystery which I shall now say unto you, and all its types and all its figures, and the manner of accomplishing its mystery,—for ye are perfect and all-perfect and ye will accomplish the whole gnosis of that mystery with its whole economy, for unto you all mysteries are entrusted, —hearken, therefore, now, that I may tell you that mystery, which is [. . . ?].

"He | then, who shall receive the one and only word of that mystery, which I have told you, if he cometh forth out of the body of the matters of the rulers, and if the retributive receivers come and free him from the body of matter of the rulers,—that is those [receivers] who free from the body all out-going souls,—when, therefore, the retributive receivers free the soul which *227. Of the ascension of the soul of him who shall receive the one and only mystery.*

hath received this one and only mystery of the Ineffable, which I have just told you, then will it straightway, if it be set free from the body of matter, become a great light-stream in the midst of those receivers, and the receivers will be exceedingly afraid of the light of that soul, and the receivers will be made powerless and fall down and desist altogether for fear of the great light which they have seen.

" And the soul which receiveth the mystery of the Ineffable, will soar into the height, being a great light-stream, and the receivers will not be able to seize it and will not know how the way is fashioned upon which it will go. For it becometh a great light-stream and soareth into the height, and no power is able to hold it down at all, nor | will they be able to come nigh it at all.

228.

" But it will pass through all the regions of the rulers and all the regions of the emanations of the Light, and it will not give answers in any region, nor giveth it any apologies, nor giveth it any tokens ; neither will any power of the rulers nor any power of the emanations of the Light be able to come nigh that soul. But all the regions of the rulers and all the regions of the emanations of the Light,—every one singeth unto it praises in their regions, in fear of the light of the stream which envelopeth that soul, until it passeth through them all, and goeth to the region of the inheritance of the mystery which it hath received,—that is to the mystery of the One and Only, the Ineffable,—and until it becometh one with its Limbs. Amēn, I say unto you : It will be in all the regions in the time a man shooteth an arrow.

" Now, therefore, amēn, I say unto you :
Every man who will receive that mystery of the
Ineffable and accomplish it in all its types and
all its figures,—he is a man in the world, but he
towereth above all angels and will tower still
more above them all.

" He is a man in the world, but he towereth
above all archangels and will tower still more
above | them all.

" He is a man in the world, but he towereth
above all tyrants and will raise himself above
them all.

" He is a man in the world, but he towereth
above all lords and will raise himself above them
all.

" He is a man in the world, but he towereth
above all gods and will raise himself above them all.

" He is a man in the world, but he towereth
above all light-givers and will raise himself above
them all.

" He is a man in the world, but he towereth
above all pure [ones] and will raise himself above
them all.

" He is a man in the world, but he towereth
above all triple-powers and will raise himself
above them all.

" He is a man in the world, but he towereth
above all forefathers and will raise himself above
them all.

" He is a man in the world, but he towereth
above all invisibles and will raise himself above
them all.

" He is a man in the world, but he towereth
above the great invisible forefather and will raise
himself above him.

" He is a man in the world, but he towereth above all those of the Midst and will raise himself above them all.

" He is a man in the world, but he towereth above the emanations of the Treasury of the Light and will raise himself above them all.

230.

" He is a man in the world, but he towereth above the Mixture | and will raise himself entirely above it.

" He is a man in the world, but he towereth above the whole region of the Treasury and will raise himself entirely above it.

" He is a man in the world, but he will rule with me in my kingdom.

" He is a man in the world, but he is king in the Light.

" He is a man in the world, but he is not one of the world.

" And amēn, I say unto you : That man is I and I am that man.

Such souls are one with the First Mystery.

" And at the dissolution of the world, that is when the universe will be raised up and when the numbering of the perfect souls will be raised up all together, and when I am king in the midst of the last Helper, being king over all the emanations of the Light and king over the seven Amēns and the five Trees and the three Amēns and the nine guards, and being king over the 'Child of the Child, that is the Twin-saviours, and being king over the twelve saviours and over the whole numbering of the perfect souls who shall receive the mysteries in the Light,—then will all men who shall receive the mysteries in the Ineffable, be fellow-kings with me and will sit on my right and on my left in my kingdom.

" And amēn, I say unto you : Those men are I, and I am they.

" On this account have I said unto you aforetime : ' Ye will sit on your | thrones on my right 231. and on my left in my kingdom and will rule with me.'

" On this account, therefore, I have not hesitated nor have I been ashamed to call you my brethren and my companions, because ye will be fellow-kings with me in my kingdom. This, therefore, I say unto you, knowing that I will give you the mystery of the Ineffable ; that is : That mystery is I, and I am that mystery.

" Now, therefore, not only will ye reign with me, but all men who shall receive the mystery of the Ineffable, will be fellow-kings with me in my kingdom. And I am they, and they are I. But my throne will tower over them. [And] because ye will suffer sorrows in the world beyond all men, until ye herald forth all the words which I shall speak unto you, your thrones shall be joined to mine in my kingdom. *Of the dignity of the thrones in the kingdom.*

" On this account I have said unto you aforetime : ' Where I shall be, there will be also my twelve ministers.' But Mary Magdalene and John, the virgin, will tower over all my disciples and over all men who shall receive the mysteries in the Ineffable. And they will be on my right and on my left. And I am they, and they are I.

" And they will be like unto you in all things save that your thrones will tower over theirs, and my throne | will tower over yours.   232.

" And all men who will find the word of the Ineffable,—amēn, I say unto you : The men

Of the gnosis
of the word
of the In-
effable.
who shall know that word, will know the gnosis of all these words which I have spoken unto you, both those of the depth and those of the height, those of the length and those of the breadth; in a word, they will know the gnosis of all these words which I have spoken unto you and which I have not yet spoken unto you, which I will speak unto you, region by region and order by order, at the expansion of the universe.

"And amēn, I say unto you: They will know in what manner the world is established, and they will know in what type all those of the height are established, and they will know out of what ground the universe hath arisen."

CHAP. 97.
When then the Saviour had said this, Mary Magdalene started forward and said: "My Lord, bear with me and be not wroth with me, if I question on all things with precision and certainty. Now, therefore, my Lord, is then another the word of the mystery of the Ineffable and another the word of the whole gnosis?"

The Saviour answered and said: "Yea, another is the mystery of the Ineffable and another the word of the whole gnosis."

And Mary answered again and said unto the Saviour: "My Lord, bear with me, if I question thee, and be not wroth with me. Now, therefore, my Lord, unless we live and know the gnosis of the whole word of the Ineffable, shall we not be able to inherit the Light-kingdom?"

233.

Of the dis-
tinction
between the
gnosis of the
universe and
the mys-
teries of the
Light.
And the Saviour answered | and said unto Mary: "Surely; for every one who shall receive a mystery of the Light-kingdom, will go and inherit up to the region up to which he hath received mysteries. But he will not know the

gnosis of the universe, wherefor all this hath
arisen, unless he knoweth the one and only word
of the Ineffable, which is the gnosis of the universe.
And again in openness: I am the gnosis of the
universe. And moreover it is impossible to
know the one and only word of the gnosis, unless
a man first receive the mystery of the Ineffable.
But all the men who shall receive mysteries
in the Light,—every one will go and inherit up
to the region up to which he hath received
mysteries.

" On this account I have said unto you aforetime : 'He who hath faith in a prophet, will
receive a prophet's reward, and he who hath
faith in a righteous [man] will receive a righteous
[man's] reward,'—that is : Every one will go
to the region up to which he hath received
mysteries. He who receiveth a lesser mystery,
will inherit the lesser mystery, and he who
receiveth a higher mystery, will inherit the higher
regions. And every one will abide in his region
in the light of my kingdom, and every one will
have power over the orders which are below
him, but he will not have the power to go to the
orders which are above him ; but he will abide in
the region of the Inheritance of the Light | of 234.
my kingdom, being in a great light immeasurable
for the gods and all the invisibles, and he will
be in great joy and great jubilation.

" But now, therefore, hearken, that I may discourse with you concerning the grandeur of those
who shall receive the mysteries of the First
Mystery.

" He, therefore, who shall receive the [first]
mystery of that First Mystery, and it shall be

Of the as-
cension of
the souls of
those who
receive the
twelve mys-
teries of the
First Mys-
tery.

at the time that he cometh out of the body of
the matter of the rulers,—then the retributive
receivers come and lead the soul of that man out
of the body. And that soul will become a great
light-stream in the hands of the retributive
receivers ; and those receivers will be afraid of
the light of that soul. And that soul will go
upwards and pass through all the regions of the
rulers and all the regions of the emanations of
the Light. And it will not give answers nor
apologies nor tokens in any single region of the
Light nor in any single region of the rulers ;
but it will pass through all the regions and cross
over them all, so that it goeth and ruleth over
all the regions of the first saviour.

" In like manner also he who shall receive the
second mystery of the First Mystery and the
third and fourth, until he shall receive the twelfth
mystery of the First Mystery, if it shall be at the
235.   time| that he cometh out of the body of the matter
of the rulers,—then the retributive receivers
come and lead the soul of that man out of the
body of matter. And those souls will become
a great light-stream in the hands of the retributive receivers ; and those receivers will be
afraid of the light of those souls and will become
powerless and fall on their faces. And those
souls will straightway soar upwards and cross
over all the regions of the rulers and all the regions
of the emanations of the Light. They will not
give answers nor apologies nor tokens in any
single region ; but they will pass through all the
regions and will cross over them all and rule
over all the regions of the twelve saviours, so that
they who receive the second mystery of the First

Mystery, will rule over all the regions of the second saviour in the inheritances of the Light.

" In like manner also those who receive the third mystery of the First Mystery and the fourth and fifth and sixth up to the twelfth,— every one will rule over all the regions of the saviour up to whom he hath received the mystery.

" And he who shall receive in sequence the twelfth mystery of the First Mystery, that is the master-mystery concerning which I discourse with you,—| and he who, therefore, shall receive 236. those twelve mysteries which belong to the First Mystery, if he goeth forth out of the world, will pass through all the regions of the rulers and all the regions of the Light, being a great light-stream, and he will moreover rule over all the regions of the twelve saviours ; but they will not be able to be like unto those who receive the one and only mystery of the Ineffable. But he who shall receive those mysteries will abide in those orders, because they are exalted, and he will abide in the orders of the twelve saviours."

It came to pass, when Jesus had finished CHAP. 98. speaking these words unto his disciples, that Mary again questioneth Mary Magdalene came forward, kissed the feet Jesus. of Jesus and said unto him : " My Lord, bear with me and be not wroth with me, if I question thee ; but have mercy upon us, my Lord, and reveal unto us all things on which we shall question thee. Now, therefore, my Lord, how doth the First Mystery possess twelve mysteries, [and] the Ineffable possess a one and only mystery ? "

Jesus answered and said unto her : " Indeed Of the three mysteries it possesseth a one and only mystery, yet that and five mystery constituteth three mysteries, although mysteries.

it is the one and only mystery ; but the type of
every one of them is different. And moreover
it constituteth five mysteries, although it is a
one and only [one] ; but the type of every one
is different. So that these five mysteries are alike

237.   with one another in the mystery | of the kingdom
in the inheritances of the Light ; but the type
of each of them is different. And their kingdom
is higher and more exalted than the whole kingdom of the twelve mysteries together of the
First Mystery ; but they are not alike in the
kingdom [with the one and only mystery] of the
First Mystery in the Light-kingdom.

"In like manner also the three mysteries
are not [?] alike in the Light-kingdom ; but
the type of every one of them is different. And
they themselves also are not alike in the kingdom
with the one and only mystery of the First
Mystery in the Light-kingdom ; and the type
of every one of the three of them, and the type
of the configuration of each of them, is different
from one another.

Of the first
mystery.

"The first [mystery of the First Mystery],—
if thou accomplishest its mystery altogether
and standest and accomplishest it finely in all
its figures, then dost thou come straightway
out of thy body, become a great light-stream
and pass through all the regions of the rulers
and all the regions of the Light, while all are in
fear of that soul, until it cometh to the region of
its kingdom.

Of the
second mys-
tery.

238.

"The second mystery of the First Mystery,
on the other hand,— | if thou accomplishest it
finely in all its figures,—the man, therefore, who
shall accomplish its mystery, if he speaketh that

mystery over the head of any man who goeth
forth out of the body, and he speaketh it into
his two ears, if indeed the man who goeth
forth out of the body hath received mysteries
for the second time and is sharing in the word
of truth,—amēn, I say unto you : That man,
if he goeth forth out of the body of matter, then
will his soul become a great light-stream and pass
through all the regions, until it cometh to the
kingdom of that mystery.

" But if that man hath received no mysteries Of its effi-
and is not sharing in the words of truth,—if uninitiated.
he who accomplisheth that mystery, speaketh
that mystery over the head of a man who cometh
forth out of the body and who hath received no
mysteries of the Light, and shareth not in the
words of truth,—amēn, I say unto you : That
man, if he cometh forth out of the body, will be
judged in no region of the rulers, nor can he be
chastized in any region at all, nor will the fire
touch him, because of the great mystery of the
Ineffable which is with him.

" And they will hasten quickly and hand him
over one to another in turn and lead him from
region to region and | from order to order, until 239.
they bring him before the Virgin of Light, while
all the regions are in fear of the mystery and the
sign of the kingdom of the Ineffable which is
with him.

" And if they bring him before the Virgin of
Light, then the Virgin of Light will see the sign
of the mystery of the kingdom of the Ineffable
which is with him ; the Virgin of Light marvelleth
and proveth him, but suffereth them not to bring
him to the Light, until he accomplisheth the total

citizenship of the light of that mystery, that is the purities of the renunciation of the world and also of the total matter therein.

" The Virgin of Light sealeth him with a higher seal, which is this [. . . ?], and letteth him in that month in which he hath come out of the body of matter, light down into a body which will be righteous and find the godhead in truth and the higher mysteries, so that he may inherit them and inherit the Light eternal, which is the gift of the second mystery of the First Mystery of the Ineffable.

Of the third mystery.

" The third mystery of that Ineffable on the other hand,—the man indeed who shall accomplish that mystery, not only if he [himself] cometh forth out of the body, will he inherit the kingdom of the mystery, but if he complete that mystery

240.

and accomplish it with | all its figures, that is if he go through with that mystery and accomplish it finely and pronounce the name of that mystery

Of its efficacy.

over a man who cometh forth out of the body and hath known that mystery,—let the former have delayed or rather not have delayed,—one who is in the dire chastisements of the rulers and in their dire judgments and their manifold fires,—amēn, I say unto you : The man who hath come forth out of the body,—if the name of this mystery is pronounced on his behalf, they will hasten quickly to bring him over and hand him over one to another, until they bring him before the Virgin of Light. And the Virgin of Light will seal him with a higher seal, which is this [. . . ?], and in that month will she let him light down into the righteous body which will find the godhead in truth and the higher mystery, so that he inherit the Light-kingdom. This, therefore, is the gift of the third mystery of the Ineffable.

" Now, therefore, every one who shall receive one of the five mysteries of the Ineffable,—if he cometh forth out of the body and inheriteth up to the region of that mystery, then is the kingdom of those five mysteries higher than the kingdom of the twelve mysteries of the First Mystery, and it is higher than all the mysteries | which are 241 below them. But those five mysteries of the Ineffable are alike with one another in their kingdom, yet are they not alike with the three mysteries of the Ineffable. *Of the three and five mysteries.*

" He on the other hand who receiveth of the three mysteries of the Ineffable, if he cometh forth out of the body, will inherit up to the kingdom of that mystery. And those three mysteries are alike with one another in the kingdom and they are higher and more exalted than the five mysteries of the Ineffable in the kingdom, but they are not alike with the one and only mystery of the Ineffable.

" He on the other hand who receiveth the one and only mystery of the Ineffable, will inherit the region of the whole kingdom according to its whole glory, as I have already told you at another time. And every one who shall receive the mystery which is in the space of the universe of the Ineffable, and all the other mysteries which are united in the Limbs of the Ineffable, concerning which I have not yet spoken unto you, and concerning their expansion and the manner of their setting-up and the type of every one, how it is and wherefor it is named the Ineffable or wherefor it standeth expanded with all its *Of the mysteries of the three spaces*

242.

Limbs and how many Limbs are in it and all its economies, | of which I will not tell you now, but when I come to the expansion of the universe I will tell you all severally,—to wit, its expansions and its description, how it is, and the aggregation [?] of all its Limbs, which belong to the economy of the One and Only, the unapproachable God in truth,—up to what region, therefore, every one shall receive the mysteries in the space of the Ineffable, up to that region will he inherit up to which he hath received. And those of the whole region of the space of that Ineffable give no answers in that region, nor give they apologies, nor give they tokens, for they are without tokens and they have no receivers, but they pass through all the regions, until they come to the region of the kingdom of the mystery which they have received.

" In like manner also those who shall receive mysteries in the second space, they have no answers nor apologies, for they are without tokens in that world, which is the space of the first mystery of the First Mystery.

" And those of the third space, which is without, which is the third space from without [? within],

243.

—every region in that space hath | its receivers and its explanations and its apologies and its tokens, which I will one day tell you when I come to speak of that mystery, that is when I shall have told you of the expansion of the universe.

Of the reign of a thou- sand years of the Light.

" Albeit at the dissolution of the universe, that is when the number of the perfect souls is completed and the mystery [through] which the universe altogether hath risen, is completed, I will pass a thousand years according to the years of the Light, being king over all the emanations of the Light and over the whole number of the perfect souls who have received all mysteries."

It came to pass, when Jesus had finished CHAP. 99. speaking these words unto his disciples, that Mary Magdalene came forward and said : " My Lord, how many years of the years of the world is a year of the Light ? "

Jesus answered and said unto Mary : " A day What is a of the Light is a thousand years in the world, Light. so that thirty-six-myriads of years and a half-myriad of years of the world are a single year of the Light.

" I shall, therefore, pass a thousand years of the Light being king in the midst of the last Helper, and being king over all the emanations of the Light and over the whole number of the perfect souls who have received the mysteries of the Light.

" And ye, my disciples, and every one who shall Of those of receive the mystery of the Ineffable, will | abide the first space in the with me on my right and on my left, being kings kingdom of with me in my kingdom. the thou- sand years.

" And they who shall receive the three mysteries 244. of that Ineffable, will be fellow-kings with you in the Light-kingdom ; but they will not be alike with you and with those who receive the mystery of the Ineffable, but they will rather abide behind you, being kings.

" And they who receive the five mysteries of the Ineffable, will also abide behind the three mysteries, being also kings.

" And moreover they who receive the twelfth mystery of the First Mystery, will also again abide behind the five mysteries of the Ineffable, being also kings according to the order of every one of them.

" And all who receive of the mysteries in all the regions of the space of the Ineffable, will also be kings and abide before those who receive the mystery of the First Mystery, expanded according to the glory of every one of them, so that those who receive the higher mysteries, will abide in the higher regions, and those who receive the lower mysteries, will abide in the lower regions, being kings in the light of my kingdom.

" These alone are the allotment of the kingdom of the first space of the Ineffable. |

245.
Of those of the second space.

" They on the other hand who receive all the mysteries of the second space, that is of the space of the First Mystery, will again abide in the light of my kingdom, expanded according to the glory of every one of them, and every one of them being in the mystery up to which he hath received. And those who receive the higher mysteries, will also abide in the higher regions, and those who receive the lower mysteries, will abide in the lower regions in the light of my kingdom.

" This is the allotment of the second king for those who receive the mystery of the second space of the First Mystery.

Of those of the third space, the first from without,

" Those on the other hand who receive the mysteries of the third space, that is of the first space from without, those again will abide behind the second king, expanded in the light of my kingdom, according to the glory of every one of them, every one abiding in the region up to which he hath received mysteries, so that those who receive the higher mysteries, will abide in the higher regions, and those who receive the lower mysteries, will abide in the lower regions.

" These are the three allotments of the Light-kingdom.

" The mysteries of these three allotments of the Light are exceedingly numerous. Ye shall find them in the two great Books of Yew. But I will give you and tell you the great mysteries | of 246 every allotment, those which are higher than every region, that is the heads according to every region and according to every order which will lead the whole race of men into the higher regions, according to the space of the Inheritance.

" Of the rest of the lower mysteries, therefore, Of the Books ye have no need; but ye will find them in the of Yew. two Books of Yew, which Enoch hath written whilst I spake with him out of the tree of gnosis and out of the tree of life in the paradise of Adam.

" Now, therefore, when I shall have explained unto you the whole expansion, I will give you and tell you the great mysteries of the three allot-ments of my kingdom, that is the heads of the mysteries which I will give you and tell you in all their figures and all their types and in their ciphers and the seals of the last space, that is the first space from without. And I will tell you the answers and the apologies and the tokens of that space.

" The second space which is within, possesseth no answers nor apologies nor tokens nor ciphers nor seals ; but it possesseth only types and figures."

When the Saviour had finished saying all this CHAP. 100. unto his disciples, | Andrew came forward and 247. said : " My Lord, be not wroth with me, but have mercy upon me and reveal unto me the mystery of the word concerning which I shall question thee, for it hath been hard for me and I have not understood it."

The Saviour answered and said unto him : " Question concerning that on which thou desirest to question, and I will reveal it unto thee face to face without similitude."

And Andrew answered and said : " My Lord, I am astonished and marvel exceedingly, how the men who are in the world and in the body of this matter, if they come forth out of this world, will pass through these firmaments and all these rulers and all lords and all gods and all these great invisibles and all those of the region of the Midst and those of the whole region of the Right and all the great [ones] of the emanations of the Light, and enter into them all and inherit the Light-kingdom. This matter, therefore, is hard for me."

When then Andrew had said this, the spirit of the Saviour was roused in him ; he cried out and said : " How long am I to endure you ? How long am I to bear with you ? Have ye then not even yet understood and are ye ignorant ? Know ye then not and do ye not understand that ye and all angels and all archangels and the gods and the lords and all the rulers and all the

great invisibles | and all those of the Midst and those of the whole region of the Right and all the great [ones] of the emanations of the Light and their whole glory,—that ye all one with another are out of one and the same paste and the same matter and the same substance, and that ye all are out of the same Mixture.

" And at the commandment of the First
Mystery the Mixture was constrained, until all
the great [ones] of the emanations of the Light and
all their glory purified themselves, and until they
purified themselves from the Mixture. And they
have not purified themselves of themselves, but
they have purified themselves by necessity
according to the economy of the One and Only,
the Ineffable.

" They indeed have not at all suffered and have
not at all changed themselves in the regions,
nor at all torn themselves asunder nor poured
themselves into bodies of different kinds and from
one into another, nor have they been in any
affliction at all.

" Ye then in particular are the refuse of the Of trans-
Treasury and ye are the refuse of the region of corporation
and purifi-
the Right and ye are the refuse of the region of cation.
those of the Midst and ye are the refuse of all
the invisibles and of all the rulers ; in a word,
ye are the refuse of all these. And ye are in
great sufferings and great afflictions in your
being poured from one into another of different
kinds of bodies | of the world. And after 249.
all these sufferings ye have struggled of yourselves and fought, having renounced the whole
world and all the matter therein ; and ye have
not left off seeking, until ye found all the mysteries
of the kingdom of the Light, which have purified
you and made you into refined light, exceedingly
purified, and ye have become purified light.

" For this cause have I said unto you aforetime : ' Seek, that ye may find.' I have, therefore, said unto you : Ye are to seek after the
mysteries of the Light, which purify the body

of matter and make it into refined light exceedingly purified.

Of the purifying mysteries.

" Amēn, I say unto you : For the sake of the race of men, because it is material, I have torn myself asunder and brought unto them all the mysteries of the Light, that I may purify them, for they are the refuse of the whole matter of their matter ; else would no soul of the total race of men have been saved, and they would not be able to inherit the kingdom of the Light, if I had not brought unto them the purifying mysteries.

" For the emanations of the Light have no need of the mysteries, for they are purified ; but it is the race of men which hath need of them, because they all are material refuse [*pl.*]. For this cause, therefore, have I said unto you aforetime :

250.

' The healthy have no need | of the physician, but the sick,'—that is : Those of the Light have no need of the mysteries, for they are purified lights ; but it is the race of men which hath need of them, for [they] are material refuse [*pl.*].

" For this cause, therefore, herald to the whole race of men, saying : Cease not to seek day and night, until ye find the purifying mysteries ; and say unto the race of men : Renounce the whole world and the whole matter therein. For he who buyeth and selleth in the world and he who eateth and drinketh of its matter and who liveth in all its cares and in all its associations, amasseth other additional matters to the rest of his matter, because this whole world and all therein and all its associations are material refuse [*pl.*], and they will make enquiry of every one concerning his purity.

" For this cause, therefore, I have said unto you aforetime : Renounce the whole world and the whole matter therein, that ye may not amass other additional matter to the rest of your matter in you. For this cause, therefore, herald it to the whole race of men, saying : Renounce the whole world and all its associations, | that 251. ye may not amass additional matter to the rest of your matter in you ; and say unto them : Cease not to seek day and night and remit not yourselves until ye find the purifying mysteries which will purify you and make you into a refined light, so that ye will go on high and inherit the light of my kingdom.

" Now, therefore, Andrew and all thy brethren thy co-disciples, because of your renunciations and all your sufferings which ye have endured in every region, and because of your changes in every region and of your being poured from one into another of different kinds of bodies and because of all your afflictions, and after all this ye have received the purifying mysteries and are become refined light exceedingly purified,—for this cause, therefore, ye will go on high and penetrate into all the regions of all the great emanations of the Light and be kings in the Light-kingdom for ever. *That all who are purified will be saved.*

" But if ye come forth out of the body and come on high and reach unto the region of the rulers, then will all the rulers be seized with shame before you, because ye are the refuse of their matter and have become light more purified than them all. And | if ye reach unto the region of 252. the Great Invisible and unto the region of those of the Midst and of those of the Right and unto *That finally they will be higher than all powers.*

the regions of all the great emanations of the
Light, then will ye be revered among them all,
because ye are the refuse of their matter and are
became light more purified than them all.   And
all the regions will sing praises before you, until
ye come to the region of the kingdom.

"This is the answer to the words on which ye
question.   Now, therefore, Andrew, art thou still
in unfaith and unknowing ? "[1]

Jesus pardoneth the ignorance of Andrew. When then the Saviour said this, Andrew knew
clearly, not only he but also all the disciples
knew with precision that they should inherit the
Light-kingdom.   They all threw themselves down
together at Jesus' feet, cried aloud, wept and
besought the Saviour, saying: "Lord, forgive
our brother the sin of unknowing."

The Saviour answered and said: "I forgive
and will forgive ; for this cause, therefore, hath
the First Mystery sent me, that I may forgive
every one his sins."

[SUB-SCRIPTION :]

A PORTION OF THE BOOKS OF THE SAVIOUR

[THE CONCLUSION OF ANOTHER BOOK]

CHAP. 101. Of the Limbs of the Ineffable. "AND those who are worthy of the mysteries
which abide in the Ineffable, which are those
which have not gone forth,—these exist before the
First Mystery, and to use a likeness and similitude,
that ye may understand it, they are as the Limbs
of the Ineffable.   And every one existeth according to the dignity of its glory : the head according

---

[1] These two sentences are placed at the end of the preceding paragraph, but clearly belong here.

to the dignity of the head and the eye according to
the dignity | of the eyes and the ear according to 253.
the dignity of the ears and the rest of the Limbs
[in like fashion] ; so that the matter is manifest :
There is a multitude of limbs but one only body.
Of this indeed have I spoken in a pattern and
similitude and likeness, but not in a form in
truth ; nor have I revealed the word in truth,
but the mystery [only] of the Ineffable.

"And all the Limbs which are in it,—according The Saviour
to the word with which I have made comparison,— is their
treasury.
that is, those which abide on the mystery of the
Ineffable, and those which abide in it, and also
the three spaces which are after them according to
the mysteries,—of all these in truth and verity I
am their treasury beside whom there is no other
treasury, who hath not his like in the world ; but
there are still words and mysteries and other
regions.

"Now, therefore, blessed is he who hath found Of the
the [words of the] mysteries [of the first space] dignity of
those who
which is from without ; and he is a god who hath have received the
found these words of the mysteries of the second mysteries.
space, which is in the midst ; and he is a saviour
and an uncontainable who hath found the words
of the mysteries of the third space, which is
within, and he is more excellent than the universe
and like unto those who are in that third space.
Because he hath found the mystery in which
they are and in which they stand,— | for this cause, 254.
therefore, is he like unto them. He on the other
hand who hath found the words of the mysteries
which I have described unto you according to a
likeness, that they are the Limbs of the Ineffable,
—amēn, I say unto you : That man who hath

found the words of these mysteries in divine truth, is the first in truth and like unto him [*sc.* the First, *i.e.* the Ineffable], for through those words and mysteries ... and the universe itself standeth through that First. For this cause he who hath found the words of those mysteries, is like unto the First. For it is the gnosis of the gnosis of the Ineffable concerning which I have discoursed with you this day."

A THIRD BOOK

Jesus continued again in the discourse and said CHAP. 102. unto his disciples: "When I shall have gone Of the pro-clamation into the Light, then herald it unto the whole of the disciples. world and say unto them: Cease not to seek day and night and remit not yourselves until ye find the mysteries of the Light-kingdom, which will purify you and make you into refined light and lead you into the Light-kingdom.

"Say unto them: Renounce the whole world What men should renounce. and the whole matter therein and all its cares and all its sins, in a word all its | associations 255. which are in it, that ye may be worthy of the mysteries of the Light and be saved from all the chastisements which are in the judgments.

"Say unto them: Renounce murmuring, that ye may be worthy of the mysteries of the Light and be saved from the fire of the dog-faced [one].

"Say unto them: Renounce eavesdropping [?], that ye may [be worthy of the mysteries of the Light] and be saved from the judgments of the dog-faced [one].

"Say unto them: Renounce litigiousness [?], that ye may be worthy of the mysteries of the Light and be saved from the chastisements of Ariël.

"Say unto them: Renounce false slander, that ye may be worthy of the mysteries of the

Light and be saved from the fire-rivers of the dog-faced [one].

" Say unto them : Renounce false witness, that ye may be worthy of the mysteries of the Light and that ye may escape and be saved from the fire-rivers of the dog-faced [one].

" Say unto them : Renounce pride and haughtiness, that ye may be worthy of the mysteries of the Light and be saved from the fire-pits of Ariël.

" Say unto them : Renounce belly-love, that ye may be worthy of the mysteries of the Light and be saved from the judgments of Amente.

" Say unto them : Renounce babbling, that ye may be worthy of the mysteries of the Light and be saved from the fires of Amente.

256. " Say unto them : | Renounce craftiness, that ye may be worthy of the mysteries of the Light and be saved from the chastisements which are in Amente.

" Say unto them : Renounce avarice, that ye may be worthy of the mysteries of the Light and be saved from the fire-rivers of the dog-faced [one].

" Say unto them : Renounce love of the world, that ye may be worthy of the mysteries of the Light and be saved from the pitch- and fire-coats of the dog-faced [one].

" Say unto them : Renounce pillage, that ye may be worthy of the mysteries of the Light and be saved from the fire-rivers of Ariël.

" Say unto them : Renounce evil conversation, that ye may be worthy of the mysteries of the Light and be saved from the chastisements of the fire-rivers . . . .

" Say unto them : Renounce wickedness, that
ye may be worthy of the mysteries of the Light
and be saved from the fire-seas of Ariël.

" Say unto them : Renounce pitilessness, that
ye may be worthy of the mysteries of the Light
and be saved from the judgments of the dragon-
faced [ones].

" Say unto them : Renounce wrath, that ye
may be worthy of the mysteries of the Light
and be saved from the fire-rivers of the dragon-
faced [ones.]

" Say unto them : Renounce cursing, that ye
may be worthy of the mysteries of the Light
and be saved from the fire-seas of the dragon-
faced [ones]. |

" Say unto them : Renounce thieving, that ye 257.
may be worthy of the mysteries of the Light
and be saved from the bubbling seas of the
dragon-faced [ones].

" Say unto them : Renounce robbery, that ye
may be worthy of the mysteries of the Light
and be saved from Yaldabaōth.

" Say unto them : Renounce slandering, that
ye may be worthy of the mysteries of the Light
and be saved from the fire-rivers of the lion-
faced [one].

" Say unto them : Renounce fighting and
strife, that ye may be worthy of the mysteries of
the Light and be saved from the seething rivers
of Yaldabaōth.

" Say unto them : Renounce all unknowing,
that ye may be worthy of the mysteries of the
Light and be saved from the servitors of Yaldabaōth and the fire-seas.

" Say unto them : Renounce evil doing, that

ye may be worthy of the mysteries of the Light and be saved from all the demons of Yaldabaōth and all his judgments.

"Say unto them: Renounce sloth, that ye may be worthy of the mysteries of the Light and be saved from the seething pitch-seas of Yaldabaōth.

"Say unto them: Renounce adultery, that ye may be worthy of the mysteries of the Light-kingdom and be saved from the sulphur- and pitch-seas of the lion-faced [one].

"Say unto them: Renounce murder, that ye may be worthy of the mysteries of the Light and be saved from the crocodile-faced ruler,—this one who is in the cold, | is the first chamber of the outer darkness.

258.

"Say unto them: Renounce pitilessness and impiety, that ye may be worthy of the mysteries of the Light and be saved from the rulers of the outer darkness.

"Say unto them: Renounce atheism, that ye may be worthy of the mysteries of the Light and be saved from the howling and grinding of teeth.

"Say unto them: Renounce [magic] potions, that ye may be worthy of the mysteries of the Light and be saved from the great cold and the hail of the outer darkness.

"Say unto them: Renounce blasphemy, that ye may be worthy of the mysteries of the Light and be saved from the great dragon of the outer darkness.

"Say unto them: Renounce the doctrines of error, that ye may be worthy of the mysteries of the Light and be saved from all the chas-

tisements of the great dragon of the outer
darkness.

" Say unto those who teach the doctrines of
error and to every one who is instructed by them :
Woe unto you, for, if ye do not repent and abandon
your error, ye will go into the chastisements
of the great dragon and of the outer darkness,
which is exceedingly evil, and never will ye be
cast [up] into the world, but will be non-existent
until the end. |

" Say unto those who abandon the doctrines 259.
of truth of the First Mystery : Woe unto you,
for your chastisement is sad compared with
[that of] all men. For ye will abide in the great
cold and ice and hail in the midst of the dragon
and of the outer darkness, and ye will never from
this hour on be cast [up] into the world, but ye
shall be frozen up [?] in that region and at the
dissolution of the universe ye will perish and become non-existent eternally.

" Say rather to the men of the world : Be *The bound-*
calm, that ye may receive the mysteries of the *aries of the*
ways of the
Light and go on high into the Light-kingdom. *worthy.*

" Say unto them : Be ye loving-unto-men,
that ye may be worthy of the mysteries of the
Light and go on high into the Light-kingdom.

" Say unto them : Be ye gentle, that ye may
receive the mysteries of the Light and go on
high into the Light-kingdom.

" Say unto them : Be ye peaceful, that ye
may receive the mysteries of the Light and go on
high into the Light-kingdom.

" Say unto them : Be ye merciful, that ye
may receive the mysteries of the Light and go on
high into the Light-kingdom.

" Say unto them : Give ye alms, that ye may receive the mysteries of the Light and go on high into the Light-kingdom.

" Say unto them : Minister unto the poor and the sick and distressed, that ye may receive the mysteries | of the Light and go on high into the Light-kingdom.

" Say unto them : Be ye loving-unto-God, that ye may receive the mysteries of the Light and go on high into the Light-kingdom.

" Say unto them : Be ye righteous, that ye may receive the mysteries [of the Light] and go on high into the Light-kingdom.

" Say unto them : Be good, that ye may receive the mysteries [of the Light] and go on high into the Light-kingdom.

" Say unto them : Renounce all, that ye may receive the mysteries of the Light and go on high into the Light-kingdom.

" These are all the boundaries of the ways for those who are worthy of the mysteries of the Light.

" Unto, such, therefore, who have renounced in this renunciation, give the mysteries of the Light and hide them not from them at all, even though they are sinners and they have been in all the sins and all the iniquities of the world, all of which I have recounted unto you, in order that they may turn and repent and be in the submission which I have just recounted unto you. Give unto them the mysteries of the Light-kingdom and hide them not from them at all ; for it is because of sinfulness that I have brought the mysteries into the world, that I may forgive all their sins which they have committed from the beginning on. For this cause

260.

Unto whom are the mysteries of the Light to be given.

The mysteries are for the forgiveness of sins.

have I said unto you aforetime : ' I am not come to call the righteous.' Now, | therefore, I have brought the mysteries that [their] sins may be forgiven for every one and they be received into the Light-kingdom. For the mysteries are the gift of the First Mystery, that he may wipe out the sins and iniquities of all sinners."

It came to pass then, when Jesus had finished saying these words unto his disciples, that Mary came forward and said to the Saviour : " My Lord, will then a righteous man who is perfected in all righteousness, and that man who hath no sin at all, will such an one be tormented in the chastisements and judgments or not ? Or will rather that man be brought into the kingdom of heaven or not ? "

And the Saviour answered and said unto Mary : " A righteous man who is perfected in all righteousness and who hath never committed any sin of any kind, and such an one who never hath received mysteries of the Light, if the time is at hand when he goeth forth out of the body, then straightway come the receivers of one of the great triple-powers,—those among whom there is a great [one],—snatch away the soul of that man from the hands of the retributive receivers and spend three days circling with it in all the creatures of the world. After three days they lead it down into the chaos, so as to lead it into all the chastisements of the judgments and to dispatch it to all the judgments. The fires of the | chaos do not trouble it greatly ; but they will trouble it partly for a short time.

" And with haste they take pity on it quickly, to lead it up out of the chaos and lead it on the way of the midst through all the rulers. And they [sc. the rulers] do not chastize it in their harsh judgments, but the fire of their regions troubleth it partly. And if it shall be brought into the region of Yachthanabas, the pitiless, then will he indeed not be able to chastize it in his evil judgments, but he holdeth it fast a short time, while the fire of his chastisements troubleth it partly.

" And again they take pity on it quickly, and lead it up out of those regions of theirs and they do not bring it into the æons, so that the rulers of the æons do not carry it away ravishingly; they bring it on the way of the sun and bring it before the Virgin of Light. She proveth it and findeth that it is pure of sins, but letteth them not bring it to the Light, because the sign of the kingdom of the mystery is not with it. But she sealeth it with a higher seal and letteth it be cast down into the body | into the æons of righteousness,—that body which will be good to find the signs of the mysteries of the Light and inherit the Light-kingdom for ever.

263.

" If on the contrary he hath sinned once or twice or thrice, then will he be cast back into the world again according to the type of the sins which he hath committed, the type of which I will tell you when I shall have told you the expansion of the universe.

" But amēn, amēn, I say unto you: Even if a righteous man hath committed no sins at all, he cannot possibly be brought into the Light-kingdom, because the sign of the kingdom of the mysteries is not with him. In a word, it is impossible to bring souls into the Light without the mysteries of the Light-kingdom."

It came to pass then, when Jesus had finished
saying these words unto his disciples, that John
came forward and said : " My Lord, suppose
a sinning and a law-breaking man is re-
plete in all iniquities, and he hath ceased from
these for the sake of the kingdom of heaven
and renounced the whole world and the whole
matter therein, and we give him from the beginning onwards the mysteries of the Light which
are in the first space from without, and if he
receiveth the mysteries, and after a little while
again if he returneth and transgresseth, and thereafter again if he turneth and ceaseth from all
sins and turneth and | renounceth the whole world 264.
and the whole matter therein, so that he cometh
again and is in great repentance, and if we
know truly in truth that he longeth after God,
so that we give him the second mystery of the
first space which is from without ;—in like manner
if he turneth anew and transgresseth and is
again in the sins of the world, and again if he
thereafter turneth and ceaseth from the sins of
the world and again renounceth the whole world
and the whole matter therein and again is in
great repentance, and we know it with certainty
that he is not a play-actor, so that we turn and
give him the mysteries of the beginning, which
[are] in the first space from without ;—in like
manner, if he turneth again and sinneth and is
in every type [of sin];—desirest thou that we
forgive him unto seven times and give him the
mysteries which are in the first space from without, unto seven times or not ? "

The Saviour answered again and said unto
John : " Not only forgive him unto seven times,

The disciples are to forgive many times seven times.
but amēn, I say unto you: Forgive him unto many times seven times, and every time give him the mysteries from the beginning onwards which are in the first space from without. Perchance ye win the soul of that brother and he inheriteth the Light-kingdom.

265.
" For this cause, therefore, when ye questioned me aforetime, | saying: ' If our brother sin against us, desirest thou that we forgive him unto seven times ? '—I answered and spake unto you in a similitude, saying: ' Not only unto seven times, but unto seventy times seven.'

" Now, therefore, forgive him many times and every time give him the mysteries which are in the first space which is from without. Perchance ye win the soul of that brother and he inheriteth the Light-kingdom.

Of the reward of the savers of souls.
" Amēn, amēn, I say unto you: He who shall keep in Life and save only one soul, besides the dignity which he possesseth in the Light-kingdom, he will receive yet another dignity for the soul which he hath saved, so that he who shall save many souls, besides the dignity which he possesseth in the Light he will receive many other dignities for the souls which he hath saved."

CHAP. 105.
John continueth his questioning.
When then the Saviour had said this, John started forward and said: " My Lord, bear with me if I question thee, for from now on I will begin to question thee on all things concerning the manner, how we are to herald it to mankind.

266.
" If, therefore, I give that brother a mystery out of the mysteries of the beginning which are in the first space from without, and if I give him many mysteries and he doeth not what | is

worthy of the kingdom of heaven,—desirest thou that we let him pass through to the mysteries of the second space ? Perchance we win the soul of that brother, and he turneth, repenteth and inheriteth the Light-kingdom. Desirest thou that we let him pass through to the mysteries [which are in the second space] or not ? "

And the Saviour answered and said unto John : "If it is a brother who is not play-acting, but in truth longeth after God, if ye have given him many times the mysteries of the beginning and because of the necessity of the elements of the Fate he hath not done what is worthy of the mysteries of the Light-kingdom, then forgive him, let him pass through and give him the first mystery which is in the second space. Perchance ye win the soul of that brother. That the mysteries shall be given again unto a re-pentant brother even up to the three of the second space.

" And if he hath not done what is worthy of the mysteries of the Light and hath committed transgression and divers sins, and thereafter hath turned again and been in great repentance and hath renounced the whole worid and ceased from all the sins of the world, and ye know with certainty that he doth not play-act but in truth longeth after God, then turn ye anew, forgive him, let him pass on through and give him the second mystery in the second | space of the First Mystery. Per- 267. chance ye win the soul of that brother and he inheriteth the Light-kingdom.

" And again if he hath not done what is worthy of the mysteries, but hath been in transgression and divers sins, and thereafter again hath turned and been in great repentance and hath renounced the whole world and the whole matter therein and ceased from the sins of the world, so that ye know truly that he is not play-acting but longeth truly after God, then turn ye anew, forgive him and receive his repentance, because the First Mystery is compassionate and merciful-minded; let also that man pass through and give him the three mysteries together which are in the second space of the First Mystery.

The limit of the power of the disciples to forgive sins.

"If that man [then] transgresseth and is in divers sins, from that moment onwards ye are not to forgive him nor to receive his repentance; but let him be among you as a stumbling-block and as a transgressor.

"For, amēn, I say unto you: Those three mysteries will be witnesses for his last repentance, and he hath not repentance from this moment onwards. For, amēn, I say unto you: The soul

268.

of that man will not | be cast back into the world above from this moment onwards, but will be in the abodes of the dragon of the outer darkness.

A former saying explained.

"For regarding the souls of such men I have spoken unto you aforetime in a similitude, saying: 'If thy brother sinneth against thee, bring him over between thee alone and him. If he hearkeneth unto thee, thou wilt win thy brother; if he hearkeneth not unto thee, take with thee yet another. If he hearkeneth not unto thee and the other, bring him to the assembly. If he hearken not unto the others, let him be for you as a trans-gressor and as a stumbling-block.'—That is: If he is not usable in the first mystery, give him the second; and if he is not usable in the second give him the three, assembled together, which is 'the assembly'; and if he is not usable in the third mystery, let him be for you as a stumbling-block and as a transgressor.

" And the word which I have spoken unto you Of the master-mystery of the forgivness of sins.
aforetime: ' So that through two to three witnesses
every word may be established,'—it is this:
Those three mysteries will witness for his last
repentance. And amēn, | I say unto you: If 269.
that man repenteth, no mystery can forgive him
his sins, nor can his repentance be received,
nor can he at all be hearkened to through any
mystery, save through the first mystery of the
First Mystery and through the mysteries of the
Ineffable. It is these alone whĭch will receive
the repentance of that man and forgive his sins;
for those mysteries in sooth are compassionate
and merciful - minded and forgiving at every
time."

When then the Saviour had said this, John CHAP. 106.
continued again and said to the Saviour: " My John continueth his questioning.
Lord, suppose an exceedingly sinful brother who
hath renounced the whole world and the whole
matter therein and all its sins and all its cares,
and we shall prove him and know that he is not
in deceit and play-acting but that in uprightness
and in truth he longeth [after God], and we know
that he hath become worthy of the mysteries
of the second space or of the third,—desirest
thou that we give him of the mysteries of the
second space and of the third, before he hath
at all received mysteries of the Inheritance of the
Light or not? Desirest thou that we give or
not?"

And the Saviour answered and said unto John Further of the forgiveness of sins.
in the midst of the disciples: " If ye know with
certainty that that man | hath renounced the 270
whole world and all its cares and all its associations
and all its sins, and if ye know in truth that he

is not in deceit, neither that he was play-acting nor that he was curious to know the mysteries, how they are brought to pass, but that he longeth after God in truth, hide them not from such an one, but give him of the mysteries of the second and third space and try even of what mystery he is worthy; and that of which he is worthy, give him and hide it not from him, for if ye hide it from him, ye may be guilty of a great condemnation.

" If ye give him once [of the mysteries] of the second space or of the third and he turneth again and sinneth, ye are to continue again the second time up to the third time. If he still sinneth, ye shall not continue to give him, for those three mysteries will be witnesses unto him for his last repentance. And amēn, I say unto you: He who shall give that man anew mysteries of the second space or of the third, is guilty of a great condemnation. But let him be for you as a transgressor and as a stumbling-block.

" Amēn, I say unto you: The soul of that man cannot be cast back into the world | from this moment onwards; but his habitation is in the midst of the jaws of the dragon of the outer darkness, the region of howling and grinding of teeth. And at the dissolution of the world his soul will be frozen up [?] and perish in the violent cold and exceedingly violent fire and will be non-existent eternally.

" Even if he yet again turneth and renounceth the whole world and all its cares and all its sins, and he is in great citizenship and great repentance, no mystery can receive from him his repentance, nor can it hearken unto him, to have mercy

271.

upon him and receive his repentance and forgive his sins, save the mystery of the First
Mystery and the mystery of the Ineffable. It
is these alone which will receive the repentance
of that man and forgive his sins; for in sooth
those mysteries are compassionate and merciful-
minded and forgiving of sins at every time."

And when the Saviour had said this, John CHAP. 107.
continued again and said: " My Lord, bear John continueth his
with me, if I question thee, and be not wroth questioning.
with me, for I question concerning all things
with surety and certainty for knowledge of the
manner, how we are to herald it to the men of
the world."

And the Saviour answered and said unto John:
" Question concerning all things on which thou
questionest, and I will reveal them unto thee,
face to face | in openness without similitude, or 272.
with surety."

And John answered and said: " My Lord,
if we go forth and herald it and come into a city
or a village, and if the men of that city come forth
to meet us without our knowing who they are,
and if they receive us unto themselves in great
deceit and great play-acting and bring us into
their house, desiring to make trial of the mysteries of the Light-kingdom, and if they play-act
with us in submission and we suppose that they
long after God, and we give them the mysteries
of the Light-kingdom, and if we thereafter know
that they have not done what is worthy of
the mystery, and we know that they have play-
acted with us, and have been deceitful against
us and that they have also made a show of the
mysteries region by region, making trial of us

and also of our mysteries,—what is then the thing which will befall such ? "

Of pre-
tenders who
receive the
mysteries.

And the Saviour answered and said unto John : " If ye come into a city or a village, where ye enter into the house and they receive you unto themselves, give them a mystery. If they are worthy, ye will win their souls and they will inherit the Light-kingdom ; but if they are not worthy but are deceitful against you, and if they also make a show of the mysteries, making trial of you and also of the mysteries, then

273.

invoke | the first mystery of the First Mystery which hath mercy on every one, and say : Thou Mystery, which we have given unto these impious and iniquitous souls who have not done what is worthy of thy mystery but have made a show of us, turn back [then] the mystery unto us and make them for ever strangers to the mystery of thy kingdom. And shake ye off the dust of your feet as a witness against them, saying : May your souls be as the dust of your house. And amēn, I say unto you : In that hour all the mysteries which ye have given unto them, will return unto you, and all the words and all the mysteries of the region up to which they have received figures, will be taken from them.

A former
saying ex-
plained.

" Concerning such men, therefore, have I aforetime spoken unto you in similitude, saying : ' Where ye enter into a house and are received, say unto them : Peace be with you. And if they are worthy, let your peace come upon them ; and if they are not worthy, let your peace return unto you,'—that is : If those men do what is worthy of the mysteries and in truth long after God, give them the mysteries of the Light-kingdom ;

but if they play-act with you and are deceitful against you, without your having known it, | and if ye give them the mysteries of the Light- 274. kingdom, and again thereafter they make a show of the mysteries and they make also trial of you and also of the mysteries, then perform the first mystery of the First Mystery, and it will turn back unto you all the mysteries which ye have given unto them, and it will make them strangers to the mysteries of the Light for ever.

" And such men will not be led back to the world from this moment onwards ; but amēn, I say unto you : Their dwelling is in the midst of the jaws of the dragon of the outer darkness. And if they still at a time of repentance renounce the whole world and the whole matter therein and all the sins of the world, and they are in entire submission to the mysteries of the Light, no mystery can hearken unto them nor forgive their sins, save this same mystery of the Ineffable, which hath mercy on every one and forgiveth every one his sins."

It came to pass, when Jesus had finished CHAP. 108. saying these words unto his disciples, that Mary Mary again questioneth adored the feet of Jesus and kissed them. Mary Jesus. said : " My Lord, bear with me, if I question thee, and be not wroth with me."

The Saviour answered and said unto Mary : " Question concerning what thou desirest to question, and I will reveal it | unto thee in 275. openness."

And Mary answered and said : " My Lord, suppose a good and excellent brother whom we have filled with all the mysteries of the Light, and that brother hath a brother or kinsman, in a word he hath in general [any] man, and this [man] is a sinner and impious or better he is no sinner, and such an one hath gone out of the body, and the heart of the good brother is grieved and mourneth over him, that he is in judgments and chastisements,—now, therefore, my Lord, what are we to do to remove him out of the chastisements and harsh judgments ? "

And the Saviour answered and said unto Mary : " Concerning this word, therefore, I have already spoken unto you at another time, but hearken that I may say it again, so that ye may be perfected in all mysteries and be called ' the perfected in every fulness.'

How the souls of those who have come out of the body may be helped by those on earth.

" Now, therefore, all men, sinners or better who are no sinners, not only if ye desire that they be taken out of the judgments and violent chastisements, but that they be removed into a righteous body which will find the mysteries of the godhead, so that it goeth on high and inheriteth the Light-kingdom,—then perform the third mystery of

276.

the Ineffable | and say : Carry ye the soul of this and this man of whom we think in our hearts, carry him out of all the chastisements of the rulers and haste ye quickly to lead him before the Virgin of Light ; and in every month let the Virgin of Light seal him with a higher seal, and in every month let the Virgin of Light cast him into a body which will be righteous and good, so that it goeth on high and inheriteth the Light-kingdom.

" And if ye say this, amēn, I say unto you : All who serve in all the orders of the judgments of the rulers, hasten to hand over that soul from one to the other, until they lead it before the Virgin of Light. And the Virgin of Light sealeth it with the sign of the kingdom of the Ineffable and handeth it over unto her receivers, and the receivers will cast it into a body which will be righteous and find the mysteries of the Light, so that it will be good and goeth on high and inheriteth the Light-kingdom. Lo, this is it on which ye question me."

And Mary answered and said : " Now, therefore, my Lord, hast thou then not brought mysteries into the world that man | may not die through the death which is appointed him by the rulers of the Fate,—be it that it is appointed one to die by the sword or die by the waters or through tortures and torturings and acts of violence which are in the law, or through any other evil death,—hast thou then not brought mysteries into the world that man may not die with them through the rulers of the Fate, but that he may die by a ·sudden death, so that he endure no sufferings through such kinds of death ? For they are exceedingly numerous who persecute us because of thee, and numerous those who persecute us because of thy name, in order that, if they torture us, we may speak the mystery and straightway go out of the body without having endured any sufferings at all."

CHAP. 109.
Mary continueth her questioning.
277.

The Saviour answered and said unto all his disciples : " Concerning this word on which ye question me, I have spoken unto you at another time ; but hearken again that I may say it unto you anew : Not only ye, but every man who will accomplish that first mystery of the First Mystery of the Ineffable,—he who, therefore, shall perform that mystery and accomplish it in all its figures and all its types and all its stations, in

How he who possesseth the mysteries can come forth out of the body without suffering.

performing it, he will not come out of the body ;
but after he hath accomplished that mystery in
278. all its figures | and all its types, thereafter then at
every time when he shall speak the name of that
mystery, he will save himself from all that which
is appointed him by the rulers of the Fate.   And
in that hour he will come forth out of the body
of the matter of the rulers, and his soul will become a great light-stream, so that it soareth on
high and penetrateth all the regions of the rulers
and all the regions of the Light, until it reacheth
the region of its kingdom.   Neither giveth it
answers nor apologies in any region at all, for it
is without tokens.''

CHAP. 110.   When then Jesus had said this, Mary continued, threw herself at Jesus' feet, kissed them
and said : '' My Lord, still will I question thee.
Reveal [it] unto us and hide [it] not from us.''

Jesus answered and said unto Mary : '' Question
on what ye question, and I will reveal [it] unto
you in openness without similitude.''

Mary con-   Mary answered and said : '' My Lord, hast
tinueth her
questioning.   thou then not brought mysteries into the world
because of poverty and riches, and because of
weakness and strength, and because of . . . and
healthy bodies, in a word because of all such, so
that, if we go into the regions of the land, and
they do not have faith in us and they hearken
not unto our words, and we perform any such
mysteries in those regions, they may know truly
279. in truth that we | herald the words [of the God]
of the universe ? ''

The Saviour answered and said unto Mary in
the midst of the disciples : '' Concerning this
mystery on which ye question me, I have given

it unto you at another time ; but I will repeat
it and speak the word unto you :

"Now, therefore, Mary, not only ye, but The mystery
every man who shall accomplish the mystery of of the raising of the
the raising of the dead,—that which healeth the dead.
demons and all pains and all sicknesses and the
blind and the lame and the maimed and the
dumb and the deaf, which I have given unto you
aforetime,—he who shall receive [that] mystery
and accomplish it, thereafter then, if he ask for all
things, for poverty and riches, for weakness and
strength, for . . . and healthy body, and for all
healings of the body and for the raising of the
dead and for healing the lame and the blind
and the deaf and the dumb and all sicknesses
and all pains,—in a word, he who shall accomplish
that mystery and ask for all the things which I
have just said, then will they quickly come to
pass for him."

When then the Saviour had said this, the The dis-
disciples came forward, cried out all together ciples became
and said : "O Saviour, thou hath made us very frenzied at
the sub-
exceedingly frenzied because of the great deeds limity of the
of which thou tellest us ; and because thou hast prospect.
borne up our souls, they have pressed to go forth
out of us | unto thee, for we issue from thee. 280.
Now, therefore, because of these great deeds of
which thou tellest us, our souls have become
frenzied and they have pressed very exceedingly,
yearning to go forth out of us on high to the
region of thy kingdom."

When then the disciples had said this, the CHAP. 111.
Saviour continued again and said unto his dis- How the
disciples
ciples : "If ye go into cities or kingdoms or shall make
countries, proclaim first unto them, saying : proclamation.

Search ever and cease not, until ye find the mysteries of the Light which will lead you into the Light-kingdom. Say unto them: Beware of the doctines of error. For many will come in my name and say: It is I. And it is not I, and they will lead many astray.

What mys-
teries they
shall give.
" Now, therefore, unto all men who come unto you and have faith in you and hearken unto your words and do what is worthy of the mysteries of the Light, give the mysteries of the Light and hide them not from them. And unto him who is worthy of the higher mysteries, give them, and to him who is worthy of the lower mysteries, give them, and hide not anything from any one.

The mystery
of the rais-
ing of the
dead not to
be given to
any.
" The mystery of the raising of the dead and of the healing of the sick, on the other hand, give unto no one nor give instruction in it, for that mystery belongeth to the rulers, it and all its namings. For this cause, therefore, give it |

281.
unto no one, nor give instruction in it until ye establish the faith in the whole world, in order that, if ye come into cities or into countries, and they do not receive you unto themselves, and do not have faith, and do not hearken unto your words, ye may raise the dead in those regions and heal the lame and the blind and manifold of sicknesses in those regions. And through all such they will have faith in you, that ye herald the God of the universe, and will have faith in all the words of you. For this cause, therefore, have I given unto you that mystery, until ye establish the faith in the whole world."

When then the Saviour had said this, he continued again in the discourse and said unto Mary: " Now, therefore, hearken, Mary, concerning the

word on which thou hast questioned me : Who
constraineth the man until he sinneth ?   Now,
therefore, hearken :

"Is the babe born, the power is feeble in it, Of the con-
and the soul is feeble in it, and also the counter- stitution of
man.
feiting spirit is feeble in it ; in a word, the three
together are feeble, without any one of them
sensing anything, whether good or evil, because
of the load of forgetfulness which is very heavy.
Moreover the body also is feeble.   And the babe
eateth of the delights of the world of the rulers ;
and the power draweth into itself from the
portion of the power which | is in the delights ; 282.
and the soul draweth into itself from the portion
of the soul which is in the delights ; and the counterfeiting spirit draweth into itself from the
portion of the evil which is in the delights and in
its lusts.   And on the other hand the body
draweth into itself the matter which senseth not,
which is in the delights.   The destiny on the
contrary taketh nothing from the delights,
because it is not mingled with them, but it
departeth again in the condition in which it
cometh into the world.

"And little by little the power and the soul and
the counterfeiting spirit grow, and every one of
them senseth according to its nature : the power
senseth to seek after the light of the height ;
the soul on the other hand senseth to seek after
the region of righteousness which is mixed, which
is the region of the commixture ; the counterfeiting spirit on the other hand seeketh after all
evils and lusts and all sins ; the body on the contrary senseth nothing unless it taketh up force
out of the matter.

" And straightway the three develop sense,
every one according to its nature. And the
retributive receivers assign the servitors to follow
them and be witnesses of all the sins which they
commit, with a view to the manner and method
how they will chastize them in the judgments.

Of the coun-
terfeiting
spirit.
283.

" And after this the counterfeiting spirit |
contriveth and senseth all sins and the evil which
the rulers of the great Fate have commanded
for the soul, and it maketh them for the soul.

" And the inner power stirreth the soul to seek
after the region of the Light and the whole godhead ; and the counterfeiting spirit leadeth away
the soul and compelleth it continually to do all
its lawless deeds, all its mischiefs and all its
sin, and is persistently allotted to the soul and
is hostile to it, and making it do all this evil
and all these sins.

" And it goadeth on the retributive servitors,
so that they are witnesses in all the sins which it
will make it do. Moreover also if it will rest in
the night [or] by day, it stirreth it in dreams or in
lusts of the world, and maketh it to lust after all
the things of the world. In a word, it driveth [?]
it into all the things which the rulers have commanded for it and it is hostile to the soul,
making it do what pleaseth it not.

" Now, therefore, Mary, this is in fact the
foe of the soul, and this compelleth it until it
doeth all sins.

284.
The state of
the sinful
soul after
death.

" Now, therefore, if | the time of that man
is completed, first cometh forth the destiny and
leadeth the man unto death through the rulers
and their bonds with which they are bound
through the Fate.

" And thereafter the retributive receivers come and lead that soul out of the body. And thereafter the retributive receivers spend three days circling round with that soul in all the regions and dispatch it to all the æons of the world. And the counterfeiting spirit and the destiny follow that soul ; and the power returneth to the Virgin of Light.

" And after three days the retributive receivers lead down that soul to the Amente of the chaos ; and when they bring it down to the chaos, they hand it over to those who chastize. And the retributive receivers return unto their own regions according to the economy of the works of the rulers concerning the coming-forth of the souls.

" And the counterfeiting spirit becometh the receiver of the soul, being assigned unto it and transferring it according to the chastisement because of the sins which it hath made it commit, and is in great enmity to the soul.

" And when the soul hath finished the chastisements in the chaos according to the sins | which it 285. hath committed, the counterfeiting spirit leadeth it forth out of the chaos, being assigned unto it and transferring it to every region because of the sins which it hath committed ; and it leadeth it forth on the way of the rulers of the midst. And when it reacheth them, [the rulers] question it on the mysteries of the destiny ; and if it hath not found them, they question their destiny. And those rulers chastize that soul according to the sins of which it is guilty. I will tell you the type of their chastisements at the expansion of the universe.

How a sinful soul is brought back to birth.

" When, therefore, the time of the chastisements of that soul in the judgments of the rulers of the midst shall be completed, the counterfeiting spirit leadeth the soul up out of all the regions of the rulers of the midst and bringeth it before the light of the sun according to the commandment of the First Man, Yew, and bringeth it before the judge, the Virgin of Light. And she proveth that soul and findeth that it is a sinning soul, and casteth her light-power into it for its standing-upright and because of the body and the community of sense,—the type of which I will tell you at the expansion of the universe. And the Virgin of Light sealeth that soul and

286.

handeth it over to one of her receivers | and will have it cast into a body which is suitable to the sins which it hath committed.

" And amēn, I say unto you : They will not discharge that soul from the changes of the body until it hath yielded its last circuit according to its merit. Of all these then will I tell you their type and the type of the bodies into which it will be cast according to the sins of each soul. All this will I tell you when I shall have told you the expansion of the universe."

CHAP. 112.
Of the ascension after death of the good soul that hath received the mysteries.

Jesus continued again in the discourse and said : " If on the contrary it is a soul which hath not hearkened unto the counterfeiting spirit in all its works, but hath become good and hath received the mysteries of the Light which are in the second space or even those which are in the third space which is within, when the time [of the coming-forth] of that soul out of the body is completed, then the counterfeiting spirit followeth that soul, it and the destiny ; and it followeth it on the way on which it will go above.

" And before it removeth itself above, it uttereth the mystery of the undoing of the seals and all the bonds of the counterfeiting spirit with which the rulers have bound it to the soul; and when it is uttered, the bonds of the counterfeiting spirit undo themselves, and it ceaseth to come into that soul and releaseth the soul according to the commandments which | the 287. rulers of the great Fate have commanded it, saying: ' Release not this soul until it tell thee the mystery of the undoing of all the seals with which we have bound thee to the soul.'

" If then the soul shall have uttered the mystery of the undoing of the seals and of all the bonds of the counterfeiting spirit, and if it ceaseth to come into the soul and ceaseth to be bound to it, then it uttereth in that moment a mystery and releaseth the destiny to its region to the rulers who are on the way of the midst. And it uttereth the mystery and releaseth the counterfeiting spirit to the rulers of the Fate to the region in which it was bound to it.

" And in that moment it becometh a great light-stream, shining exceedingly, and the retributive receivers who have led it forth out of the body, are afraid of the light of that soul and fall on their faces. And in that moment that soul becometh a great light-stream, it becometh entirely wings of light, and penetrateth all the regions of the rulers and all the orders of the Light, until it reacheth the region of its kingdom up to which it hath received mysteries.

" If on the other hand it is a soul which hath

Of the state
after death
of one who
hath re-
ceived the
mysteries,
and yet hath
transgressed.
288.
received mysteries in the first space which is
without, and if after it | hath received the
mysteries it hath accomplished them, it [then]
turneth and committeth sin after the accomplishing of the mysteries, and if the time of the
coming-forth of that soul is completed, then the
retributive receivers come to lead that soul out
of the body.

"And the destiny and the counterfeiting
spirit follow that soul. Because the counterfeiting spirit is bound to it with the seals and the
bonds of the rulers, it followeth thus that soul
which travelleth on the ways with the counterfeiting spirit.

"It uttereth the mystery of the undoing of
all the bonds and all the seals with which the
rulers have bound the counterfeiting spirit to
the soul. And when the soul uttereth the
mystery of the undoing of the seals, straightway
the bonds of the seals which are bound in the
counterfeiting spirit to the soul undo themselves.
And when the soul uttereth the mystery of the
undoing of the seals, straightway the counterfeiting spirit undoeth itself and ceaseth to be
assigned to the soul. And in that moment
the soul uttereth a mystery and restraineth the
counterfeiting spirit and the destiny and dis-
chargeth them which follow it. But no one of
them is in its power ; | but it is in their power.

"And in that moment the receivers of that soul
come with the mysteries which it hath received,
come and snatch that soul out of the hands of
the retributive receivers, and the [latter] receivers
go back to the works of the rulers for the purpose
of the economy of the leading-forth of the souls.

" And the receivers of that soul on the other hand who belong to the Light, become wings of light for that soul and become vestures of light for it and they do not lead it into the chaos, because it is not lawful to lead into the chaos souls which have received mysteries, but they lead it on the way of the rulers of the midst. And when it reacheth the rulers of the midst, those rulers meet the soul, they being in great fear and violent fire and with different faces, in a word in great immeasurable fear.

" And in that moment the soul uttereth the mystery of their apology. And they are exceedingly afraid and fall on their faces, being in fear of the mystery which it hath uttered, and of their apology. | And that soul surrendereth their 290. destiny, saying unto them : Take your destiny ! I come not to your regions from this moment onwards. I have become a stranger unto you for ever, being about to go unto the region of my inheritance.

The apology of the rulers of the ways of the midst.

" And when the soul shall have said this, the receivers of the Light fly with it on high and lead it into the æons of the Fate, it giving every region its apology and its seals,—which I will tell you at the expansion of the universe. And it giveth the counterfeiting spirit to the rulers and telleth them the mystery of the bonds with which it is bound to it, and sayeth unto them : There have ye your counterfeiting spirit ! I come not to your region from this moment onwards. I have become a stranger unto you for ever. And it giveth every one his seal and his apology.

The apology of the rulers of the Fate.

" And when the soul shall have said this, the receivers of the Light fly with it on high and lead

291.
Of the as-
cension of
that soul
into the In
heritance.

it | out of the æons of the Fate and lead it up into
all the æons [above], it giving to every region its
apology and the apology of all the regions and
the seals to the tyrants of the king, the Adamas.
And it giveth the apology of all the rulers of all
the regions of the Left,—whose collective apologies and seals I will one day tell you when I shall
tell you the expansion of the universe.

" And moreover those receivers lead that soul
to the Virgin of Light and that soul giveth the
Virgin of Light the seals and the glory of the
songs of praise.   And the Virgin of Light and also
the seven other virgins of the Light together prove
that soul and find together their signs in it and
their seals and their baptisms and their chrism.
And the Virgin of Light | sealeth that soul and
the receivers of the Light baptize that soul and
give it the spiritual chrism ; and every one of
the virgins of the Light sealeth it with her seals.

292

" And moreover the receivers of the Light
hand it over to the great Sabaōth, the Good,
who is at the gate of the Life in the region of
those of the Right, who is called ' Father.'   And
that soul giveth him the glory of his songs of
praise and his seals and his apologies.   And
Sabaōth, the Great and Good, sealeth it with his
seals.   And the soul giveth its science and the
glory of the songs of praise and the seals to the
whole region of those of the Right.   They all
seal it with their seals ; and Melchisedec, the
great Receiver of the Light who is in the region of
those of the Right, sealeth that soul and all the
receivers of Melchisedec seal that soul and lead it
into the Treasury of the Light.

" And it giveth the glory and the honour and

the laud of the songs of praise and all the seals of all the regions of the Light. And all those of the region of the Treasury of the Light seal it with their seals and it goeth unto the region of the Inheritance."

When then the Saviour had said this unto his CHAP. 113. disciples | he said unto them : " Understand ye 293. in what manner I discourse with you ? "

And Mary again started forward and said : Mary inter-" Yea, my Lord, I understand in what manner preteth from former say-thou dost discourse with me, and I will compre- ings. hend them all [sc. thy words]. Now, therefore, concerning these words which thou sayest, my mind hath brought forward four thoughts in me and my light-man hath led me and exulted and seethed, desiring to come forth out of me and enter into thee. Now, therefore, my Lord, hearken that I may tell thee the four thoughts which have arisen in me.

" The first thought hath arisen in me concerning the word which thou hast spoken : ' Now, therefore, the soul giveth the apology and seal unto all the rulers who are in the region of the king, the Adamas, and giveth the apology and the honour and the glory of all their seals and the songs of praise to the region of the Light,'—concerning this word then thou hast spoken unto us aforetime, when they brought thee the piece of The piece money and thou didst see that it was of silver and of money which was copper and didst ask : ' Whose is this image ? ' brought unto They said : ' The king's.' And when thou Jesus. sawest that it was of silver and copper mixed, thou saidst : ' Give therefore the king's unto the king and God's unto God,'—that is : If the soul receiveth mysteries, it giveth the apology to all the rulers and to the region | of the king, the Adamas ; and the soul giveth the honour and the glory to all those of the region of the Light. And the word : ' It hath glistened, when thou didst see that it is made up of silver and copper,'—it is the type thereof, that in it [*sc.* the soul] is the power of the Light, which is the refined silver, and that in it is the counterfeiting spirit, which is the material copper. This, my Lord, is the first thought.

" The second thought is on the other hand that which thou hast just said unto us concerning the soul which receiveth the mysteries : ' If it cometh into the region of the rulers of the way of the midst, they come forth to meet it in exceedingly great fear and they are afraid of it. And the soul giveth the mystery of the fear unto them and they are afraid before it. And it giveth the destiny to its region, and it giveth the counterfeiting spirit to its own region, and it giveth the apology and the seals to every one of the rulers who are on the ways, and it giveth the honour and the glory and the laud of the seals and the songs of praise to all those of the region of the Light,'— concerning this word, my Lord, thou hast spoken aforetime through the mouth of our brother

A saying of Paul.

Paul : ' Give tax to whom tax is due, give fear to whom fear is due, give tribute to whom tribute is due, give honour to whom honour is due, and give laud to whom laud is due, and owe not any

295.

other anything,' | —that is, my Lord : The soul which receiveth mysteries, giveth apology to all regions. This, my Lord, is the second thought.

" The third thought on the other hand concerning the word which thou hast aforetime spoken unto us : ' The counterfeiting spirit is hostile to The foes of the soul, making it do all sins and all mischiefs, one's own house. and it transferreth it in the chastisements because of all the sins which it hath made it commit ; in a word, it is hostile to the soul in every way,'—concerning this word, therefore, thou hast said unto us aforetime : ' The foes of the man are the dwellers in his house,'—that is : The dwellers in the house of the soul are the counterfeiting spirit and the destiny, which are hostile to the soul the whole time, making it commit all sin and all iniquities. Lo this, my Lord, is the third thought.

" The fourth thought on the other hand concerning the word which thou hast said : ' If the soul goeth forth out of the body and travelleth on the way with the counterfeiting spirit, and if it hath not found the mystery of the undoing of all the bonds and the seals which are bound to the counterfeiting spirit, so that it may cease to haunt or be assigned to it,—if it then hath not found it, the counterfeiting spirit leadeth the soul to the Virgin of Light, the judge ; and the judge, the Virgin of Light, proveth the soul and findeth | that it hath sinned and, as she also hath not found 296. the mysteries of the Light with it, she handeth it over to one of her receivers, and her receiver leadeth it and casteth it into the body, and it cometh not out of the changes of the body before it hath yielded its last circuit,'—concerning this word, then, my Lord, thou hast said unto us aforetime : ' Be reconciled with thy foe as long A former as thou art on the way with him, lest perchance saying concerning rebirth. thy foe hand thee over to the judge and the judge hand thee over to the servant and the servant cast thee into prison, and thou shalt not come forth out of that region till thou hast yielded the last farthing.'

" Because of this manifestly is thy word : Every soul which cometh forth out of the body and travelleth on the way with the counterfeiting spirit and findeth not the mystery of the undoing of all the seals and all the bonds, so that it may undo itself from the counterfeiting spirit which is bound to it,—that soul which hath not found mysteries of the Light and hath not found the mysteries of detachment from the counterfeiting spirit which is bound to it,—if then it hath not found it, the counterfeiting spirit leadeth that soul to the Virgin of Light, and the Virgin of Light, yea that judge, handeth over that

297. soul | to one of her receivers, and her receiver casteth it into the sphere of the æons, and it cometh not out of the changes of the body before it hath yielded the last circuit which is appointed for it.   This then, my Lord, is the fourth thought.''

CHAP. 114. It came to pass then, when Jesus had heard Mary say these words, that he said : " Well said, all-blessed Mary, spiritual [one].   These are the solutions of the words which I have spoken.''

Mary con- Mary answered and said : " Still, my Lord,
tinueth to do I question thee, because from now on I will
question
Jesus. begin to question thee on all things with sureness. For this cause, therefore, my Lord, be patient with us and reveal unto us all things on which we shall question thee for the sake of the manner, how my brethren are to herald it to the whole race of men.''

And when she had said this to the Saviour,

the Saviour answered and said unto her in great compassion towards her : " Amēn, amēn, I say unto you : Not only will I reveal unto you all things on which ye shall question me, but from now on I will reveal unto you other things on which· ye have not thought to question, which have not entered into the heart of man, and which also all the gods, who are below man, know not. Now, therefore, Mary, question on what thou mayest question, and I will reveal it unto thee face to face without similitude."

And Mary answered and said : " My Lord, CHAP. 115. in what type then do | the baptisms forgive sins ? 298. I heard thee say : ' The retributive servitors follow the soul, being witnesses to it for all the sins which it committeth, that they may convict it in the judgments.' Now, therefore, my Lord, do the mysteries of the baptisms wipe out the sins which are in the hands of the retributive servitors, so that they forget them ? Now, therefore, my Lord, tell unto us the type, how they forgive sins ; nay, we desire to know it with sureness."

And the Saviour answered and said unto Mary : Of the re- " Finely hast thou spoken. The servitors indeed tributive servitors. are they who bear witness to all sins ; but they abide in the judgments, seizing the souls and convicting all the souls of sinners who have received no mysteries ; and they keep them fast in the chaos, chastizing them. And those retributive receivers cannot overstep the chaos to reach to the orders which are above the chaos, and convict the souls which come forth out of those regions. Now then it is not lawful to use force on the souls which receive mysteries, and lead them into the chaos, so that the retributive servitors may convict them. But the retributive servitors convict the | souls of the sinners and they keep fast those who have received no mysteries which may lead them out of the chaos. The souls on the other hand which receive mysteries,—they have no power of convicting them, because they do not come forth out of their regions, and also, if they come forth into their regions, they are not able to obstruct them ; nay, they cannot lead them into that chaos.

" Hearken moreover that I may tell you the word in truth, in what type the mystery of baptism forgiveth sins. Now, therefore, if the souls sin when they are still in the world, the retributive servitors indeed come and are witnesses of all the sins which the soul committeth, lest in sooth they should come forth out of the regions of the chaos, in order that they may convict them in the judgments which are outside the chaos. And the counterfeiting spirit becometh witness of all the sins which the soul shall commit, in order that it may convict it in the judgments which are outside the chaos, not only that it may bear witness of them, but—all the sins of the souls—it sealeth the sins and maketh them fast on to the soul, in order that all the rulers of the chastisements of the sinners may recognize it, that it is a sinning soul, and that they may know of the number of sins which it hath committed, by the seals which the counterfeiting spirit hath made fast on to it, so that it shall be chastized according to | the number of sins which it hath committed. This do they with all sinning souls.

" Now, therefore, he who shall receive the

299.

How the soul of the sinner is stamped with his sins.

300.

mysteries of the baptisms, then the mystery of them becometh a great, exceedingly violent, wise fire and it burneth up the sins and entereth into the soul secretly and consumeth all the sins which the counterfeiting spirit hath made fast on to it. And when it hath finished purifying all the sins which the counterfeiting spirit hath made fast on to the soul, it entereth into the body secretly and pursueth all the pursuers secretly and separateth them off on the side of the portion of the body. For it pursueth the counterfeiting spirit and the destiny and separateth them off from the power and from the soul and putteth them on the side of the body, so that it separateth off the counter-feiting spirit and the destiny and the body into one portion; the soul and power on the other hand it separateth into another. The mystery of baptism on the contrary remaineth in the midst of the two, continually separating them from one another, so that it maketh them clean and puri-fieth them, in order that they may not be stained by matter.

How the baptisms purify sins.

The separation of the portions by the mystery of baptism.

" Now, therefore, Mary, this is the way in which the mysteries of the baptisms forgive sins and all iniquities."

When then | the Saviour had said this, he said unto his disciples : " Understand ye in what manner I discourse with you ? "

CHAP. 116.

301.

Then Mary started forward and said : " Yea, my Lord, in truth I enquire closely into all the words which thou sayest. Concerning the word then of the forgiveness of sins thou hast spoken unto us in similitude aforetime, saying : ' I am come to cast fire on the earth,' and again : ' What will I that it burn ? ' And again thou hast distin-

Mary inter-preteth the same from a former saying.

guished it clearly, saying : ' I have a baptism, to baptize in it ; and how shall I endure until it is accomplished ? Think ye I am come to cast peace on the earth ? Nay, but I am come to cast division. For from now on five will be in one house ; three will be divided against two, and two against three.' This, my Lord, is the word which thou hast spoken clearly.

" The word indeed which thou hast spoken : ' I am come to cast fire on the earth, and what will I that it burn ? '—that is, my Lord : Thou hast brought the mysteries of the baptisms into the world, and thy pleasure is that they should consume all the sins of the soul and purify them. And thereafter again thou hast distinguished it clearly, saying : ' I have a baptism, to baptize in it ; and | how shall I endure until it is accomplished ? '—that is : Thou wilt not remain in the world until the baptisms are accomplished and purify the perfect souls.

" And moreover the word which thou hast spoken unto us aforetime : ' Think ye I am come to cast peace on the earth ? Nay, but I am come to cast division. For from now on five will be in one house ; three will be divided against two, and two against three,'—that is : Thou hast brought the mystery of the baptisms into the world, and it hath effected a division in the bodies of the world, because it hath separated the counterfeiting spirit and the body and the destiny into one portion ; the soul and the power on the other hand it hath separated into another portion ; —that is : Three will be against two, and two against three."

And when Mary had said this, the Saviour

said : " Well said, thou spiritual and light-pure Mary. This is the solution of the word."

Mary answered again and said : " My Lord, CHAP. 117. I will still continue to question thee. Now, Mary further questioneth therefore, my Lord, bear with me questioning Jesus thee. Lo, in openness have we known the type in which the baptisms forgive sins. Now on the other hand the mystery of these three spaces and the mysteries of this First Mystery and the mysteries of the Ineffable, in what type do they forgive sins ? Do they forgive in the type | of 303. the baptisms, or not ? "

The Saviour answered again and said : " Nay, Of the for-giveness of but all the mysteries of the three spaces forgive sins accord-the soul in all the regions of the rulers all the sins ing to the higher mys-which the soul hath committed from the begin- teries. ning onwards. They forgive it, and moreover they forgive the sins which it thereafter will commit, until the time up to which every one of the mysteries shall be effective,—the time up to which every one of the mysteries shall be effective I will tell you at the expansion of the universe.

" And moreover the mystery of the First Mystery and the mysteries of the Ineffable for-give the soul in all the regions of the rulers all the sins and all the iniquities which the soul hath committed ; and [not only] do they forgive it all, but they impute unto it no sin from this hour unto all eternity, because of the gift of that great mystery and its prodigiously great glory."

When then the Saviour had said this, he said CHAP. 118. unto his disciples : " Understand ye in what manner I speak with you ? "

And Mary answered again and said : " Yea, my Lord, already have I seized on all the words

which thou sayest. Now, therefore, my Lord,
concerning the word which thou sayest : | ' All
the mysteries of the three spaces forgive sins
and cover their [sc. the souls'] iniquities,'—
David, the prophet, then hath prophesied aforetime concerning this word, saying : ' Blessed
are they whose sins are forgiven and whose iniquities are covered.'

" And the word which thou hast spoken: ' The
mystery of the First Mystery and the mystery of
the Ineffable forgive all men who shall receive
those mysteries, not only the sins which they
have committed from the beginning onwards,
but also they impute them not to them from
this hour unto all eternity,' — concerning this
word David hath prophesied aforetime, saying : ' Blessed are those to whom the Lord God
will not impute sins,'—that is : Sins will not
be imputed from this hour to those who have
received the mysteries of the First Mystery
and who have received the mystery of the Ineffable."

He said : " Well said, Mary, thou spiritual
and light-pure Mary. This is the solution of
the word."

And Mary continued again and said : " My
Lord, if the man receiveth mysteries from the
mysteries | of the First Mystery and again turneth
and sinneth and transgresseth, and if he thereafter again turneth and repenteth and prayeth
in any [mystery] of his mystery, will it be forgiven him, or not ? "

The Saviour answered and said unto Mary :
" Amēn, amēn, I say unto you : Every one who
shall receive the mysteries of the First Mystery,

305.

if he again turneth and transgresseth twelve times Of forgiveness even unto twelve times of those who and again twelve times repenteth, praying in the mystery of the First Mystery, it will be forgiven. have received the mysteries of the First Mystery.

" But if after the twelve times he again transgresseth and turneth and transgresseth, it will not be forgiven him for ever, so that he should turn himself to any [mystery] of his mystery ; and this [man] hath not repentance unless he receiveth the mysteries of the Ineffable, which have compassion at every time and forgive at every time."

Mary continued again and said : " My Lord, CHAP. 119. but if on the other hand they who have received the mysteries of the First Mystery, turn and transgress, and if they come out of the body before they have repented, will they inherit the kingdom or not, because indeed they have received the gift of the First Mystery ? "

The Saviour answered and said unto Mary : Of such initiated who sin and die without repentance. 306. " Amēn, amēn, I say unto you : Every man who hath received mysteries in the First Mystery, having transgressed for the first and the second and the third time, and if he cometh out of the body before he hath repented, his judgment is far sorer than all the judgments ; for his dwelling is in the midst of the jaws of the dragon of the outer darkness, and at the end of all this he will be frozen up [?] in the chastisements and perish for ever, because he hath received the gift of the First Mystery and hath not abided in it [sc. the gift].

Mary answered and said : " My Lord, all men Of the unending forgiveness of those who have received the mystery of the Ineffable. who shall receive the mysteries of the mystery of the Ineffable, and have turned again, have transgressed and have ceased in their faith, and again thereafter, when they are still in life, have turned and have repented, how many times will it be forgiven them?"

The Saviour answered and said unto Mary: "Amēn, amēn, I say unto you: To every man who shall receive the mysteries of the Ineffable, not only if he transgresseth once, turneth again and repenteth, will it be forgiven, but if at any time he transgresseth, and if, when still in life, he turneth again and repenteth, without play-acting, and again if he turneth and repenteth and prayeth in any of his mysteries, then will it be forgiven him, because he hath received of the gift of | the mysteries of the Ineffable, and moreover because those mysteries are compassionate and forgive at every time."

307.

And Mary answered again and said unto Jesus: "My Lord, those who shall receive the mysteries of the Ineffable, and have again turned, have transgressed and have ceased in their faith and are moreover come out of the body before they have repented, what will befall such?"

Of such ini-
tiated who
sin and die
without re-
pentance.

And the Saviour answered and said unto Mary: "Amēn, amēn, I say unto you: All men who shall receive the mysteries of the Ineffable,—blessed indeed are the souls which shall receive of those mysteries; but if they turn and transgress and come out of the body before they have repented, the judgment of those men is sorer than all the judgments, and it is exceedingly violent, even if those souls are new and it is their first time for coming into the world. They will not return to the changes of the bodies from that hour onwards and will not be able to do anything, but they will be cast out into the outer darkness and perish and be non-existent for ever."

And when the Saviour had said this, he said CHAP. 120. unto his disciples : " Understand ye in what manner I speak with you ? "

Mary answered | and said : " I have seized on 308. the words which thou hast said. Now, there- Mary interfore, my Lord, this is the word which thou hast same from said : ' They who shall receive the mysteries of saying. a former the Ineffable,—blessed indeed are those souls ; but if they turn, transgress, and cease in their faith, and if they go forth out of the body without having repented, they are no more fit from this hour onwards to return to the changes of the body, nor for anything at all, but they are cast out into the outer darkness, they will perish in that region and be non-existent for ever,'—concerning [this] word thou hast spoken unto us aforetime, saying : ' Salt is good ; but if the salt becometh sterile, with what are they to salt it ? It is fit neither for the dunghill nor for the earth ; but they throw it away,'—that is : Blessed are all the souls which shall receive of the mysteries of the Ineffable ; but if they once transgress, they are not fit to return to the body henceforth from this hour onwards nor for anything at all, but they are cast into the outer darkness and perish in that region."

And when she had said this, the Saviour said : " Well said, thou spiritual light-pure Mary. This is the solution of the word."

And Mary continued again | and said : " My 309. Lord, all men who have received the mysteries of the First Mystery and the mysteries of the Ineffable, those who have not transgressed. but whose faith in the mysteries was in sincerity, without play-acting,—they then have again sinned through the compulsion of the Fate and have again turned and repented and again prayed in any of the mysteries, how often will it be forgiven them ? "

Of the unending compassion of the great mysteries for the repentant.

And the Saviour answered and said unto Mary in the midst of his disciples : " Amēn, amēn, I say unto you : All men who shall receive the mysteries of the Ineffable and moreover the mysteries of the First Mystery, sin every time through the compulsion of the Fate, and if they, when they are still in life, turn and repent and abide in any of their mysteries, it will be forgiven them at every time, because those mysteries are compassionate and forgiving for all time. For this cause then have I said unto you before : Those mysteries will not only forgive them their sins which they have committed from the beginning onwards, but they do not impute them to them from this hour onwards,—of which I have said unto you that they receive repentance at any time, and that they also will forgive the sins which they commit anew.

Of the unrepentant.
310.

" If on the other hand those who shall receive mysteries of | the mystery of the Ineffable and of the mysteries of the First Mystery, turn and sin and come out of the body without having repented, then they will be even as those will be who have transgressed and not repented. Their dwelling also is in the midst of the jaws of the dragon of the outer darkness and they will perish and be non-existent for ever. For this cause have I said unto you : All men who shall receive the mysteries, if they knew the time when they come out of the body, would watch themselves and not sin, in order that they may inherit the Light-kingdom for ever."

When then the Saviour had said this unto his CHAP. 121. disciples, he said unto them : " Understand ye in what manner I speak with you ? "

Mary answered and said : " Yea, my Lord, Mary inter-with precision have I precisely followed all the preteth from a former words which thou hast said. Concerning this saying. word then thou hast spoken unto us aforetime : ' If the house-holder knew at what hour in the night the thief cometh to break into the house, he would keep awake and not suffer the man to break into his house.' "

When then Mary had said this, the Saviour said : " Well said, thou spiritual Mary. This is the word."

The Saviour continued again and said unto his disciples : " Now, therefore, herald ye unto all men who shall receive mysteries in the Light, and speak | unto them, saying : Keep watch over 311. yourselves and sin not, lest ye heap evil on evil and go out of the body without having repented and become strangers to the Light-kingdom for ever."

When the Saviour had said this, Mary answered and said : " My Lord, great is the compassion of those mysteries which forgive sins at every time."

The Saviour answered and said unto Mary in If even men the midst of the disciples : " If to-day a king on earth are compassion-who is a man of the world, giveth a gift to men of ate, how much more his like, and also forgiveth murderers and those then the highest mys-who have intercourse with males, and the rest of teries ? the very grievous sins which are deserving of death,—if it becometh him who is a man of the

world, to have done this, much more then have
the Ineffable and the First Mystery, who are the
lords of the universe, the authority to act in all
things as it pleaseth them, that they forgive
every one who shall receive mysteries.

" Or if on the other hand a king to-day in-
vesteth a soldier with a royal vesture and sendeth
him into foreign regions, and he committeth
murders and other grievous sins which are deserving of death, then they will not impute them
to him, and are not able to do him any evil because he is invested with the royal vesture,—how
much more then those who wear the mysteries
of the vestures of the Ineffable and those of the
First Mystery, who are lords over all those of
the height and all those of the depth ! "

Thereafter Jesus saw a woman who came to
make repentance. | He had baptized her three
times, and yet she had not done what was worthy
of the baptisms.   And the Saviour desired to try
Peter, to see if he was compassionate and forgiving, as he had commanded them.   He said unto
Peter : " Lo, three times have I baptized this
soul, and yet at this third time she hath not done
what is worthy of the mysteries of the Light.
Wherefor then doth she make her body good for
nothing ?   Now, therefore, Peter, perform the
mystery which cutteth off the souls from the
inheritances of the Light ; perform that mystery
in order that it may cut off the soul of this woman
from the Inheritance of the Light."

When then the Saviour had said this, he
tried [Peter] to see whether he was compassionate
and forgiving.

When then the Saviour had said this, Peter

said : " My Lord, let her yet this time, that we may give her the higher mysteries ; and if she is fit, then hast thou let her inherit the Light-kingdom, but if she is not fit, then hast thou [to] cut her off from the Light-kingdom."

When then Peter had said this, the Saviour knew that Peter was compassionate as he and forgiving.

When then all this was said, the Saviour said unto his disciples : " Have ye understood all these words and the type | of this woman ? "   313.

Mary answered and said : " My Lord, I have understood the mysteries of the things which have fallen to this woman's lot. Concerning the things then which have fallen to her lot, thou hast spoken unto us aforetime in similitude, saying : ' A man owned a fig-tree in his vineyard ; and he came to look for its fruit, and he found not a single one on it. He said to the vine-dresser : Lo, three years do I come to look for fruit on this fig-tree, and I have not any produce at all from it. Cut it down then ; why doth it make the ground also good for nothing ? But he answered and said unto him : My lord, have patience with it still this year, until I dig round it and give it dung ; and if it beareth in another year, thou hast let it, but if thou dost not find any [fruit] at all, then hast thou [to] cut it down.' Lo, my Lord, this is the solution of the word."

Mary interpreteth the incident from a former saying.

The Saviour answered and said unto Mary : " Well said, spiritual [one]. This is [the solution of] the word."

Mary continued again and said unto the Saviour : " My Lord, a man who hath received mysteries and hath not done what is worthy of

CHAP. 123.

them, but he hath turned and hath sinned, thereafter he hath again repented and hath been in great repentance,—is it then lawful for my brethren to renew for him the mystery which he hath received, or | rather give him a mystery out of the lower mysteries,—is it lawful, or not?"

The Saviour answered and said unto Mary: "Amēn, amēn, I say unto you: Neither the mystery which he hath received, nor the lower hearken unto him, to forgive his sins; but it is the mysteries which are higher than those which he hath received, which hearken unto him and forgive his sins. Now, therefore, Mary, let thy brethren give him the mystery which is higher than that which he hath received, and they are to accept his repentance from him and forgive his sins,—the latter indeed, because he hath received it once more, and the former, because he hath towered over them [the lower mysteries] upward,—the latter indeed hearkeneth not unto him to forgive his sin; but it is the mystery which is higher than that which he hath received, that forgiveth his sins. But if on the other hand he hath received the three mysteries in the two spaces or in the third from within, and he hath turned and transgressed, no mystery hearkeneth unto him to help him in his repentance, neither the higher nor the lower, save the mystery of the First Mystery and the mysteries of the Ineffable, —it is they which hearken unto him and accept his repentance from him."

Mary answered and said: " My Lord, a man who hath received mysteries up to two or three | in the second or third space, and he hath not transgressed, but is still in his faith in uprightness and without play-acting, [what will befall him] ? "

And the Saviour answered and said unto Mary : *There is no limit to the number of mysteries the faithful may receive.* " Every man who hath received mysteries in the second and in the third space, and hath not transgressed, but is still in his faith without play-acting, it is lawful for such an one to receive mysteries in the space which pleaseth him, from the first to the last, because they have not transgressed."

Mary continued again and said : " My Lord, CHAP. 124. a man who hath known the godhead and hath received of the mysteries of the Light, and hath turned and transgressed and done lawlessly and hath not turned to repent, and a man on the other hand who hath not found the godhead nor known it, and that man is a sinner and moreover impious, and they both have come out of the body,—which of them will get more suffering in the judgments ? "

The Saviour answered again and said unto *The fate of the gnostic who sinneth is more terrible than that of the ignorant sinner.* Mary : " Amēn, amēn, I say unto thee : The man who hath known the godhead and hath received the mysteries of the Light, and sinned and hath not turned to repent, he will get suffering in the chastisements of the judgments in great sufferings and | judgments exceedingly far *316.* more in comparison with the impious and law-breaking man who hath not known the godhead. Now, therefore, who hath ears to hear, let him hear."

When then the Saviour had said this, Mary *Mary interpreteth the same from a former saying.* started forward and said : " My Lord, my light-man hath ears, and I have understood the whole word which thou hast spoken. Concerning this word then thou hast spoken unto us in a similitude : ' The slave who knew the will of his lord and made not ready nor did the will of his lord, will receive great blows ; but he who knew not and did not, will be deserving of less. For from every one to whom more is entrusted, of him will more be demanded, and to whom much is handed over, of him much is required,'—that is, my Lord : He who knew the godhead and hath found the mysteries of the Light and hath transgressed, will be chastized in a far greater chastisement than he who hath not known the godhead. This, my Lord, is the solution of the word."

CHAP. 125. Mary continued again and said unto the Saviour: "My Lord, if the faith and the mysteries shall have revealed themselves,—now, therefore, if souls come into the world in many circuits and are neglectful of receiving mysteries, hoping that, if they come into the world at any other circuit, they will receive them, will they not then be **317.** in danger | of not succeeding in receiving the mysteries ? "

Of those who procrastin- ate, saying they have many births before them. The Saviour answered and said unto his disciples : " Herald unto the whole world and say unto men : Strive thereafter that ye may receive the mysteries of the Light in this time of affliction and enter into the Light-kingdom. Join not one day to another, or one circuit to another, hoping that ye may succeed in receiving the mysteries if ye come into the world in another circuit.

" And these know not when the number of the perfect souls will be at hand ; for if the number of the perfect souls shall be at hand, I will now shut the gates of the Light, and no one from this hour onwards will enter in, nor will

any one hereafter go forth, for the number of the
perfect souls is completed and the mystery of the
First Mystery is completed, for the sake of which
the universe hath arisen,—that is : I am that
Mystery.

" And from this hour onwards no one will be Of the time
able to enter into the Light and no one be able to of the com-
go forth. For at the completion of the time of pletion.
the number of the perfect souls, before I have set
fire to the world, in order that it may purify the
æons and the veils and the firmaments and the
whole earth and also all the matters which are on
it, mankind | will be still existing. 318.

" At that time then the faith will reveal Those who
itself still more and the mysteries in those days. procrastin-
And many souls will come by means of the circuits cluded from
of the changes of the body, and coming back into the Light.
the world are some of those in this present time
who have hearkened unto me, how I taught, who
at the completion of the number of the perfect
souls will find the mysteries of the Light and
receive them and come to the gates of the Light
and find that the number of the perfect souls
is complete, which is the completion of the First
Mystery and the gnosis of the universe. And
they will find that I have shut the gates of the
Light and that it is impossible that any one
should enter in or that any one should go forth
from this hour.

" Those souls then will knock at the gates of Their en-
the Light, saying : Lord, open unto us ! And I treaties at
will answer unto them : I know you not, whence Light.
ye are. And they will say unto me : We have
received of thy mysteries and fulfilled thy whole
teaching and thou hast taught us on the high

ways. And I will answer and say unto them: I know you not, who ye are, ye who are doers of iniquity and of evil even unto now. Wherefor go into the outer darkness. And | from that hour they will go into the outer darkness, there where is howling and grinding of teeth.

319.

" For this cause then, herald unto the whole world and say unto them: ' Strive thereafter, to renounce the whole world and the whole matter therein, that ye may receive the mysteries of the Light before the number of the perfect souls is completed, in order that they may not make you stop before the gates of the Light and lead you away into the outer darkness.'

" Now, therefore, who hath ears to hear, let him hear."

Mary inter-preteth the same.

When then the Saviour had said this, Mary started forward again and said: " My Lord, not only hath my light-man ears, but my soul hath heard and understood all the words which thou sayest. Now, therefore, my Lord, concerning the words which thou hast spoken: ' Herald unto the men of the world and say unto them: Strive thereafter, to receive the mysteries of the Light, in this time of affliction, that ye may inherit the Light-kingdom. . . .

.   .   .   .   .   .

[A CONSIDERABLE LACUNA HERE OCCURS IN THE TEXT.]

.   .   .   .   .   .

A FOURTH BOOK

And Mary continued again and said unto Jesus : " In what type is the outer darkness ; or rather how many regions of chastisement are there in it ? "

And Jesus answered and said unto Mary : " The outer darkness is a great dragon, whose tail is in his mouth, outside the whole world and surrounding the whole world. And there are many regions of chastisement within it. There are twelve mighty | chastisement-dungeons and a ruler is in every dungeon and the face of the rulers is different one from another.

" And the first ruler, who is in the first dungeon, hath a crocodile's face, whose tail is in his mouth. And out of the jaws of the dragon cometh all ice and all dust and all cold and all different diseases. This [is] he who is called with his authentic name in his region ' Enchthonin.'

" And the ruler who is in the second dungeon,— a cat's face is his authentic face. This [is] he who is called in his region ' Charachar.'

" And the ruler who is in the third dungeon,— a dog's face is his authentic face. This [is] he who is called in his region ' Archarōch.'

" And the ruler who is in the fourth dungeon,— a serpent's face is his authentic face. This [is] he who is called in his region ' Achrōchar.'

" And the ruler who is in the fifth dungeon,—a black bull's face is his authentic face. This [is] he who is called in his region ' Marchŭr.'

" And the ruler who is in the sixth dungeon,—a wild boar's face is his authentic face. This [is] he who is called in his region ' Lamchamōr.'

" And the ruler who is in the seventh dungeon,

321. |·—a bear's face is his authentic face. This [is] he who is called in his region with his authentic name ' Luchar.'

" And the ruler of the eighth dungeon,—a vulture's face is his authentic face, whose name in his region is called ' Laraōch.'

" And the ruler of the ninth dungeon,—a basilisk's face is his authentic face, whose name in his region is called ' Archeōch.'

" And in the tenth dungeon is a multitude of rulers, and every one of them hath seven dragon's heads in his authentic face. And he who is over them all is in his region with his name called ' Xarmarōch.'

" And in the eleventh dungeon is a multitude of rulers,—and every one of them hath seven cat-faced heads in his authentic face. And the great one over them is called in his region ' Rōchar.'

" And in the twelfth dungeon is an exceedingly great multitude of rulers, and every one of them hath seven dog-faced heads in his authentic face. And the great one over them is called in his region ' Chrēmaōr.'

" These rulers then of these twelve dungeons are inside the dragon of the outer darkness, each

322. and every one | of them hath a name every hour, and every one of them changeth his face every

hour.   And moreover every one of these dungeons Of the doors of the dungeons.
hath a door opening upwards, so that the dragon
of the outer darkness hath twelve dark dungeons,
and every dungeon hath a door opening upwards.   And an angel of the height watcheth
each of the doors of the dungeons,—whom
Yew, the First Man, the overseer of the Light, The angels who watch the doors.
the envoy of the First Commandment, hath
established as watchers of the dragon, so that
the dragon and the rulers of his dungeons which
are in him, may not mutiny."

When the Saviour had said this, Mary Mag- CHAP. 127.
dalene answered and said: " My Lord, will then
the souls which shall be led into that region, be
led through these twelve doors of the dungeons,
every one according to the judgment of which it
is deserving ? "

The Saviour answered and said unto Mary : What souls pass into the dragon, and how.
" No soul at all will be led into the dragon
through these doors.   But the soul[s] of the blas-
phemers and of those who are in the doctrines of
error and of all who teach doctrines of error, and
of those who have intercourse with males, and
of those stained and impious men and of atheists
and murderers and adulterers and sorcerers,—all
such souls then, if while still in life they do not
repent but | remain persistently in their sin, and 323
all the souls which have stayed behind without,—
that is those which have had the number of the
circuits which are appointed them in the sphere,
without having repented,—well, at their last
circuit will those souls, they and all the souls of
which I have just told you, be led out of [?] the
jaws of the tail of the dragon into the dungeons
of the outer darkness.   And when those souls

have been led into the outer darkness into the jaws of his tail, he turneth his tail into his own mouth and shutteth them in. Thus will the souls be led into the outer darkness.

The nature of the names of the dragon.

" And the dragon of the outer darkness hath twelve authentic names on his doors, a name on every one of the doors of the dungeons. And these twelve names are different one from another; but the twelve are one in the other, so that he who speaketh one name, speaketh all. These then will I tell you at the expansion of the universe. Thus then is fashioned the outer darkness,—that is the dragon."

When then the Saviour had said this, Mary answered and said | unto the Saviour: " My Lord, are then the chastisements of that dragon far more terrible compared with all the chastisements of the judgments ? "

324.

Of the severity of the chastise. ments of the dragon.

The Saviour answered and said unto Mary : " Not only are they more painful compared with all the chastisements of the judgments, but all the souls which are led into that region, will be frozen up [?] in the violent cold and the hail and exceedingly violent fire which is in that region, but also at the dissolution of the world, that is at the ascension of the universe, those souls will perish through the violent cold and the exceedingly violent fire and be non-existent for ever."

Mary answered and said : " Woe unto the souls of sinners ! Now, therefore, my Lord, is the fire in the world of mankind fiercer, or the fire in Amente ? "

Of the de. grees of the fires of the chastise. ments.

The Saviour answered and said unto Mary : " Amēn, I say unto thee : The fire in Amente is nine times fiercer than the fire in mankind.

" And the fire in the chastisements of the great chaos is nine times more violent than that in Amente.

" And the fire in the chastisements of the rulers who [are] on the way of the midst, is nine times more violent than the fire of the chastisements in the great chaos.

" And the fire | in the dragon of the outer dark- 325. ness and in all the chastisements in him is seventy times more violent than the fire in all the chastisements and in all the judgments of the rulers who [are] on the way of the midst."

And when the Saviour had said this unto Mary, CHAP. 128. she smote her breast, she cried out and wept, The dis-she and all the disciples together, and said : the fate of " Woe unto sinners, for their chastisements are sinners. exceedingly numerous ! "

Mary came forward, she fell down at the feet of Jesus, kissed them and said : " My Lord, bear with me if I question thee, and be not wroth with me, that I trouble thee oft ; for from now on I will begin to question thee on all things with determination."

The Saviour answered and said unto Mary : " Question concerning all things on which thou desirest to question, and I will reveal them unto thee in openness without similitude."

Mary answered and said : " My Lord, if a good Mary further man hath accomplished all the mysteries and he questioneth Jesus. hath a kinsman, in a word he hath a man, and that man is an impious [one] who hath committed all sins and is deserving of the outer darkness, and he hath not repented, or he hath completed his number of circuits in the changes of the body, and that man hath done nothing useful,

and he hath come out of the body, and we have
known certainly of him, that he hath sinned | and
is deserving of the outer darkness,—what are
we to do with him, to save him from the chastisements of the dragon of the outer darkness, and
that he may be removed into a righteous body
which shall find the mysteries of the Light-
kingdom, in order that it may be good and go
on high and inherit the Light-kingdom ? "

How to save
the souls of
sinners.

The Saviour answered and said unto Mary :
" If a sinner is deserving of the outer darkness, or
hath sinned according to the chastisements of
the rest of the chastisements and hath not repented, or a sinning man who hath completed
his number of circuits in the changes of the body
and hath not repented,—if then these men of
whom I have spoken, shall come out of the body
and be led into the outer darkness, now, therefore, if ye desire to remove them out of the
chastisements of the outer darkness and all the
judgments and to remove them into a righteous
body which shall find the mysteries of the Light,
that it may go on high and inherit the Light-
kingdom,—then perform this same mystery of
the Ineffable which forgiveth sins at every time,
and when ye have finished performing the mystery
then say :

A summary
of the for-
mulæ.

" The soul of such or such a man of whom
I think in my heart,—if it is in the region of the
chastisements of the dungeons of the outer darkness, or if it is in the rest of the chastisements of
the dungeons of the outer darkness and in the rest
of the chastisements | of the dragons,—then is it
to be removed out of them all. And if it hath
completed its number of its circuits of the changes,

then is it to be led before the Virgin of Light, and
the Virgin of Light is to seal it with the seal of
the Ineffable and cast it down in whatever month
into a righteous body which shall find the mysteries
of the Light, so that it may be good, go on high
and inherit the Light-kingdom. And moreover
if it hath completed the circuits of changes, then
is that soul to be led before the seven virgins
of the Light who [are set] over the baptisms, and
they are to apply them to the soul and seal it
with the sign of the kingdom of the Ineffable
and lead it into the orders of the Light.

" This then will ye say when ye perform the
mystery.

" Amēn, I say unto you : The soul for which ye
shall pray, if it indeed is in the dragon of the outer
darkness, he will draw his tail out of his mouth
and let go that soul. And moreover if it is in
all the regions of the judgments of the rulers,
amēn, I say unto you : The receivers of Melchisedec will with haste snatch it away, whether
the dragon let it go or it is in the judgments of
the rulers ; in a word, the receivers of Melchisedec |
will snatch it away out of all the regions in which 328.
it is, and will lead it into the region of the Midst
before the Virgin of Light, and the Virgin of Light
proveth it and seeth the sign of the kingdom of
the Ineffable which is on that soul.

" And if it hath not yet completed its number
of circuits in the changes of the soul, or [in the
changes] of the body, the Virgin of Light sealeth
it with an excellent seal and hasteth to have it
cast down in any month into a righteous body
which shall find the mysteries of the Light, be
good and go on high into the Light-kingdom.

" And if that soul hath had its number of the circuits, then the Virgin of Light proveth it, and doth not have it chastized, because it hath had its number of circuits, but handeth it over to the seven virgins of the Light.　And the seven virgins of the Light prove that soul, baptize it with their baptisms and give it the spiritual chrism and lead it into the Treasury of the Light and put it in the last order of the Light until the ascension of all the perfect souls.　And when they prepare to draw apart the veils of the region of those of the Right, they cleanse that soul anew and purify it and put it in the orders of the first saviour who [is] in the | Treasury of the Light."

329.

CHAP. 129.　It came to pass then, when the Saviour had finished speaking these words unto his disciples, that Mary answered and said unto Jesus : " My Lord, I have heard thee say : ' He who shall receive of the mysteries of the Ineffable or who shall receive of the mysteries of the First Mystery, —they become flames of light-beams and light-streams and penetrate all the regions until they reach the region of their inheritance.' "

Of the light-beams and light-streams.　The Saviour answered and said unto Mary : " If they receive the mystery when still in life, and if they come out of the body, they become light-beams and light-streams and penetrate all the regions until they reach the region of their inheritance.

" But if they are sinners and are come out of the body and have not repented, and if ye perform for them the mystery of the Ineffable, in order that they may be removed out of all the chastisements and be cast into a righteous body, which is good and inheriteth the Light-kingdom or is

brought into the last order of the Light, then they
will not be able to penetrate the regions, because
they do not perform the mystery [themselves].
But the receivers of Melchisedec follow them and
lead them before the Virgin of Light. And | the 330.
servitors of the judges of the rulers make frequent
haste to take those souls and hand them over
from one to the other until they lead them before
the Virgin of Light."

And Mary continued and said unto the Saviour : CHAP. 130.
" My Lord, if a man hath received the mysteries Mary plead-
of the Light which [are] in the first space from who have
without, and when the time of the mysteries up mysteries.
to which they reach, is completed, and if that
man continueth anew to receive mysteries of
the mysteries which [are] within the mysteries
which he hath already received, and moreover
that man hath become negligent, not having
prayed in the prayer which taketh away the evil
of the victuals which he eateth and drinketh,
and through the evil of the victuals he is bound to
the axle of the Fate of the rulers and through the
necessity of the elements he hath sinned anew
after the completion of the time up to which the
mystery reacheth,—because he hath become
negligent and hath not prayed in the prayer
which taketh away the evil of the souls and purifieth them,—and that man is come out of the
body before he hath repented anew and anew
received the mysteries of the mysteries which [are]
within the mysteries which he hath already received,—those which accept repentance from him
and forgive his sins,—and when he | came forth 331.
out of the body and we knew with certainty
that they have carried him into the midst of the

dragon of the outer darkness because of the sins which he committed, and that that man hath no helper in the world nor any one compassionate, that he should perform the mystery of the Ineffable until he should be removed out of the midst of the dragon of the outer darkness and led into the Light-kingdom,—now, therefore, my Lord, what will befall him until he save himself from the chastisements of the dragon of the outer darkness? By no means, O Lord, abandon him, because he hath endured sufferings in the persecutions and in the whole godhood in which he is.

" Now, therefore, O Saviour, have mercy with me, lest one of our kinsmen should be in such a type, and have mercy with all the souls which shall be in this type ; for thou art the key which openeth the door of the universe and shutteth the door of the universe, and thy mystery comprehendeth them all. Have then mercy, O Lord, with such souls. For they have called on the name of thy mysteries, [were it but] for one single day, and have truly had faith in them and were not in play-acting. Give them then, O Lord, a gift in thy goodness and give them rest in thy mercy."

When then Mary had said this, the Saviour called her most exceedingly blessed because of the words | which she had spoken. And the Saviour was in great compassion and said unto Mary : " Unto all men who shall be in this type of which thou hast spoken, unto them while they [are] still in life, give ye the mystery of one of the twelve names of the dungeons of the dragon of the outer darkness,—those which I will give you when I have ended explaining unto you the uni-

332.

verse from within without and from without within.

" And all men who shall find the mystery of one of the twelve names of that dragon of the outer darkness, and all men even if they are very great sinners, and they have first received the mysteries of the Light and thereafter have transgressed, or they have performed no mystery at all, then if they have completed their circuits in the changes, and if such men go forth out of the body without having repented anew, and if they are led into the chastisements which [are] in the midst of the dragon of the outer darkness, and remain in the circuits and remain in the chastisements in the midst of the dragon,—these, if they know the mystery of one of the twelve names of the angels while they are in life and are in the world, and if they speak one of their names while they are in the midst of the chastisements of the dragon,—then, at the hour when they shall speak it, the whole dragon will be tossed about and most exceedingly convulsed, and the door of the dungeon in which the souls | of those men are, openeth itself upward, and the ruler of the dungeon in which those men are, casteth the souls of those men out of the midst of the dragon of the outer darkness, because they have found the mystery of the name of the dragon.

" And when the ruler casteth out souls, straightway the angels of Yew, the First Man, who watch the dungeons of that region, hasten to snatch away those souls to lead them before Yew, the First Man, the Envoy of the First Commandment. And Yew, the First Man, seeth the souls and proveth them ; he findeth that they have com-

Of the efficacy of the names of the twelve angels.

333.

The souls who know the names escape and are taken to Yew.

pleted their circuits and that it is not lawful to bring them anew into the world, for it is not lawful to bring anew into the world all souls which are cast into the outer darkness. [But] if they have not yet completed their number of circuits in the changes of the body, the receivers of Yew keep them with them until they perform for them the mystery of the Ineffable, and remove them into a good body which shall find the mysteries of the Light and inherit the Light-kingdom.

Of their subsequent fate.

334.

" But if Yew proveth them and findeth that they have completed their circuits and that it is not lawful to [re]turn them anew to the world, and that also the sign of the Ineffable | is not with them, then Yew hath compassion upon them and leadeth them before the seven virgins of the Light. They baptize them with their baptisms, but they do not give them the spiritual chrism. And they lead them into the Treasury of the Light, but they do not put them in the orders of the Inheritance, because no sign and no seal of the Ineffable is with them. But they save them from all chastisements and put them into the light of the Treasury, separated and apart by themselves alone until the ascension of the universe. And at the time when they will draw apart the veils of the Treasury of the Light, they cleanse those souls anew and purify them most exceedingly and give them anew mysteries and put them in the last order which [is] in the Treasury, and those souls will be saved from all the chastisements of the judgments."

And when the Saviour had said this, he said unto his disciples : " Have ye understood in what manner I discourse with you ? "

Mary then answered and said : " My Lord, Mary inter-
this is the word which thou hast spoken unto us preteth the same from
aforetime, in a similitude, saying : ' Make to a former saying.
yourselves a friend out of the Mamōn of unrighteousness, so that if ye remain behind, he may
receive you into | the everlasting tents.' Who 335.
then is the Mamōn of unrighteousness, if not the
dragon of the outer darkness ? This is the
word : He who shall understand the mystery
of one of the names of the dragon of the outer
darkness, if he remaineth behind in the outer
darkness or if he hath completed the circuits of
the changes, and speaketh the name of the dragon,
he will be saved and go up out of the darkness
and be received into the Treasury of the Light.
This is the word, my Lord."

The Saviour answered again and said unto
Mary : " Well said, spiritual and pure [one].
This is the solution of the word."

Mary continued again and said : " My Lord, CHAP. 131.
doth the dragon of the outer darkness come into
this world or doth he not come ? "

The Saviour answered and said unto Mary : Of the light
" When the light of the sun is outside [? above the of the sun and the
world], he covereth the darkness of the dragon ; darkness of the dragon.
but if the sun is below the world, then the dark-
ness of the dragon abideth as veiling of the sun
and the breath of the darkness cometh into the
world in form of a smoke in the night,—that is,
if the sun withdraweth into himself his rays,
then indeed the world is not able to endure the
darkness of the dragon in its true form ; otherwise would it be dissolved and go to ruin withal."

When the Saviour had said this, Mary continued again and said unto the Saviour : " My

336. Lord, still do I question thee and | hide [it] not from me. Now, therefore, my Lord, who compelleth then the man until he sinneth ? ''

The Saviour answered and said unto Mary : '' It is the rulers of the Fate who compel the man until he sinneth.''

Mary answered and said unto the Saviour : '' My Lord, surely the rulers do not come down to the world and compel the man until he sinneth ? ''

Of the cup of forgetfulness. The Saviour answered and said unto Mary : '' They do not come down in this manner into the world. But the rulers of the Fate, when an old soul is about to come down through them, then the rulers of that great Fate who [are] in the regions of the head of the æons,—which is that region which is called the region of the kingdom of Adamas, and which is that region which is in face of the Virgin of Light,—then the rulers of the region of that head give the old soul a cup of forgetfulness out of the seed of wickedness, filled with all the different desires and all forgetfulness. And straightway, when that soul shall drink out of the cup, it forgetteth all the **337.** regions to which it hath gone, | and all the chastisements in which it hath travelled. And *Of the counterfeiting spirit.* that cup of the water of forgetfulness becometh body outside the soul, and it resembleth the soul in all [its] figures and maketh [itself] like it,— which is what is called the counterfeiting spirit.

Of the fashioning of a new soul. '' If on the other hand it is a new soul which they have taken out of the sweat of the rulers and out of the tears of their eyes, or far rather out of the breath of their mouths,—in a word, if it is one of the new souls or one of such souls, if it is one out of the sweat, then the five great

rulers of the great Fate take up the sweat of all
the rulers of their æons, knead it together withal,
portion it and make it into a soul. Or far
rather if it is refuse of the purification of the
Light, then Melchisedec taketh it up from the
rulers. The five great rulers of the great Fate
knead the refuse together, portion it and make
it into different souls, so that every one of the
rulers of the æons, every one of them putteth his
portion into the soul. For this cause they knead
it jointly, so that all may [par]take of the soul.

" And the five great rulers, if they portion it
and make it into souls, bring it out of the sweat |
of the rulers. But if it is one out of the refuse 338.
of the purification of the Light, then Melchisedec,
the great Receiver of the Light, taketh it [sc. the
refuse] up from the rulers, or far rather if it is out
of the tears of their eyes or out of the breath of
their mouth,—in a word, out of such souls, when
the five rulers portion it and make it into different
souls,—or far rather if it is an old soul, then the
ruler who is in the head of the æons, himself
mixeth the cup of forgetfulness with the seed of
wickedness, and he mixeth it with every one of
the new souls at the time when he is in the region
of the head. And that cup of forgetfulness
becometh the counterfeiting spirit for that soul,
and bideth outside the soul, being a vesture for
it and resembling it in every way, being envelope
as vesture outside it.

" And the five great rulers of the great Fate Of the in-
of the æons and the ruler of the disk of the sun breathing of
and the ruler of the disk of the moon inbreathe the power.
within into that soul, and there cometh forth out
of them a portion out of my power which the

last Helper hath cast into the Mixture. And the portion of that power remaineth within in the

soul, | unloosed and existing on its own authority for the economy unto which it hath been inset, to give sense unto the soul, in order that it may seek after the works of the Light of the Height always.

" And that power is like the species of the soul in every form and resembleth it. It cannot be outside the soul, but remaineth inside it, as I have commanded it from the beginning. When I willed to cast it into the first Commandment, I gave it commandment to remain outside [? inside] the souls for the economy of the First Mystery.

" And so I will tell you at the expansion of the universe all these words concerning the power and also concerning the soul, after what type they are fashioned, or what ruler fashioneth them, or what are the different species of the souls. And so will I tell you at the expansion of the universe how many fashion the soul. And I will tell you the name of all of them who fashion the soul. And I will tell you the type, how the counterfeiting spirit and the destiny have been prepared. And I will tell you the name of the soul before it is purged, and moreover its name when it hath been purged and become pure. And I will tell you the name of the counterfeiting spirit; and I will tell you the name of the destiny. And I will tell you the name of all the bonds with which

the rulers bind the counterfeiting spirit | to the soul. And I will tell you the name of all the decans who fashion the soul in the bodies of the soul in the world; and I will tell you in what manner the souls are fashioned. And I will tell you the type of every one of the souls ; and I will tell you the type of the souls of the men and of those of the birds and of those of the wild beasts and of those of the reptiles. And I will tell you the type of all the souls and of those of all the rulers which are sent into the world, in order that ye may be completed in all gnosis. All this will I tell you at the expansion of the universe. And after all this I will tell you wherefor all this hath come to pass.

" Hearken, therefore, that I may discourse with you concerning the soul according as I have said : The five great rulers of the great Fate of the æons and the rulers of the disk of the sun and the rulers of the disk of the moon breathe into that soul, and there cometh out of them a portion of my power, as I have just said. And the portion of that power remaineth within the soul, so that the soul can stand. And they put | the counterfeiting spirit outside the soul, watching it and assigned to it ; and the rulers bind it to the soul with their seals and their bonds and seal it to it, that it may compel it always, so that it continually doeth its mischiefs and all its iniquities, in order that it may be their slave always and remain under their sway always in the changes of the body ; and they seal it to it that it may be in all the sin and all the desires of the world.

Of the light-power and the counter-feiting spirit.

341.

" For this cause, therefore, have I in this manner brought the mysteries into this world which undo all the bonds of the counterfeiting spirit and all the seals which are bound to the soul,—those which make the soul free and free it from its

The parents we are to abandon.

parents the rulers, and make it into refined light and lead it up into the kingdom of its father, the first Issue, the First Mystery, for ever.

" For this cause therefore, have I said unto you aforetime : ' He who doth not abandon father and mother and come and follow after me, is not worthy of me.' I have, therefore, said at that time : Ye are to abandon your parents the rulers, that I may make you sons of the First Mystery for ever."

CHAP. 132.
342.
Salome is in doubt.

And when | the Saviour had said this, Salome started forward and said : " My Lord, if our parents are the rulers, how standeth it written in the Law of Moses : ' He who shall abandon his father and his mother, let him die the death ' ? Hath not thus the Law made statement thereon ? "

And when Salome had said this, the light-power in Mary Magdalene bubbled up in her and she said to the Saviour : " My Lord, give commandment unto me that I discourse with my sister Salome to tell her the solution of the word which she hath spoken."

It came to pass then, when the Saviour had heard Mary say these words, that he called her most exceedingly blessed. The Saviour answered and said unto Mary : " I give commandment unto thee, Mary, that thou speak the solution of the word which Salome hath spoken."

Mary re-moveth the doubt of Salome.

And when the Saviour had said this, Mary started forward to Salome, embraced her and said unto her : " My sister Salome, concerning the word which thou hast spoken : It standeth written in the Law of Moses : ' He who shall abandon his father and his mother, let him die the death,'—now, therefore, my sister Salome,

the Law hath not said this concerning the soul
nor concerning the body nor concerning the
counterfeiting spirit, for all these are sons | of 343.
the rulers and are out of them. But the Law
hath said this concerning the power which hath
came forth out of the Saviour, and which is the
light-man within us to-day. The Law hath moreover said : Every one who shall remain without
the Saviour and all his mysteries, his parents,
will not only die the death but go to ruin in
destruction."

When then Mary had said this, Salome
started forward to Mary and embraced her anew.
Salome said : " The Saviour hath power to make
me understanding like thyself."

It came to pass, when the Saviour had heard
the words of Mary, that he called her most
exceedingly blessed. The Saviour answered and
said unto Mary in the midst of his disciples:
" Hearken, therefore, Mary, who it is who compelleth the man until he sinneth.

" Now, therefore, the rulers seal the counter- Of the
feiting spirit to the soul, [but] so that it doth not charge given
to the coun-
agitate it every hour, making it do all sins and all terfeiting
iniquities. And they give commandment more- spirit.
over unto the counterfeiting spirit, saying : ' If
the soul cometh out of the body, do not agitate
it, being assigned to it and transferring it to all
the regions of the judgments, region by region,
on account of all the sins which thou hast made it
do, in order that it may be chastized in all the
regions of the judgments, so that it may not be
able to go | on high to the Light and return into 344.
changes of the body.'

" In a word, they give commandment to the

counterfeiting spirit, saying : ' Do not agitate it at all at any hour unless it doth not speak mysteries and undo all the seals and all the bonds with which we have bound thee to it. [But] if it sayeth the mysteries and undoeth all the seals and all the bonds and [sayeth] the apology of the region, and if it cometh, then let it go forth, for it belongeth to those of the Light of the Height and hath become a stranger unto us and unto thee, and thou wilt not be able to seize it from this hour onwards. If on the contrary it sayeth not the mysteries of the undoing of thy bonds and of thy seals and of the apologies of the region, then seize it and let it not out ; thou shalt transfer it to the chastisements and all the regions of the judgments on account of all the sins which thou hast made it do. After this lead [such souls] before the Virgin of Light, who sendeth them once more into the circuit.'

Of the charge given to the servitors.

" The rulers of the great Fate of the æons hand these over to the counterfeiting spirit ; and the rulers summon the servitors of their æons, to the number of three-hundred-and-sixty-and-five, and give them the soul and the counterfeiting spirit, which are bound to one another. The counterfeiting spirit is the without of the soul, and the compound of the power is the within of the soul, being within both of them, in order that they

345.

may be able to stand, for | it is the power which keepeth the two up-right. And the rulers give commandment to the servitors, saying unto them : ' This is the type which ye are to put into the body of the matter of the world.' They say unto them indeed : ' Put the compound of the power, the within of the soul, within them

all, that they may be able to stand, for it is their
up-rightness, and after the soul put the counterfeiting spirit.'

" Thus they give commandment to their ser- Of concep-
vitors, that they may deposit it into the bodies
of the antitype. And following this fashion the
servitors of the rulers bring the power and the
soul and the counterfeiting spirit, bring them
down to the world, and pour [them] out into
the world of the rulers of the midst. The rulers
of the midst look after the counterfeiting spirit ;
and also the destiny, whose name is Moira, leadeth
the man until it hath him slain through the death
appointed unto him, which the rulers of the great
Fate have bound to the soul. And the servitors
of the sphere bind the soul and the power and
the counterfeiting spirit and the destiny. And
they portion them all and make them into two
portions and seek after the man and also after
the woman in the world to whom they have
given signs, in order that they may | send them 346.
into them. And they give one portion to the man
and one portion to the woman in a victual of
the world or in a breath of the air or in water or
in a kind which they drink.

" All this I will tell unto you and the species
of every soul and the type, how they enter into
the bodies, whether of men or of birds or of
cattle or of wild beasts or of reptiles or of all the
other species in the world. I will tell you their
type, in what type they enter into men ; I will
tell it you at the expansion of the universe.

" Now, therefore, when the servitors of the
rulers cast the one portion into the woman and
the other into the man in the fashion which I

Of the compulsion of the parents. have told you, then the servitors secretly compel them, even if they are removed at very great distance from one another, so that they concert to be in a concert of the world. And the counterfeiting spirit which is in the man, cometh to the portion which is entrusted to the world in the matter of his body, and lifteth it and casteth it down into the womb of the woman [into the portion] which is entrusted to the seed of wickedness.

Of the process of gestation. " And in that hour the three-hundred-and-sixty-and-five servitors of the rulers go into her womb and take up their abode in it. The servitors bring the two portions the one to the other, and

347. moreover the servitors withhold | the blood of all the food of the woman which she will eat and which she will drink, and they withhold [it] in the womb of the woman up to forty days. And after forty days they knead the blood of the power of all the food and knead it well in the woman's womb.

" After forty days they spend another thirty days in building its members in the image of the body of the man ; each buildeth a member. I will tell you the decans who will build it [sc. the body] ; I will tell them you at the expansion of the universe.

Of the incarnation of the soul. " If then after this the servitors shall have completed the whole body and all its members in seventy days, after this the servitors summon into the body which they have built,—first indeed they summon the counterfeiting spirit ; thereafter they summon the soul within them ; and thereafter they summon the compound of the power into the soul ; and the destiny they put outside

them all, as it is not blended with them, [but]
following them and accompanying them.

" And after this the servitors seal them one *Of the seal-*
to the other with all the seals which the rulers *ing of the*
plasm.
have given them. [And] they seal the day on
which they have taken up their abode in the womb
of the woman,—they seal [it] on the left hand | of 348.
the plasm ; and they seal the day on which they
have completed the body, on the right hand ;
and they seal the day on which the rulers have
handed it over to them, on the middle of the skull
of the body of the plasm ; and they seal the day
on which the soul hath come forth out of the
rulers, they seal it on the [left of] the skull of the
plasm ; and they seal the day on which they
kneaded the members and separated them for
a soul, they seal it on the right of the skull of the
plasm ; and the day on which they have bound
the counterfeiting spirit to it [the soul], they seal
on the back of the skull of the plasm ; and the
day on which the rulers have breathed the power
into the body, they seal on the brain which is
in the midst of the head of the plasm and also
on the inside [? the heart] of the plasm ; and the
number of years which the soul will spend in
the body, they seal on the forehead which is on
the plasm. And so they seal all those seals on
the plasm. I will tell you the names of all these
seals at the expansion of the universe ; and after
the expansion of the universe I will tell you wherefor all hath come to pass. And, if ye could
understand it, I am that mystery.

" Now, therefore, the servitors complete the
whole man. And of all these seals with which
they have sealed the body, | the servitors carry the 349.

whole peculiarity and bring it to all the retributive rulers who [are] over all the chastisements of the judgments; and these hand it over to their receivers, in order that they may lead their souls out of the bodies,—they hand over to them the peculiarity of the seals, in order that they may know the time when they are to lead the souls out of the bodies, and in order that they may know the time when they are to bring to birth the body, so that they may send their servitors in order that they may draw near and follow the soul and bear witness of all the sins it shall do,—they and the counterfeiting spirit,—on account of the manner and way, how they shall chastize it in the judgment.

Of the destiny.

"And when the servitors have given the peculiarity of the seals to the retributive rulers, they withdraw themselves to the economy of their occupations which is appointed unto them through the rulers of the great Fate. And when the number of months of the birth of the babe is completed, the babe is born. Small in it is the compound of the power, and small in it is the soul; and small in it is the counterfeiting spirit. The destiny on the contrary is large, as it is not mingled into the body for their economy, but followeth the soul | and the body and the counterfeiting spirit, until the time when the soul shall come forth out of the body, on account of the type of death by which it shall slay it [the body] according to the death appointed for it by the rulers of the great Fate.

350.

Of how a man cometh by his death.

"Is he to die by a wild beast, the destiny leadeth the wild beast against him until it slay him; or is he to die by a serpent, or is he to fall into a pit by mischance, or is he to hang himself, or is he to die in water, or through such [kinds of death], or through another death which is worse or better than this,—in a word, it is the destiny which forceth his death upon him. This is the occupation of the destiny, and it hath no other occupation but this. And the destiny followeth every man until the day of his death."

Mary answered and said : " To all men then CHAP. 133. who are in the world, will all which is appointed them through the Fate, whether good or bad or sin or death or life,—in a word, will all which is appointed them through the rulers of the Fate, have to come unto them ? "

The Saviour answered and said unto Mary : There is no " Amēn, I say unto you : All which is appointed escape from the destiny. unto every one through the Fate, whether all good or all sins,—in a word, all which is appointed them, cometh unto them.

" For this cause, therefore, have I brought | the 351 keys of the mysteries of the kingdom of heaven ; Of the keys of the mys- otherwise no flesh in the world would be saved. teries. For without mysteries no one will enter into the Light-kingdom, be he a righteous or a sinner.

" For this cause, therefore, have I brought the keys of the mysteries into the world, that I may free the sinners who shall have faith in me and hearken unto me, so that I may free them from the bonds and the seals of the æons of the rulers and bind them to the seals and the vestures and the orders of the Light, in order that he whom I shall free in the world from the bonds and the seals of the æons of the rulers, may be freed in the Height from the bonds and seals of the æons of the rulers, and in order that he whom I

shall bind in the world to the seals and the vestures
and the orders of the Light, may be bound in the
Light-land to the orders of the inheritances of
the Light.

"For the sake of sinners, therefore, have I
torn myself asunder at this time and have brought
them the mysteries, that I may free them from the
æons of the rulers and bind them to the inheritances of the Light, and not only the sinners, but
also the righteous, in order that I may give them
the mysteries and that they may be taken into
the Light, for without mysteries they cannot | be
taken into the Light.

352.

The mys-
teries are
for all men.

"For this cause, therefore, I have not hidden
it, but I have cried it aloud clearly. And I have
not separated the sinners, but I have cried it
aloud and said it unto all men, unto sinners and
righteous, saying: 'Seek that ye may find,
knock that it may be opened unto you; for
every one who seeketh in truth, will find, and who
knocketh, to him it will be opened.' For I have
said unto all men: They are to seek the mysteries
of the Light-kingdom which shall purify them and
make them refined and lead them into the Light.

A prophecy
of John the
Baptizer.

"For this cause, therefore, hath John the
Baptizer prophesied concerning me, saying: 'I
indeed have baptized you with water unto repentance for forgiveness of your sins. He who
cometh after me, is stronger than me. Whose
fan is in his hand, and he will purify his floor.
The chaff indeed he will consume with un-
quenchable fire, but the wheat he will gather into
his barn.' The power in John hath prophesied
concerning me, knowing that I would bring the
mysteries into the world and purify the sins of

the sinners who shall have faith in me and hearken
unto me, and make them into refined light and
lead them into the Light."

When then Jesus had said this, Mary answered CHAP. 134.
and said : " My Lord, if men go to seek and they
come upon the doctrines of error, | whence then 353.
are they to know whether they belong to thee
or not ? "

The Saviour answered and said unto Mary :
" I have said unto you aforetime : ' Be ye as
skilful money-changers. Take the good, throw
the bad away.'

" Now, therefore, say unto all men who would The crite-
seek the godhead : ' If north wind cometh, orthodoxy.
then ye know that there will be cold ; if south
wind cometh, then ye know that there will be
burning and fervent heat.' Now, therefore, say
unto them : ' If ye have known the face of the
heaven and of the earth from the winds, then
know ye exactly, if then any come now unto you
and proclaim unto you a godhead, whether their
words have harmonized and fitted with all your
words which I have spoken unto you through two
up to three witnesses, and whether they have harmonized in the setting of the air and of the
heavens and of the circuits and of the stars and
of the light-givers and of the whole earth and all
on it and of all waters and all in them.' Say
unto them : ' Those who shall come unto you,
and their words fit and harmonize in the whole
gnosis with that which I have said unto you, I
will receive as belonging unto us.' This is what
ye shall say unto men, if ye make proclamation
unto them in order that they may guard them-
selves from the doctrines of error. |

" Now, therefore, for the sake of sinners have I rent myself asunder and am come into the world, that I may save them. For even for the righteous, who have never done any evil and have not sinned at all, it is necessary that they should find the mysteries which are in the Books of Yew, which I have made Enoch write in Paradise, discoursing with him out of the tree of the Gnosis and out of the tree of the Life. And I made him deposit them in the rock Ararad, and set the ruler Kalapataurôth, who is over Skemmût, on whose head is the foot of Yew, and who surroundeth all æons and Fates,—I set up that ruler as watcher over the Books of Yew on account of the flood, and in order that none of the rulers may be envious of them and destroy them. These will I give you, when I shall have told you the expansion of the universe."

When then the Saviour had said this, Mary answered and said : " My Lord, who now then is the man in the world who hath not sinned at all, who is pure of iniquities ? For if he is pure of one, he will not be able to be pure of another, so that he may find the mysteries which are in the Books of Yew ? For I say : A man in this world will not be able to be pure of sins; for if he is pure of one, he will not be able to be pure of another."

Few only
will accom-
plish the
mystery of
the First
Mystery.
355.

The Saviour answered and said unto Mary : " I say unto you : They will find one in a thousand and two in ten-thousand for the accomplishment | of the mystery of the First Mystery. This will I tell unto you when I have explained to you the expansion of the universe. For this cause, there-fore, I have rent myself asunder and have brought the mysteries into the world, because all are under sin and all are in need of the gift of the mysteries."

Mary answered and said unto the Saviour : CHAP. 135. "My Lord, before thou didst come to the region of the rulers and before thou didst come down into the world, hath no soul entered into the Light?"

The Saviour answered and said unto Mary : No soul had entered into "Amēn, amēn, I say unto you : Before I did come the Light before the coming of the First Mystery. into the world, no soul hath entered into the Light. And now, therefore, when I am come, I have opened the gates of the Light and opened the ways which lead to the Light. And now, therefore, let him who shall do what is worthy of the mysteries, receive the mysteries and enter into the Light."

Mary continued and said : "But, my Lord, I have heard that the prophets have entered into the Light."

The Saviour continued and said unto Mary : Of the prophets. "Amēn, amēn, I say unto you : No prophet hath entered into the Light; but the rulers of the æons have discoursed with them out of the æons and given them the mystery of the æons. And when I came to the regions of the æons, I have turned Elias and sent him into the body of John the Baptizer, and the rest also I turned into righteous bodies, which will find the mysteries | of the Light, 356. go on high and inherit the Light-kingdom.

"Unto Abraham on the other hand and Isaac Of the patriarchs. and Jacob I have forgiven all their sins and their iniquities and have given them the mysteries of the Light in the æons and placed them in the region of Yabraōth and of all the rulers who have repented. And when I go into the Height and am on the point of going into the Light, I will carry their souls with me into the Light. But, amēn, I say unto you, Mary : They will not go into the Light before I have carried thy soul and those of all thy brethren into the Light.

Of the souls of the righteous from Adam to Jesus.

" The rest of the patriarchs and of the righteous from the time of Adam unto now, who are in the æons and all the orders of the rulers, when I came to the region of the æons, I have through the Virgin of Light made to turn into bodies which will all be righteous,—those which will find the mysteries of the Light, enter in and inherit the Light-kingdom."

Mary answered and said : " Blessed are we before all men because of these splendours which thou hast revealed unto us."

The Saviour answered and said unto Mary and all the disciples : " I will still reveal unto you all the splendours of the Height, from the interiors of the interiors to the exteriors of the exteriors, | that ye may be perfected in all gnosis and in all fulness and in the height of the heights and the depths of the depths."

357.

The disciples know of a surety that Jesus is the Great Initiator.

And Mary continued and said to the Saviour : " Lo, my Lord, we have openly, exactly and clearly known that thou hast brought the keys of the mysteries of the Light-kingdom, which forgive souls sins and purify them and make them into refined light and lead them into the Light."

[SUB-SCRIPTION :]

A PORTION OF THE BOOKS OF THE SAVIOUR

A FIFTH BOOK

It came to pass then, when Jesus our Lord had been crucified and had risen from the dead on the third day, that his disciples gathered round him, adored him and said : " Our Lord, have mercy upon us, for we have abandoned father and mother and the whole world and have followed thee."

At that time Jesus stood with his disciples on the water of the Ocean and made invocation with this prayer, saying : " Hear me, my Father, father of all fatherhood, boundless Light : *aeēiouō iaō aōi ōia psinōther thernōps nōpsither zagourē pagourē nethmomaōth nepsiomaōth marachachtha thōbarrabau tharnachachan zorokothora ieou* [= *Yew*] *sabaōth.*"

And while Jesus said this, | Thomas, Andrew, James and Simon the Cananite were in the west with their faces turned towards the east, and Philip and Bartholomew were in the south turned towards the north, and the rest of the disciples and the women-disciples stood back of Jesus. But Jesus stood at the altar.

And Jesus made invocation, turning himself towards the four corners of the world with his disciples, who were all clad in linen garments, and saying : " *iaō iaō iaō.*" This is its interpretation : *iōta*, because the universe hath gone

295

forth ; *alpha,* because it will turn itself back again ; *ōmega,* because the completion of all the completeness will take place.

And when Jesus had said this, he said : " *iaphtha iaphtha mounaēr mounaēr ermanouēr ermanouēr.*" That is: " O father of all fatherhood of the boundless [spaces], hear me for the sake of my disciples whom I have led before thee, that they may have faith in all the words of thy truth, and grant all for which I shall invoke thee ; for I know the name of the father of the Treasury of the Light."

Again did Jesus,—that is Aberamenthō,— make invocation, speaking the name of the father of the Treasury of the Light, and said : " Let all the mysteries of the rulers and the authorities and the angels and the archangels and all powers

and | all things of the invisible god Agrammachamarei and Barbēlō draw near the Leech [Bdella] on one side and withdraw to the right."

And in that hour all the heavens went to the west, and all the æons and the sphere and their rulers and all their powers flew together to the west to the left of the disk of the sun and the disk of the moon.

The figures
of the disk
of the sun
and of the
moon.

And the disk of the sun was a great dragon whose tail was in his mouth and who reached to seven powers of the Left and whom four powers in the form of white horses drew.

And the base of the moon had the type of a ship which a male and a female dragon steered and two white bulls drew. The figure of a babe was on the stern of the moon who guided the dragons who robbed the light from the rulers. And on its prow was a cat's face.

And the whole world and the mountains and the seas fled together to the west to the left.

And Jesus and his disciples remained in the midst in an aëry region on the ways of the way of the midst, which lieth below the sphere. And they came to the first order of the way of the midst. And Jesus stood in the air of its region with his disciples. Jesus and the disciples are transported to the ways of the midst.

The disciples of Jesus said unto him: " What is this region | in which we are ? " 360.

Jesus said : " These are the regions of the way of the midst. For it came to pass, when the rulers of Adamas mutinied and persistently practised congress, procreating rulers, archangels, angels, servitors and decans, that Yew, the father of my father, came forth from the Right and bound them to a Fate-sphere. Of the repentant and unrepentant rulers.

" For there are twelve æons ; over six Sabaōth, the Adamas, ruleth, and his brother Yabraōth ruleth over the other six. At that time then Yabraōth with his rulers had faith in the mysteries of the Light and was active in the mysteries of the Light and abandoned the mystery of congress. But Sabaōth, the Adamas, and his rulers have persisted in the practice of congress.

" And when Yew, the father of my father, saw that Yabraōth had faith, he carried him and all the rulers who had had faith with him, took him unto himself out of the sphere and led him into a purified air in face of the light of the sun between the regions of those of the midst and between [?] the regions of the invisible god. He posted him there with the rulers who had had faith in him.

" But he carried Sabaōth, the Adamas, and his

rulers who had not been active in the mysteries of the Light, but have been persistently active in the mysteries of congress, and inbound them into the sphere.

Of the hierarchies of the un- repentant rulers and the names of their five regents.

361.
" He bound eighteen-hundred rulers in every æon, and set three-hundred-and-sixty | over them, and he set five other great rulers as lords over the three-hundred-and-sixty and over all the bound rulers, who in the whole world of mankind are called with these names: the first is called Kronos, the second Arēs, the third Hermēs, the fourth Aphroditē, the fifth Zeus."

CHAP. 137.

Of the powers which Yew bound into the five regents.
Jesus continued and said: " Hearken then, that I may tell you their mystery. It came to pass then, when Yew had thus bound them, that he drew forth a power out of the great In- visible and bound it to him who is called Kronos. And he drew another power out of Ipsantachoun- chaïnchoucheōch, who is one of the three triple- powered gods, and bound it to Arēs. And he drew a power out of Chaïnchōōōch, who also is one of the three triple-powered gods, and bound it to Hermēs. Again he drew a power out of the Pistis, the Sophia, daughter of Barbēlō, and bound it to Aphroditē.

Of the func- tions of Zeus, the chief regent.
" And moreover he perceived that they needed a helm to steer the world and the æons of the sphere, so that they might not wreck it [the world] in their wickedness. He went into the Midst, drew forth a power out of the little Sabaōth, the Good, him of the Midst, and bound it to Zeus, because he is a good [regent], so that he may steer them in his goodness. And he set thus estab-
362.
lished the circling of his order, | that he should spend thirteen [? three] months in every æon,

confirming [it], so that he may set free all the
rulers over whom he cometh, from the evil of
their wickedness. And he gave him two æons,
which are in face of those of Hermēs, for his
dwelling.

" I have told you for the first time the names The incorrup-
of these five great rulers with which the men of of the re-
the world are wont to call them. Hearken now gents.
then that I may tell you also their incorruptible
names, which are: Ōrimouth correspondeth to
Kronos; Mounichounaphōr correspondeth to
Arēs; Tarpetanouph correspondeth to Hermēs;
Chōsi correspondeth to Aphroditē; Chōnbal correspondeth to Zeus. These are their incorruptible names."

And when the disciples had heard this, they CHAP. 138.
fell down, adored Jesus and said: " Blessed are
we beyond all men, because thou hast revealed
unto us these great wonders."

They continued, besought him and said: " We
beseech thee, reveal unto us: What are then these
ways ? "

And Mary drew nigh unto him, fell down, Mary ques-
adored his feet and kissed his hands and said: Jesus on the
" Yea, my Lord, reveal unto us: What is the ways of the
use of the ways of the midst ? For we have heard
from thee that they are set over great chastisements. How then, my Lord, will we remove
or escape from them ? Or in what way do they
seize the souls ? Or | how long a time do they 363.
spend in their chastisements ? Have mercy upon
us, our Lord, our Saviour, in order that the receivers of the judgments of the ways of the midst
may not carry off our souls and judge us in their
evil judgments, so that we ourselves may inherit

the Light of thy father and not be wretched and destitute of thee."

Of the mysteries which Jesus will give unto his disciples.
When then Mary said this weeping, Jesus answered in great compassion and said unto them: " Truly, my brethren and beloved, who have abandoned father and mother for my name's sake, unto you will I give all mysteries and all gnoses.

" I will give you the mystery of the twelve æons of the rulers and their seals and their ciphers and the manner of invocation for reaching their regions.

" I will give you moreover the mystery of the thirteenth æon and the manner of invocation for reaching their regions, and I will give you their ciphers and their seals.

" And I will give you the mystery of the baptism of those of the Midst and the manner of invocation for reaching their regions, and I will announce unto you their ciphers and their seals.

" And I will give you the baptism of those of the Right, our region, and its ciphers and its seals and the manner of invocation for reaching thither.

" And I will give you the great mystery of
364.
the Treasury of the Light and | the manner of invocation for reaching thither.

" I will give you all the mysteries and all the gnoses, in order that ye may be called 'children of the fulness, perfected in all the gnoses and all the mysteries.' Blessed are ye beyond all men on earth, for the children of the Light are come in your time."

CHAP. 139.
Jesus continued in the discourse and said: " It came to pass then thereafter, that the father of my father,—that is Yew,—came and took

other three-hundred-and-sixty rulers from the Of the con-
rulers of Adamas who had not had faith in the stitution of the way of
mystery of the Light, and bound them into these the midst.
aërial regions, in which we are now, below the
sphere. He established another five great rulers
over them,—that is these who are on the way of
the midst.

"The first ruler of the way of the midst is Of Paraplēx.
called Paraplēx, a ruler with a woman's shape,
whose hair reacheth down to her feet, under whose
authority stand five-and-twenty archdemons
which rule over a multitude of other demons.
And it is those demons which enter into men
and seduce them, raging and cursing and slandering; and it is they which carry off hence and in
ravishment the souls and dispatch them through
their dark smoke and their evil chastisements."

Mary said : | " I shall behave badly to question 365.
thee. Be not wroth with me if I question on
all things."

Jesus said: " Question what thou wilt."

Mary said : " My Lord, reveal unto us in what
manner they carry off hence the souls in ravishment, that also my brethren may understand it."

Jesus,—that is Aberamenthō,—said : "Since Of Yew and
indeed the father of my father,—that is Yew,— Melchisedec.
is the fore-minder of all the rulers, gods and
powers who have arisen out of the matter of the
Light of the Treasury, and Zorokothora Melchisedec is the envoy to all the lights which are purified
in the rulers, leading them into the Treasury of
the Light,—these two alone are the great Lights,
and their ordinance is that they down go to the
rulers and purify them, and that Zorokothora
Melchisedec carrieth away the purification of

the lights which they have purified in the rulers and leadeth them into the Treasury of the Light, —when the cipher and the time of their ordinance cometh, that they go down to the rulers and oppress and constrain them, carrying away the purification from the rulers.

" But straightway when they shall cease from the oppressing and constraining and return to the regions of the Treasury of the Light, it cometh to pass that, if they reach the regions of the Midst, Zorokothora Melchisedec carrieth off the lights and leadeth them unto | the gate of those of the Midst and leadeth them into the Treasury of the Light, and that Yew withdraweth himself into the regions of those of the Right.

" Up to the time of the cipher for them to come forth again, the rulers mutiny through the wrath of their wickedness, going straightway up to the lights, because they [Yew and Melchisedec] are not with them at that time, and they carry off the souls which they may be able to snatch away in ravishment, and destroy them through their dark smoke and their evil fire.

" At that time then this authority, with name Paraplēx, along with the demons which stand under her, carrieth off the souls of the violently passionate, of cursers and of slanderers and dispatcheth them through the dark smoke and destroyeth them through her evil fire, so that they begin to be undone and dissolved. One-hundred-and-thirty-and-three years and nine months do they spend in the chastisements of her regions, while she tormenteth them in the fire of her wickedness.

" It cometh to pass then after all these times,

(marginal notes)

366.

How the demon rulers carry off souls.

The chastisements of Paraplēx.

when the sphere turneth itself and the little
Sabaōth, Zeus, cometh to the first of the æons
of the sphere, which is called in the world the
Ram of Boubastis, that is of Aphroditē ; [and]
when she [Boubastis] cometh to the seventh
house of the sphere, that is to the Balance, then
the veils which are between those of the Right
and those of the Left, draw themselves aside,
and there looketh from the height out of those
of the Right the | great Sabaōth, the Good ; and 367
the whole world and the total sphere [become
alarmed] before he hath looked forth. And he
looketh down on the regions of Paraplēx, so that
her regions may be dissolved and perish. And
all the souls which are in her chastisements, are
carried and cast back [up] into the sphere anew,
because they are ruined in the chastisements of
Paraplēx."

" He continued in the discourse and said : " The
second order is called Ariouth the Æthiopian, a
female ruler, who is entirely black, under whom
stand fourteen other [arch]demons which rule
over a multitude of other demons. And it is
those demons which stand under Ariouth the
Æthiopian, that enter into strife-seekers until they
stir up wars and murders arise, and they harden
their heart and seduce it to wrath in order that
murders may arise.

CHAP. 140.
Of Ariouth the
Æthiopian.

" And the souls which this authority will carry
off in ravishment, pass one-hundred-and-thirteen
years in her regions, while she tormenteth them
through her dark smoke and her wicked fire, so
that they come nigh unto destruction.

" And thereafter, when the sphere turneth itself, and the little Sabaōth, the Good, who is called

in the world Zeus, cometh, and he cometh to the fourth æon of the sphere, that is the Crab, and Boubastis, who is called in the world Aphroditê, cometh into the tenth æon of the sphere which

is called the | Goat, at that time the veils which are between those of the Left and those of the Right, draw themselves aside, and Yew looketh forth to the right; the whole world becometh alarmed and is agitated together with all the æons of the sphere. And he looketh on the dwellings of Ariouth the Æthiopian, so that her regions are dissolved and ruined, and all the souls which are in her chastisements are carried off and cast back into the sphere anew, because they are ruined through her dark smoke and her wicked fire."

He continued further in his discourse and said : " The third order is called Triple-faced Hekatê, and there are under her authority seven-and-twenty [arch]demons, and it is they which enter into men and seduce them to perjuries and lies and to covet that which doth not belong to them.

" The souls then which Hekatê beareth hence in ravishment, she handeth over to her demons which stand under her, in order that they may torment them through her dark smoke and her wicked fire, they being exceedingly afflicted through the demons. And they spend one-hundred-and-five years and six months, being chastized in her wicked chastisements; and they begin to be dissolved and destroyed.

" And thereafter, when the sphere turneth itself, and the little Sabaôth, the Good, he of the Midst, who is called in the world Zeus, cometh,

and he cometh to the | eighth æon of the sphere

which is called the Scorpion, and when Boubastis, whom they call Aphroditē, cometh, and
she cometh to the second æon of the sphere which
is called the Bull, then the veils which are between
those of the Right and those of the Left draw
themselves aside and Zorokothora Melchisedec
looketh out of the height; and the world and the
mountains are agitated and the æons become
alarmed. And he looketh on all the regions of
Hekatē, so that her regions are dissolved and
destroyed, and all the souls which are in her chastisements, are carried off and cast back anew into
the sphere, because they are dissolved in the fire
of her chastisements."

He continued and said : " The fourth order Of Parhedrōn
is called Parhedrōn Typhōn, who is a mighty Typhōn.
ruler, under whose authority are two-and-thirty
demons. And it is they which enter into men
and seduce them to lusting, fornicating, adultery
and to the continual practice of intercourse. The
souls then which this ruler will carry off in ravishment, pass one-hundred-and-twenty-and-eight
years in his regions, while his demons torment
them through his dark smoke and his wicked fire,
so that they begin to be ruined and destroyed.

" It cometh to pass then, when the sphere
turneth itself and the little Sabaōth, | the Good, 370.
he of the Midst, who is called Zeus, cometh, and
when he cometh to the ninth æon of the sphere
which is called the Archer, and when Boubastis,
who is called in the world Aphroditē, cometh,
and she cometh to the third æon of the sphere
which is called the Twins, then the veils which are
between those of the Left and those of the
Right, draw themselves aside, and there looketh

forth Zarazaz, whom the rulers call with the name of a mighty ruler of their regions ' Maskelli,' and he looketh on the dwellings of Parhedrōn Typhōn, so that his regions are dissolved and destroyed. And all the souls which are in his chastisements are carried and cast back anew into the sphere, because they are reduced through his dark smoke and his wicked fire."

Of Yachthan-abas.

Again he continued in the discourse and said unto this disciples : " The fifth order, whose ruler is called Yachthanabas, is a mighty ruler under whom standeth a multitude of other demons. It is they which enter into men and bring it about that they have respect of persons,— treating the just with injustice, and favour the cause of sinners, taking gifts for a just judgment and perverting it, forgetting the poor and needy, —they [the demons] increasing the forgetfulness in their souls and the care for that which |

371.

bringeth no benefit, in order that they may not think of their life, so that when they come out of the body, they are carried in ravishment.

" The souls then which this ruler will carry off in ravishment, are in his chastisements one-hundred-and-fifty years and eight months ; and he destroyeth them through his dark smoke and his wicked fire, while they are exceedingly afflicted through the flames of his fire.

" And when the sphere turneth itself and the little Sabaōth, the Good, who is called in the world Zeus, cometh, and he cometh to the eleventh æon of the sphere which is called the Water-man, and when Boubastis cometh to the fifth æon of the sphere which is called the Lion, then the veils which are between those of the Left and those of the Right, draw themselves aside, and there looketh out of the height the great Iaõ, the Good, he of the Midst, on the regions of Yachthanabas, so that his regions are dissolved and destroyed. And all the souls which are in his chastisements are carried off and cast back anew into the sphere, because they are ruined in his chastisements.

" These then are the doings of the ways of the midst concerning which ye have questioned me."

And when the disciples had heard this, they fell down, adored him and said : " Help us now, Lord, and have mercy upon us, in order that we may be preserved from these wicked chastisements which are prepared for the sinners. Woe | unto them, woe unto the children of men ! For they grope as the blind in the darkness and see not. Have mercy upon us, O Lord, in this great blindness in which we are. And have mercy upon the whole race of men ; for they have lain in wait for their souls, as lions for their prey, making it [sc. the prey] ready as food for their [sc. the rulers'] chastisements because of the forgetfulness and unknowing which is in them. Have mercy then upon us, our Lord, our Saviour, have mercy upon us and save us in this great stupefaction."

Jesus said unto his disciples : " Be comforted and be not afraid, for ye are blessed, because I will make you lords over all these and put them in subjection under your feet. Remember that I have already said unto you before I was crucified : ' I will give you the keys of the kingdom of heaven.' Now, therefore, I say unto you : I will give them unto you."

CHAP. 141.
The disciples beseech Jesus to have mercy upon sinners.

372.

Jesus encourageth his disciples.

Jesus and
his disciples
ascend
higher.
When then Jesus said this, he chanted a song of praise in the great name. The regions of the ways of the midst hid themselves, and Jesus and his disciples remained in an air of exceedingly strong light.

He breath-
eth into
their eyes.
Jesus said unto his disciples : " Draw near unto me." And they drew near unto him. He turned himself towards the four corners of the world, said the great name over their heads, blessed them and breathed into their eyes.

Jesus said unto them : " Look up and see what ye may see."

373.
Their eyes
are opened.
And they raised their eyes and saw a | great, exceedingly mighty light, which no man in the world can describe.

He said unto them anew : " Look away out of the light and see what ye may see."

They said : " We see fire, water, wine and blood."

Jesus ex-
plaineth the
vision of fire
and water,
and wine
and blood.
Jesus,—that is Aberamenthō,—said unto his disciples : " Amēn, I say unto you : I have brought nothing into the world when I came, save this fire, this water, this wine and this blood. I have brought the water and the fire out of the region of the Light of the lights of the Treasury of the Light ; and I have brought the wine and the blood out of the region of Barbēlō. And after a little while my father sent me the holy spirit in the type of a dove.

" And the fire, the water and the wine are for the purification of all the sins of the world. The blood on the other hand was for a sign unto me because of the human body which I received in the region of Barbēlō, the great power of the invisible god. The breath on the other hand advanceth towards all souls and leadeth them unto the region of the Light.

" For this cause have I said unto you: ' I am come to cast fire on the earth,'—that is: I am come to purify the sins of the whole world with fire. *The same explained from former sayings.*

" And for this cause have I said to the Samaritan woman: ' If thou knewest of the gift of God, and who it is who saith unto thee: Give me to drink,—thou wouldst ask, and he would give thee | living water, and there would be in thee a spring which welleth up for everlasting life.' *374.*

" And for this cause I took also a cup of wine, blessed it and give it unto you and said: ' This is the blood of the covenant which will be poured out for you for the forgiveness of your sins.'

" And for this cause they have also thrust the spear into my side, and there came forth water and blood.

" And these are the mysteries of the Light which forgive sins ; that is to say, these are the namings and the names of the Light."

It came to pass then thereafter that Jesus gave command : " Let all the powers of the Left go to their regions." And Jesus with his disciples remained on the Mount of Galilee. The *Jesus and his disciples descend to earth.* disciples continued and besought him : " For how long then hast thou not let our sins which we have committed, and our iniquities be forgiven and made us worthy of the kingdom of thy father ? "

And Jesus said unto them : " Amēn, I say

Jesus pro-
miseth to
give them
the mystery
of the for-
giveness of
sins.

unto you : Not only will I purify your sins, but
I will make you worthy of the kingdom of my
father. And I will give you the mystery of the
forgiveness of sins, in order that to him whom ye
shall forgive on earth, it will be forgiven in heaven,
and he whom ye shall bind on earth, will be
bound in heaven. I will give you the mystery
of the kingdom of heaven, in order that ye yourselves may perform them [*sc.* the mysteries] for
men."

CHAP. 142.
375.
The mystic
offering.

And Jesus | said unto them : " Bring me fire
and vine branches." They brought them unto
him. He laid out the offering, and set down two
wine-vessels, one on the right and the other on
the left of the offering. He disposed the offering
before them, and set a cup of water before the
wine-vessel on the right and set a cup of wine
before the wine-vessel on the left, and laid loaves
according to the number of the disciples in the
middle between the cups and set a cup of water
behind the loaves.

Jesus stood before the offering, set the disciples
behind him, all clad with linen garments, and in
their hands the cipher of the name of the father
of the Treasury of the Light, and he made in-
The invoca-
tion. vocation thus, saying : " Hear me, O Father,
father of all fatherhood, boundless Light: *iaō
iouō iaō aōi ōia psinōther therōpsin ōpsither
nephthomaōth nephiomaōth marachachtha marmar-
achtha iēana menaman amanēi (of heaven) israi
amēn amēn soubaibai appaap amēn amēn deraarai
(behind) amēn amēn sasarsartou amēn amēn
koukiamin miai amēn amēn iai iai touap amēn
amēn amēn main mari mariē marei amēn amēn
amēn.*

" Hear me, O Father, father of all fatherhood. I invoke you yourselves, ye forgivers of sins, ye purifiers of iniquities. | Forgive the sins of 376. the souls of these disciples who have followed me, and purify their iniquities and make them worthy to be reckoned with the kingdom of my father, the father of the Treasury of the Light, for they have followed me and have kept my commandments.

" Now, therefore, O Father, father of all fatherhood, let the forgivers of sins come, whose names are these : *siphirepsnichieu zenei berimou sochabrichēr euthari na nai (have mercy upon me) dieisbalmērich meunipos chirie entair mouthiour smour peuchēr oouschous minionor isochobortha.*

" Hear me, invoking you, forgive the sins of these souls and blot out their iniquities. Let them be worthy to be reckoned with the kingdom of my father, the father of the Treasury of the Light.

" I know thy great powers and invoke them : *auēr bebrō athroni ē oureph ē ōne souphen knitou- sochreōph mauōnbi mneuōr souōni chōcheteōph chōche eteōph memōch anēmph.*

" Forgive [*sing.*] the sins of these souls, blot out their iniquities which they have knowingly and unknowingly committed, which they have committed in fornication and adultery unto this day ; forgive them then and make them worthy to be reckoned with the kingdom of my father, so that they are worthy to receive of this offering, holy Father.

" If thou then, Father, hast heard me and for- given the sins of these souls | and blotted out 377. their iniquities, and hast made them worthy to

be reckoned with thy kingdom, mayest thou give
me a sign in this offering."

And the sign which Jesus had said [? besought]
happened.

The rite is consummated. Jesus said unto his disciples : " Rejoice and
exult, for your sins are forgiven and your ini-
quities blotted out, and ye are reckoned with the
kingdom of my father."

And when he said this, the disciples rejoiced
in great joy.

Directions as to the future use of the rite. Jesus said unto them : " This is the manner
and way and this is the mystery which ye are to
perform for the men who have faith in you,
in whom is no deceit and who hearken unto you
in all good words. And their sins and their
iniquities will be blotted out up to the day on
which ye have performed for them this mystery.
But hide this mystery and give it not unto all
men, but unto him who shall do all the things
which I have said unto you in my commandments.

" This then is the mystery in truth of the
baptism for those whose sins are forgiven and
whose iniquities are blotted out. This is the
baptism of the first offering which showeth the
way to the region of Truth and to the region of
the Light."

CHAP. 143. Of three other mystic rites. Thereafter his disciples said unto him : " Rabbi,
reveal unto us the mystery of the Light of thy
father, since we heard thee say : ' There is still
a fire-baptism and there is still a baptism of the
holy spirit of the Light, and there is | a spiritual
chrism ; these lead the souls into the Treasury
of the Light.' Tell us, therefore, their mystery,
so that we ourselves may inherit the kingdom of
thy father."

378.

Jesus said unto them : " There is no mystery Of the high-
est mys-
teries and
of the great
name.
which is more excellent than these mysteries on
which ye question, in that it will lead your souls
into the Light of the lights, into the regions of
Truth and Goodness, into the region of the Holy
of all holies, into the region in which there is
neither female nor male, nor are there forms in
that region, but a perpetual indescribable Light.
Nothing more excellent is there, therefore, than
these mysteries on which ye question, save only
the mystery of the seven Voices and their nine-
and-forty powers and their ciphers. And there
is no name which is more excellent than them all,
the name in which are all names and all lights
and all powers.

" Who then knoweth that name, if he cometh Of the
efficacy of
that name.
out of the body of matter, nor smoke nor darkness
nor authority nor ruler of the Fate-sphere nor
angel nor archangel nor power can hold down the
soul which knoweth that name ; but if it cometh
out of the world and sayeth that name to the
fire, it is quenched and the darkness withdraweth.

" And if it sayeth it to the demons | and to 379.
the receivers of the outer darkness and their rulers
and their authorities and their powers, they will
all sink down and their flame will burn and they
will cry out : ' Holy, holy art thou, most holy
of all holies.'

" And if one sayeth that name to the receivers
of the wicked chastisements and their authorities
and all their powers and also to Barbēlō and the
invisible god and the three triple-powered gods,
straightway if one will say this name in those
regions, they will all fall one on another, will
be undone and destroyed and cry out : ' O Light

of all lights, which is in the boundless lights, remember us and purify us.' "

And when Jesus had finished saying these words, all his disciples cried out, wept with loud sobbing, saying : . . .

.   .   .   .   .   .

[LACUNA OF EIGHT LEAVES.]

.   .   .   .   .   .

A SIXTH BOOK

. . . .

. . . [and lead them forth to the fire-rivers
and fire-seas] and take vengeance on it therein
for another six months and eight days. Thereafter they lead it up on the way of the midst,
and every one of the rulers of the way of the
midst chastizeth it in his chastisements another
six months and eight days. Thereafter they lead
it to the Virgin of Light, who judgeth the good
and the evil, that she may judge it. And when
the sphere turneth itself, she handeth it over to
her receivers, that they may cast it into the
æons of the sphere. And the servitors of the
sphere lead it forth to a water which is below
the sphere ; and it becometh | a seething fire 380.
and eateth into it, until it purifieth it utterly.

"And then cometh Yaluham, the receiver of
Sabaōth, the Adamas, who handeth the souls the
cup of forgetfulness, and he bringeth a cup filled
with the water of forgetfulness and handeth
it to the soul, and it drinketh it and forgetteth
all regions and all the regions to which it hath
gone. And they cast it down into a body which
will spend its time continually troubled in its
heart.

"This is the chastisement of the curser."

Mary continued and said : "My Lord, the man

who persistently slandereth, if he cometh out of the body, whither shall he get or what is his chastisement ? "

Jesus said : "A man who persistently slandereth, if his time is completed through the sphere, that he cometh out of the body, then Abiout and Charmōn, the receivers of Ariēl, come, lead his soul out of the body and spend three days going round with it and instructing it concerning the creatures of the world.

" Thereafter they lead it below into Amente before Ariēl, and he chastizeth it in his chastisements eleven months and twenty-and-one days.

" Thereafter they lead it into the chaos before Yaldabaōth and his forty-and-nine demons, and every one of his demons fall upon it another eleven months and twenty-and-one days, scourging it with fiery whips.

381. " Thereafter | they lead it into fire-rivers and boiling fire-seas, to take vengeance on it therein another eleven months and twenty-and-one days.

" And thereafter they carry it on to the way of the midst, and every one of the rulers on the way of the midst chastizeth it in his chastisements another eleven months and twenty-and-one days.

" Thereafter they carry it to the Virgin of Light, who judgeth the righteous and the sinners, that she may judge it. And when the sphere turneth itself, she handeth it over to her receivers, that they may cast it into the æons of the sphere. And the servitors of the sphere will lead it to a water which is below the sphere ; and it becometh a seething fire and eateth into it until it purifieth it utterly.

"And Yaluham, the receiver of Sabaōth, the Adamas, bringeth the cup of forgetfulness and handeth it to the soul, and it drinketh it and forgetteth all regions and all things and all the regions through which it hath gone. And they deliver it unto a body which will spend its time being afflicted.

" This is the chastisement of the slanderer."

Mary said : " Woe, woe, unto sinners ! "   CHAP. 145.

Salome answered and said : " My Lord Jesus, a murderer who hath never committed any sin but murdering, if he cometh out of the body, what is his chastisement ? "

Jesus answered and said : " A murderer who hath never committed any sin but murdering, if his time is completed through the sphere, that he cometh out of the body, the receivers of Yaldabaōth come and lead his soul out of the body and bind it by its feet to a great demon with a horse's face, and he spendeth three days circling round with it in the world.   Of the chastisement of the murderer. 382.

" Thereafter they lead it into the regions of the cold and of the snow, and they take vengeance on it there three years and six months.

" Thereafter they lead it down into the chaos before Yaldabaōth and his forty-and-nine demons, and every one of his demons scourgeth it another three years and six months.

" Thereafter they lead it down into the chaos before Persephonē and take vengeance on it with her chastisements another three years and six months.

" Thereafter they carry it on to the way of

the midst, and every one of the rulers of the way
of the midst taketh vengeance on it with the chastisements of its regions another three years and
six months.

" Thereafter they lead it unto the Virgin of
Light, who judgeth the righteous and the sinners,
that she may judge it. And when the sphere
turneth itself, she commandeth that it shall be
cast into the outer darkness until the time when
the darkness of the midst shall be up-raised ; it
[the soul] will be destroyed and dissolved.

" This is the chastisement of the murderer."

CHAP. 146.
383.
Peter pro-
testeth
against the
women.
Peter said : " My Lord, let the women | cease
to question, in order that we also may question."

Jesus said unto Mary and the women : " Give
opportunity to your men brethren, that they also
may question."

Peter answered and said : " My Lord, a robber
and thief, whose sin is this persistently, when he
cometh out of the body, what is his chastisement ? "

Of the chas-
tisement of
the thief.
Jesus said : " If the time of such an one is
completed through the sphere, the receivers of
Adōnis come after him, and lead his soul out of
the body, and they spend three days circling round
with it and instructing it concerning the creatures
of the world.

" Thereafter they lead it down into the Amente
before Ariēl, and he taketh vengeance on it in
his chastisements three months, eight days and
two hours.

" Thereafter they lead it into the chaos before
Yaldabaōth and his forty-and-nine demons, and
every one of his demons taketh vengeance on it
another three months, eight days and two hours.

" Thereafter they lead it on to the way of the midst, and every one of the rulers of the way of the midst taketh vengeance on it through his dark smoke and his wicked fire another three months, eight days and two hours.

" Thereafter they lead it up unto the Virgin of Light, who judgeth the righteous and the sinners, that she may judge it. And when the sphere turneth itself, she handeth it over to her receivers, that they may cast it into the æons of the sphere. And they lead it forth into a water which is below the sphere; | and it becometh a seething 384. fire and eateth into it until it purifieth it utterly.

" Thereafter cometh Yaluham, the receiver of Sabaôth, the Adamas, bringeth the cup of forgetfulness and handeth it unto the soul; and it drinketh it and forgetteth all things and all the regions to which it had gone. And they cast it into a lame, halt and blind body.

" This is the chastisement of the thief."

Andrew answered and said : " An arrogant, overweening man, when he cometh out of the body, what will happen to him ? "

Jesus said : " If the time of such an one is completed through the sphere, the receivers of Ariêl come after him and lead out his soul [out of the body] and spend three days travelling round in the world [with it] and instructing it concerning the creatures of the world. *Of the chastisement of the arrogant.*

" Thereafter they lead it down into the Amente before Ariêl ; and he taketh vengeance on it with his chastisements twenty months.

" Thereafter they lead it into the chaos before Yaldabaôth and his forty-and-nine demons ; and he and his demons, one by one, take vengeance on it another twenty months.

"Thereafter they carry it on to the way of the midst; and every one of the rulers of the way of the midst taketh vengeance on it another twenty months.

"And thereafter they lead it unto the Virgin of Light, that she may judge it. And when the sphere turneth itself, she handeth it over to her receivers, that they may cast it into the æons of the sphere. And the servitors of the sphere |
385.
lead it into a water which is below the sphere; and it becometh a seething fire and eateth into it until it purifieth it.

"And Yaluham, the receiver of Sabaôth, the Adamas, cometh and bringeth the cup with the water of forgetfulness and handeth it to the soul; and it drinketh and forgetteth all things and all the regions to which it had gone. And they cast it up into a lame and deformed body, so that all despise it persistently.

"This is the chastisement of the arrogant and overweening man."

Thomas said: "A persistent blasphemer, what is his chastisement?"

Of the chas-
tisement of
the blas-
phemer.
Jesus said: "If the time of such an one is completed through the sphere, the receivers of Yaldabaôth come after him and bind him by his tongue to a great demon with a horse's face; they spend three days travelling round with him in the world, and take vengeance on him.

"Thereafter they lead him into the region of the cold and of the snow, and take vengeance on him there eleven years.

"Thereafter they lead him down into the

chaos before Yaldabaôth and his forty-and-nine
demons, and every one of his demons taketh
vengeance on him another eleven years.

" Thereafter they lead him into the outer
darkness until the day when the great ruler
with the dragon's face | who encircleth the dark- 386.
ness, shall be judged. And that soul becometh
frozen up [?] and destroyed and dissolved.

" This is the judgment of the blasphemer."

Bartholomew said : " A man who hath inter- CHAP. 147.
course with a male, what is his vengeance ? "

Jesus said: " The measure of the man who Of the chas-
hath intercourse with males and of the man $\begin{smallmatrix}\text{tisement of}\\\text{him who}\end{smallmatrix}$
with whom he lieth, is the same as that of the $\begin{smallmatrix}\text{hath inter-}\\\text{course with}\end{smallmatrix}$
blasphemer.   males.

" When then the time is completed through
the sphere, the receivers of Yaldabaôth come
after their soul, and he with his forty-and-nine
demons taketh vengeance on it eleven years.

" Thereafter they carry it to the fire-rivers
and seething pitch-seas, which are full of demons
with pigs' faces. They eat into them and take
vengeance on [?] them in the fire-rivers another
eleven years.

" Thereafter they carry them into the outer
darkness until the day of judgment when the
great darkness is judged ; and then they will be
dissolved and destroyed."

Thomas said : " We have heard that there are
some on the earth who take the male seed and
the female monthly blood, and make it into a
lentil porridge and eat it, | saying: ' We have 387.
faith in Esau and Jacob.' Is this then seemly or
not ? "

Jesus was wroth with the world in that hour

Of the chas-
tisement of
a foul act of
sorcery.

and said unto Thomas : " Amēn, I say : This sin is more heinous than all sins and iniquities. Such men will straightway be taken into the outer darkness and not be cast back anew into the sphere, but they shall perish, be destroyed in the outer darkness in a region where there is neither pity nor light, but howling and grinding of teeth. And all the souls which shall be brought into the outer darkness, will not be cast back anew, but will be destroyed and dissolved."

John answered [and said] : " A man who hath committed no sin, but done good persistently, but hath not found the mysteries to pass through the rulers, when he cometh out of the body, what will happen unto him ? "

Of the after-
death state
of the
righteous
man who
hath not
been ini-
tiated.

Jesus said : " If the time of such an one is completed through the sphere, the receivers of Bainchōōōch, who is one of the triple-powered gods, come after his soul and lead his soul with joy and exultation and spend three days circling round with it and instructing it concerning the creations of the world with joy and exultation.

" Thereafter they lead it down into the Amente and instruct it concerning the instruments of chastisement in the Amente ; but they will not take vengeance on it therewith. But they will only instruct it concerning them, and the smoke of the flame of the chastisements | catcheth it only a little.

388.

" Thereafter they carry it up unto the way of the midst and instruct it concerning the chastise-ments of the ways of the midst, the smoke from the flame catching it a little.

" Thereafter they lead it unto the Virgin of Light, and she judgeth it and depositeth it with

the little Sabaōth, the Good, him of the Midst,
until the sphere turneth itself, and Zeus and
Aphroditē come in face of the Virgin of Light,
while Kronos and Arēs come behind her.

" At that hour she taketh that righteous soul
and handeth it over to her receivers, that they
may cast it into the æons of the sphere. And
the servitors of the sphere lead it forth into a
water which is below the sphere ; and a seething
fire ariseth and eateth into it until it purifieth it
utterly.

" Thereafter cometh Yaluham, the receiver of
Sabaōth, the Adamas, who giveth the cup of
forgetfulness unto the souls, and he bringeth
the water of forgetfulness and handeth it to the
soul ; [and it drinketh it] and forgetteth all
things and all the regions to which it had gone.

" Thereafter there cometh a receiver of the little Of the cup
Sabaōth, the Good, him of the Midst.   He himself of wisdom.
bringeth a cup filled with thoughts and wisdom,
and soberness is in it ; [and] he handeth it to the
soul.   And they cast it into a body which can
neither sleep nor forget because of the cup of
soberness which hath been handed unto it ; but |
it will whip its heart persistently to question about 389.
the mysteries of the Light until it find them,
through the decision of the Virgin of Light, and
inherit the Light for ever."

Mary said : " A man who hath committed all CHAP. 148.
sins and all iniquities and hath not found the
mysteries of the Light, will he receive the chastisements for them all at once ? "

Jesus answered : " Yea, he will receive it ; A sinner
if he hath committed three sins, he will receive suffereth for
chastisement for three." ate sin.

John said : " A man who hath committed all sins and all iniquities, but at last hath found the mysteries of the Light, is it possible for him to be saved ? "

Jesus said : " Such a man who hath committed all sins and all iniquities, and he findeth the mysteries of the Light, and performeth and fulfilleth them and ceaseth not nor doeth sins, will inherit the Treasury of the Light."

Jesus said unto his disciples : " When the sphere turneth itself, and Kronos and Arēs come behind the Virgin of Light and Zeus and Aphroditē come in face of the Virgin, they being in their own æons, then the veils of the Virgin draw themselves aside and she falleth into joy in that hour when she seeth these two light-stars before her. And all the souls which she shall cast at that hour into the circuit of the æons of the sphere, that they

may come into the world, will be righteous and good and find at this time the mysteries of the Light ; she sendeth them anew that they may find the mysteries of the Light.

" If on the other hand Arēs and Kronos come in face of the Virgin and Zeus and Aphroditē behind her, so that she seeth them not, then all the souls which she shall cast in that hour into the creatures of the sphere, will be wicked and wrathful and do not find the mysteries of the Light."

When then Jesus said this unto his disciples in the midst of the Amente, the disciples cried and wept, [saying]: " Woe, woe unto sinners, on whom the negligence and the forgetfulness of the rulers lie until they come out of the body and are led to these chastisements ! Have mercy upon us, have mercy upon us, son of the Holy

[One], and have compassion with us, that we may
be saved from these chastisements and these
judgments which are prepared for the sinners ;
for we also have sinned, our Lord and our Light."

[A LATER POSTSCRIPT]

.   .   .   .   .   .

. . . the righteous [man].   They went forth three The pro-
by three to the four zones of heaven and they clamation
                                                of the
proclaimed the goodness of the kingdom in the apostles.
whole world, the Christ inworking with them
through the words of confirmation and the signs
and the wonders which followed them.   And thus
was known the kingdom of God on the whole
earth and in the whole world of Israel as a
witness for all the nations which are from the
rising unto the setting [of the sun].

.   .   .   .   .   .

.   .   .   .   .   .

[Two Lines erased.]

THE END.